COMEDY

COMEDY

AN ESSAY ON COMEDY
George Meredith

★

LAUGHTER
Henri Bergson

INTRODUCTION AND
APPENDIX: "THE MEANINGS OF COMEDY"
BY WYLIE SYPHER

The Johns Hopkins University Press
Baltimore and London

Published in 1956 as a Doubleday Anchor Book
Johns Hopkins Paperbacks edition, 1980
Second printing, 1983

The Johns Hopkins University Press,
Baltimore, Maryland 21218
The Johns Hopkins Press Ltd., London

The translation of Bergson's Laughter *in this Johns
Hopkins edition is used by arrangement with the Presses
Universitaires de France.*

LIBRARY OF CONGRESS CATALOGING IN
PUBLICATION DATA
Sypher, Wylie, ed., *Comedy.*
Reprint of the 1st ed. published by Doubleday, Garden
    City, N. Y.
Bibliography: p. 259
1. Comedy.   2.   Laughter.   I.   Meredith, George,
1828–1909.   An essay on comedy.   1980.   II.
Bergson, Henri Louis, 1859–1941.   Fire.   English.
1980.   III.   Title.
[PN1922.S9   1980]   809.2′523   79–3701
ISBN 0–8018–2327–7

Contents

Introduction—Wylie Sypher vii

AN ESSAY ON COMEDY—*George Meredith* 3

LAUGHTER—*Henri Bergson*
 I. The Comic in General 61
   The Comic Element in Forms
    and Movements 74
   Expansive Force of the Comic 84
 II. The Comic Element in Situations and
   the Comic Element in Words 104
 III. The Comic in Character 146

Appendix: THE MEANINGS OF COMEDY—*Wylie Sypher*
 I. Our New Sense of the Comic 193
 II. The Ancient Rites of Comedy 214
 III. The Guises of the Comic Hero 226
 IV. The Social Meanings of Comedy 241

Notes 256
Bibliographical Note 259

Everyone who has read Marcel Proust's novels, especially *The Past Recaptured*, knows something of the philosophy of Henri Bergson, for Proust fulfilled in art several of the notions of time and intuition and memory Bergson developed in his influential books like *Time and Free Will*, *Creative Evolution*, and *The Two Sources of Morality and Religion*, all of them accepting "vitalism" instead of "mechanism" as the explanation of human experience. Bergson had begun as a mathematician before he read deeply in Herbert Spencer, then finally emerged as the most celebrated modern philosopher of "intuition." At Bergson's death in 1941 Paul Valéry paid national tribute to the Frenchman who, like Pascal, made reason poetic and believed that intuition, not logic, "attains the absolute." Bergson's volatile and difficult ideas are more accessible in his essay on *Laughter* (1900) than in his philosophic works, famous as they are. This essay began to take form as early as 1884 in his academic lecture on *Le Rire: de quoi rit-on? pourquoi rit-on?*

Just seven years previously, in February, 1877, the English novelist George Meredith had, somewhat nervously, read to the London Institution a paper on *The Idea of Comedy and the Uses of the Comic Spirit* [*An Essay on Comedy*]. As lecturer, of course, Meredith could hardly compete with Bergson, who as appointee at the École Normale Supérieure and at the Collège de France drew overflowing, indeed reverential, crowds to hear his quietly spoken attacks on materialism and mechanism in modern thought. Yet Meredith's essay has become one of the classic documents on comedy. As novelist, Meredith has never enjoyed great popularity, perhaps because of his mannered prose. Admittedly, however, his glittering *Ordeal of Richard Feverel* and *The Egoist* are among the most spirited, artfully paced social satires in British fiction, and something of the rarity of style and substance in these novels reappears in *The Idea of Comedy*. Thus, as is the case with Bergson, we can more easily approach Meredith through this little essay than through most of his major works.

The relation between Bergson's essay on comedy and Meredith's is not simply chronological: essentially both were reacting against the coarse logic, the "machinery," of the nineteenth century, against everything cut-and-dried. Bergson believed that life is a "vital impulse," an *élan vital*, not to be understood by the reason alone. For him, life is instinct, and the real meanings of experience must be sought along the fringe of intuitions surrounding every clear idea. In *The Two Sources of Morality and Religion* he claims that morality itself springs from intuition, not reason, and that the letter kills the spirit. This theme is carried over into the essay on *Laughter,* for he sees the comical as something mechanical encrusted on the living—"movement without life." The absurdity of logical systems was already proved in Meredith's *Richard Feverel* (1859), in which Sir Austin tries to rear his son on the high scientific principle that "Sin is an alien element in our blood." The inevitable and human outcome is that the System seems to triumph—just when it is about to fall. Sir Austin sees Richard destroy himself and his wife, along with the logical System: "Richard was no longer the Richard of his creation: his pride and his joy: but simply a human being with the rest." So Sir Austin concludes: "It is useless to base any System on a human being."

Meredith's essay needs to be supplemented by the "Prelude" he wrote to *The Egoist* (1879), which rephrases his theory of comedy and serves as a half-poetic comment on Bergson's views also. Here, like Bergson, he finds comedy a cure for "the malady of sameness, our modern malady," especially the sameness that drove us "in a body to Science the other day for an antidote." But science can tell us little of human life, simply because "we have little to learn of apes"; like Bergson, Meredith rejects the naïve nineteenth-century faith in laws of evolution. To cure our sameness, we must learn "to be alive, to be quick in the soul," and "there should be diversity in the companion-throbs of your pulses." Comedy teaches us to look at life exactly as it *is*, undulled by scientific theories. Comedy banishes "monstrous monotonousness." It teaches us to be responsive, to be honest, to interrogate ourselves and correct our pretentiousness. So the comic spirit is "born of our united social intelligence," which shows us "our individual countenances," and thus keeps us alive. The comic spirit is "the ultimate civilizer" in a dull, insensitive world. She watches our vanity, our sentimentalism, with a birch rod; she strips us of our affectations. "In Comedy is the singular scene of charity issuing of disdain under the stroke of honorable laughter."

Bergson would heartily agree, however his views may differ in detail. For both writers are really concerned with one *kind* of comedy—a kind that above all others was needed in the nineteenth century—

comedy of manners. And they both read into comedy of manners new "social" meanings.

This should not surprise us, since all the great writers of the nineteenth century—Stendhal and Thoreau, Mill and Dostoevsky, Arnold and Flaubert —sooner or later found themselves facing a cultural crisis in the middle-class: how to guard the person himself from his society. One cannot read Bergson's essay without remembering what Marx said in 1848: that the middle class has deprived man of his individuality and made him an appendage to the machine. Bergson, like Meredith, saw this very danger and remarked that "regulating life as a matter of business routine is more widespread than might be imagined." This "mechanization" (the word is Bergson's) is the quintessence of pedantry, which is "nothing else than art pretending to outdo nature." Bergson spent all his philosophy protesting against the mechanical, seeking to discern in us "the individuality that escapes our ken," attempting to protect what is inward and spontaneous from what is automatic. To Bergson laughter is an exposure of our *ready-made* gestures and values, and the comic figure is one who is not a man but, instead, a clockwork apparatus leading the special kind of life a puppet seems to have—"the malady of sameness," Meredith called it.

Bergson finds, also, that our mechanical behavior is one result of the division of labor (here let us invoke Adam Smith, not Marx). In his closing pages Bergson presents us with the modern comic type— the professional man who acts with rigidity. He thinks with the automatism of his business code; he has the egoism of the expert, the inhumanity of those who dwell inside the "small societies formed on the surface of Society at large." This comic figure

is identified by his "professional callousness," his inelasticity—which is a mode of pride. The automatic
responses of this egoist make him appear, when we
look at him attentively, like a ready-made product
standardized for the market. The motor-efficiencies
of the specialist (and we are now all specialists)
give him the aspect of one who is absent-minded,
or who is insensitive, incapable of authentic personality. He lives by formulas, not by animation, and
his behavior is a series of repetitions. But life should
be a negation of repetition. So we laugh at him.
Society holds over him the "threat of correction"
whenever he proves himself unadaptable. Here
Bergson could have relied upon Darwin's theory
that in the course of biological evolution the unadaptable perish. However, Bergson would be less
sympathetic to Darwin than to someone like John
Ruskin, who said the same thing about the ready-
made personalities of the nineteenth-century: "No
such thing as a Man," exclaimed Ruskin in *Fors
Clavigera,* "but only a Mechanism . . . you feel
yourself to be only a machine . . . and necessarily
recognize only major machinery as regulating *you.*"

  In his other works Bergson proposed again and
again that the meaning of human life is known only
by intuition, wrought only in the private existence
of the soul. Life is a vitality, a spontaneous, changing, personal response to each situation in which we
find ourselves. We cannot even define our deepest
experiences by reason, but live them in a special
psychological field Bergson called "duration" to distinguish it from clock-time, which measures our
history only from the outside. What is alive lives by
inward discoveries and intensities, not in the external world regulated by clock and calendar. What is
alive is not mechanical. What is mechanical suffers

a death of the heart. Bergson's comic figure of man lives in the world outside, in the field of vocation and specialized reaction. "And thus," said Browning in a poem, "we half-men struggle." To Browning's lurid eye the effort of these half-men was not comedy but melodrama. But Bergson sees us half-men as playing the comedy of modern life—for Bergson is really writing about comedy, not merely laughter.

His idea of comedy is but one aspect, then, of his larger philosophy of vitalism, and we can explain why his theory of the comic is very precise and, unlike the British appetite for humor, somewhat narrow. To Bergson's notion, a comic impasse occurs wherever a human being ceases to behave like a human being—that is, whenever he "resembles a piece of clockwork wound up once for all and capable of working automatically," but is incapable of living. The instant this automatic figure (who makes gestures but who cannot act of his own personal will) appears under the glare of our intelligence, he looks ridiculous, particularly when he is caught at an intersection of events where his automatic response is seen to be inadequate. Then he is isolated, in all his mechanical idiocy, facing unexpected demands; and we behold him as if he were set, like a type displayed, on a stage where he forfeits our sympathy. Comedy requires, for Bergson as it does for Stendhal, an insensitivity on the part of the beholder—an "anesthesia of the heart," which numbs our pity and allows us to examine, unsociably, someone who suddenly looks like a puppet. Together with other Frenchmen, Bergson looks backward to the bright theatre of Molière; but he finds his modern comic hero in the hollow man who is insulated by the confines of his business, speaking only the jargon of his enterprise, which he takes—"seriously" —as a substitute for living.

This sort of limitation or (what indeed it is) vanity is the point where, Bergson says, comic art touches life itself; and the spectacle of such vanity suggests that the automatic response is a vice, like "a curvature in the soul." Yet in closing Bergson makes the disconcerting statement that there is a difference between comedy and art, notably tragic art. Comedy oscillates between art and life because it looks at life from outside, and because laughter is an undulation on only the surface of existence. Bergson mentions, but refuses to consider further, the pessimism "which becomes the more pronounced as the laugher more closely analyzes his laughter." Tragedy, he says, is a heightened vision of life because it represents, as comedy cannot, the full life-history of a soul. Comedy is a "game" that imitates life; but only with the gestures of "types," not living beings. The automatic gesture can, however, reveal vice "in all its nakedness."

This brings us to Meredith's opinion that our vanities, pompousness, and kindred follies are the special sins chastened by the comic spirit in any cultivated society of men and women. For Meredith, too, comedy is a game; yet even if it is played in the narrow field of the drawing room, it is art. Meredith assigns to comedy richer values than does Bergson. Meredith demands no anesthesia of the heart, perhaps because he writes in the margins of that broad tradition of British humor, tolerant, outgoing, tinged by pathos since the days of Chaucer. Meredith is able to take the-world-as-it-is more genially than Bergson: "And to love Comedy," he insists, "you must know the real world, and know men and women well enough not to expect too much of them, though you may still hope for good." Meredith can "warmly" understand the plight of a Misanthrope like Molière's Alceste. It is not unexpected that Meredith should, like Bergson, turn to Molière to find the quintessence of comedy; but it is curious that Meredith should seem to appreciate Molière more cordially than Bergson. Is it because Meredith does not isolate Molière's characters from life and compassion, and because he feels that there are shadows of tragedy in the laugh of a great humorist? He knows that laughter is a complicated reaction, and that comedy can refine a human dilemma to a degree of pain. Meredith's comic spirit can regard man's failings over a wider range than mere mechanical absurdities. Meredith dares turn the eye of comedy inward upon vanities that are not exposed to the public. Too derisive a laughter spoils his comic effect. He is very sensitive to the intimate comedy we are playing alone, inside our vulnerable selves.

Thus Meredith finds in Molière a luminous sanity that is nothing less than a standard of morality: Molière has "the wit of wisdom," throwing fresh light everywhere. Meredith explains that the life of comedy "is in the idea"—and "the idea" is a vision of how ridiculously we behave when we are uncivilized; that is, when we are not sane. Whenever we are self-deceived, overblown, blinded by our pedantries, we deserve the scourge of the satirist or the grave verdict of the moralist. But Meredith's comic spirit is able to chasten us without rancor or sanctimony, for under the laugh this spirit exacts from us there is a taste of ashes—the ashes of humility, a pessimistic concession that mortals are apt to be fools in all sorts of ways, and we too, but for the grace of God. To Meredith's way of thinking, your

talent for comedy is measured by your "being able
to detect the ridicule of them you love, without loving them less: and more by being able to see yourself somewhat ridiculous in dear eyes, and accepting the correction their image of you proposes." So
the kindliness is not chilled; for when that happens,
we have slipped into the harsh grip of satire.

Yet comedy passes moral judgments, since our
vanities are barbarous. Witness Meredith's rebuke
to Sir Willoughby Patterne in *The Egoist*. This
glossy hero always assumed he had but to choose
among the ladies aspiring to be Lady Patterne. But
Sir Willoughby finds, to his affliction, that Clara
Middleton disengages herself, and he can save the
mere shell of his prestige only by exerting desperate
pressure upon Laetitia Dale to accept him. The fate
of the inordinate Sir Willoughby shows how comedy
reduces imposing figures. Here Meredith is at one
with Bergson, who thinks that "the specific remedy
for vanity is laughter, and that the one failing that
is essentially laughable is vanity." We master this
egoism by a watchful sanity that is morality in gay
disguise. The censure passed by the comic spirit is
civilized because it spares us "the bitter craving to
strike heavy blows." Meredith's comic faun is a sun-
lit creature who bids us love, and passionately love,
so long as we do not deceive ourselves by pretending
to feel what we do not feel; one foot's length of
pretence, and the lover's foot is caught in a trap.
The malice of this faun is honorable because it is
generous, granting the laughter no exemption from
the folly of the victim at whom he laughs. The joy
of Meredith's comedy is thoughtful; its mirth is not
noisy—a finely tempered smile, perhaps.

For all this, Meredith really gives us only slight,
scattered remarks compared with Bergson, whose

idea of comedy grows with the subtle but inevitable logic of living things into an intricate and poetic definition. The truth is that the two essays should be read together: since if Meredith does not have this logical finesse, he has the high-spirited affections that are congenial to the very temper of comedy. Meredith seems to find comedy more touchingly inherent in life than Bergson, who for all his wisdom imposes a silence on our pity. Meredith's laughter is somewhat more charitable and subdued by modesty. Neither Meredith nor any true Englishman could grant Bergson that "the comic appeals to the intelligence pure and simple." In fact, Bergson goes on to warn, "Laughter is incompatible with emotion. Depict some fault, however trifling, in such a way as to arouse sympathy, fear, or pity; the mischief is done, it is impossible for us to laugh." Nevertheless Bergson and Meredith are in deep agreement. Both, inclined to think of comedy as being comedy of manners, would have the comedian shun what is gross. Both take comedy as a game played in society. Both use it as a discipline of the self.

Bergson says that comedy can make us human and natural in the midst of mechanical societies. And Meredith implies that comedy can enlighten us and redeem us from our worst stupidity—the original sin of pride, or complacency. Both, in sum, believe that comedy is a premise to civilization. That is why these two essays, each in its own imaginative way, prove that comedy is not only a social game, but art.

WYLIE SYPHER

AN ESSAY ON COMEDY

★

George Meredith

Good comedies are such rare productions that, notwithstanding the wealth of our literature in the comic element, it would not occupy us long to run over the English list. If they are brought to the test I shall propose, very reputable comedies will be found unworthy of their station, like the ladies of Arthur's Court when they were reduced to the ordeal of the mantle.

There are plain reasons why the comic poet is not a frequent apparition, and why the great comic poet remains without a fellow. A society of cultivated men and women is required, wherein ideas are current, and the perceptions quick, that he may be supplied with matter and an audience. The semi-barbarism of merely giddy communities, and feverish emotional periods, repel him; and also a state of marked social inequality of the sexes; nor can he whose business is to address the mind be understood where there is not a moderate degree of intellectual activity.

Moreover, to touch and kindle the mind through laughter demands, more than sprightliness, a most subtle delicacy. That must be a natal gift in the comic poet. The substance he deals with will show him a startling exhibition of the dyer's hand, if he is without it. People are ready to surrender themselves to witty thumps on the back, breast, and sides; all except the head—and it is there that he aims. He must be subtle to penetrate. A corresponding acuteness must exist to welcome him. The necessity for the two conditions will explain how it is that we count him during centuries in the singular number.

'*C'est une étrange entreprise que celle de faire rire les honnêtes gens,*' Molière says; and the difficulty of the undertaking cannot be overestimated.

Then again, he is beset with foes to right and left, of a character unknown to the tragic and the lyric poet, or even to philosophers.

We have in this world men whom Rabelais would call 'agelasts'; that is to say, non-laughers—men who are in that respect as dead bodies, which, if you prick them, do not bleed. The old gray boulder-stone, that has finished its peregrination from the rock to the valley, is as easily to be set rolling up again as these men laughing. No collision of circumstances in our mortal career strikes a light for them. It is but one step from being agelastic to misogelastic, and the μισόγελως, the laughter-hating, soon learns to dignify his dislike as an objection in morality.

We have another class of men who are pleased to consider themselves antagonists of the foregoing, and whom we may term 'hypergelasts'; the excessive laughers, ever-laughing, who are as clappers of a bell, that may be rung by a breeze, a grimace; who are so loosely put together that a wink will shake them.

C'est n'estimer rien qu'estimer tout le monde;

and to laugh at everything is to have no appreciation of the comic of comedy.

Neither of these distinct divisions of non-laughers and over-laughters would be entertained by reading *The Rape of the Lock,* or seeing a performance of *Le Tartuffe.* In relation to the stage, they have taken in our land the form and title of Puritan and

Bacchanalian; for though the stage is no longer a public offender, and Shakespeare has been revived on it, to give it nobility, we have not yet entirely raised it above the contention of these two parties. Our speaking on the theme of comedy will appear almost a libertine proceeding to one, while the other will think that the speaking of it seriously brings us into violent contrast with the subject.

Comedy, we have to admit, was never one of the most honored of the Muses. She was in her origin, short of slaughter, the loudest expression of the little civilization of men. The light of Athene over the head of Achilles illuminates the birth of Greek tragedy. But comedy rolled in shouting under the divine protection of the Son of the Wine-jar, as Dionysus is made to proclaim himself by Aristophanes. Our second Charles was the patron, of like benignity, of our Comedy of Manners, which began similarly as a combative performance, under a license to deride and outrage the Puritan, and was here and there Bacchanalian beyond the Aristophanic example—worse, inasmuch as a cynical licentiousness is more abominable than frank filth. An eminent Frenchman judges, from the quality of some of the stuff dredged up for the laughter of men and women who sat through an Athenian comic play, that they could have had small delicacy in other affairs, when they had so little in their choice of entertainment. Perhaps he does not make sufficient allowance for the regulated license of plain-speaking proper to the festival of the god, and claimed by the comic poet as his inalienable right, or for the fact that it was a festival in a season of license, in a city accustomed to give ear to the boldest utterance of both sides of a case. However that may be, there can be no question that the men and women who sat through the acting of Wycherley's *Country Wife* were past blushing. Our tenacity of national impressions has caused the word 'theatre' since then to prod the Puritan nervous system like a satanic instrument; just as one has known anti-papists for whom Smithfield was redolent of a sinister smoke, as though they had a later recollection of the place than the lowing herds. Hereditary Puritanism regarding the stage is met, to this day, in many families quite undistinguished by arrogant piety. It has subsided altogether as a power in the profession of morality; but it is an error to suppose it extinct, and unjust also to forget that it had once good reason to hate, shun, and rebuke our public shows.

We shall find ourselves about where the comic spirit would place us, if we stand at middle distance between the inveterate opponents and the drum-and-fife supporters of comedy. '[*Celui qui s'arrête*] *fait remarquer l'emportement des autres, comme un point fixe,*' as Pascal says. And were there more in this position, comic genius would flourish.

Our English idea of a comedy of manners might be imaged in the person of a blowsy country girl— say Hoyden, the daughter of Sir Tunbelly Clumsey, who, when at home, never disobeyed her father except in the 'eating of green gooseberries'—transforming to a varnished city madam, with a loud laugh and a mincing step; the crazy ancestress of an accountably fallen descendant. She bustles prodigiously, and is punctually smart in her speech, always in a fluster to escape from Dulness, as they say the dogs on the Nile-banks drink at the river running to avoid the crocodile. If the monster catches her, as at times he does, she whips him to a froth, so that those who know Dulness only as a thing of ponderousness shall fail to recognize him in that light and airy shape.

When she has frolicked through her five acts, to surprise you with the information that Mr. Aimwell is converted by a sudden death in the world outside the scenes into Lord Aimwell, and can marry the lady in the light of day, it is to the credit of her vivacious nature that she does not anticipate your calling her Farce. Five is dignity with a trailing robe; whereas one, two, or three acts would be short skirts, and degrading. Advice has been given to householders that they should follow up the shot at a burglar in the dark by hurling the pistol after it, so that if the bullet misses, the weapon may strike, and assure the rascal he has it. The point of her wit is in this fashion supplemented by the rattle of her tongue, and effectively, according to the testimony of her admirers. Her wit is at once, like steam in an engine, the motive force and the warning whistle of her headlong course; and it vanishes like the track of steam when she has reached her terminus, never troubling the brains afterward; a merit that it shares with good wine, to the joy of the Bacchanalians.

As to this wit, it is warlike. In the neatest hands it is like the sword of the cavalier in the Mall, quick to flash out upon slight provocation, and for a similar office—to wound. Commonly its attitude is entirely pugilistic; two blunt fists rallying and countering. When harmless, as when the word 'fool' occurs, or allusions to the state of husband, it has the sound of the smack of harlequin's wand upon clown, and is to the same extent exhilarating. Believe that idle, empty laughter is the most desirable of recreations, and significant comedy will seem pale and shallow in comparison. Our popular idea would be hit by the sculptured group of Laughter holding both his

sides, while Comedy pummels, by way of tickling
him. As to a meaning, she holds that it does not
conduce to making merry; you might as well carry
cannon on a racing-yacht. Morality is a duenna to
be circumvented. This was the view of English comedy of a sagacious essayist, who said that the end of
a comedy would often be the commencement of a
tragedy, were the curtain to rise again on the per-
formers. In those old days female modesty was protected by a fan, behind which—and it was of a
convenient semicircular breadth—the ladies present
in the theatre retired at a signal of decorum, to peep,
covertly askant, or with the option of so peeping,
through a prettily-fringed eyelet-hole in the eclips-
ing arch.

> Ego limis specto
> sic per flabellum clanculum.
> —TERENCE.

That fan is the flag and symbol of the society giving
us our so-called Comedy of Manners, or comedy of
the manners of South-Sea islanders under city ve-
neer; and, as to comic idea, vacuous as the mask
without the face behind it.

Elia, whose humor delighted in floating a galleon
paradox, and wafting it as far as it would go, bewails
the extinction of our artificial comedy, like a poet
sighing over the vanished splendor of Cleopatra's
Nile-barge; and the sedateness of his plea, for a
cause condemned even in his time to the peniten-
tiary, is a novel effect of the ludicrous. When the
realism of those 'fictitious, half-believed personages,'
as he calls them, had ceased to strike, they were
objectionable company, uncaressable as puppets.
Their artifices are staringly naked, and have now
the effect of a painted face, viewed, after warm

hours of dancing, in the morning light. How could the Lurewells and the Plyants ever have been praised for ingenuity in wickedness? Critics apparently sober, and of high reputation, held up their shallow knaveries for the world to admire. These Lurewells, Plyants, Pinchwifes, Fondlewifes, Miss Prue, Peggy, Hoyden, all of them save charming Millamant, are dead as last year's clothes in a fashionable fine lady's wardrobe; and it must be an exceptionably abandoned Abigail of our period that would look on them with the wish to appear in their likeness. Whether the puppet-show of Punch and Judy inspires our street-urchins to have instant recourse to their fists in a dispute, after the fashion of every one of the actors in that public entertainment who gets possession of the cudgel, is open to question; it has been hinted; and angry moralists have traced the national taste for tales of crime to the smell of blood in our nursery-songs. It will at any rate hardly be questioned that it is unwholesome for men and women to see themselves as they are, if they are no better than they should be; and they will not, when they have improved in manners, care much to see themselves as they once were. That comes of realism in the comic art; and it is not public caprice, but the consequence of a bettering state. The same of an immoral may be said [as] of realistic exhibitions of a vulgar society.

The French make a critical distinction in *ce qui remue* from *ce qui émeut*—that which agitates from that which touches with emotion. In the realistic comedy it is an incessant *remuage;* no calm—merely bustling figures—and no thought. Excepting Congreve's *Way of the World,* which failed on the stage, there was nothing to keep our comedy alive on its merits; neither, with all its realism, true portraiture, nor much quotable fun, nor idea; neither salt nor soul.

The French have a school of stately comedy to which they can fly for renovation whenever they have fallen away from it; and their having such a school is mainly the reason why, as John Stuart Mill pointed out, they know men and women more accurately than we do. Molière followed the Horatian precept, to observe the manners of his age, and give his characters the color befitting them at the time. He did not paint in raw realism. He seized his characters firmly for the central purpose of the play, stamped them in the idea, and, by slightly raising and softening the object of study (as in the case of the ex-Huguenot, Duc de Montausier, for the study of the Misanthrope, and, according to Saint-Simon, the Abbé Roquette for Tartuffe), generalized upon it so as to make it permanently human. Concede that it is natural for human creatures to live in society, and Alceste is an imperishable mark of one, though he is drawn in light outline, without any forcible human coloring.

Our English school has not clearly imagined society; and of the mind hovering above congregated men and women it has imagined nothing. The critics who praise it for its downrightness, and for bringing the situations home to us, as they admiringly say, cannot but disapprove of Molière's comedy, which appeals to the individual mind to perceive and participate in the social. We have splendid tragedies, we have the most beautiful of poetic plays, and we have literary comedies passingly pleasant to read, and occasionally to see acted. By literary comedies, I mean comedies of classic inspiration, drawn chiefly from Menander and the Greek New Comedy through Terence; or else comedies of the poet's personal conception, that have had no model in life, and are humorous exaggerations, happy or otherwise. These are the comedies of Ben Jonson, Massinger, and Fletcher. Massinger's Justice Greedy we can all of us refer to a type, 'with good capon lined,' that has been, and will be; and he would be comic, as Panurge is comic, but only a Rabelais could set him moving with real animation. Probably Justice Greedy would be comic to the audience of a country booth, and to some of our friends. If we have lost our youthful relish for the presentation of characters put together to fit a type, we find it hard to put together the mechanism of a civil smile at his enumeration of his dishes. Something of the same is to be said of Bobadill, swearing 'by the foot of Pharaoh'; with a reservation, for he is made to move faster, and to act. The comic of Jonson is a scholar's excogitation of the comic; that of Massinger a moralist's.

Shakespeare is a well-spring of characters which are saturated with the comic spirit; with more of what we will call blood-life than is to be found anywhere out of Shakespeare; and they are of this world, but they are of the world enlarged to our embrace by imagination, and by great poetic imagination. They are, as it were—I put it to suit my present comparison—creatures of the woods and wilds, not in walled towns, not grouped and toned to pursue a comic exhibition of the narrower world of society. Jaques, Falstaff and his regiment, the varied troop of clowns, Malvolio, Sir Hugh Evans and Fluellen (marvelous Welshmen!) Benedick and Beatrice, Dogberry, and the rest, are subjects of a special study in the poetically comic.

His comedy of incredible imbroglio belongs to the literary section. One may conceive that there was a natural resemblance between him and Menander, both in the scheme and style of his lighter plays. Had Shakespeare lived in a later and less emotional, less heroical, period of our history, he might have turned to the painting of manners as well as humanity. Euripides would probably, in the time of Menander, when Athens was enslaved but prosperous, have lent his hand to the composition of romantic comedy. He certainly inspired that fine genius.

Politically, it is accounted a misfortune for France that her nobles thronged to the Court of Louis Quatorze. It was a boon to the comic poet. He had that lively quicksilver world of the animalcule passions, the huge pretensions, the placid absurdities, under his eyes in full activity; vociferous quacks and snapping dupes, hypocrites, posturers, extravagants, pedants, rose-pink ladies and mad grammarians, sonnetteering marquises, highflying mistresses, plain-minded maids, interthreading as in a loom, noisy as at a fair. A simply bourgeois circle will not furnish it, for the middle class must have the brilliant, flippant, independent upper for a spur and a pattern; otherwise it is likely to be inwardly dull, as well as outwardly correct. Yet, though the King was benevolent toward Molière, it is not to the French Court that we are indebted for his unrivaled studies of mankind in society. For the amusement of the Court the ballets and farces were written, which are dearer to the rabble upper, as to the rabble lower, class than intellectual comedy. The French bourgeoisie of Paris were sufficiently quick-witted and enlightened by education to welcome great works like *Le Tartuffe*, *Les Femmes Savantes*, and *Le Misanthrope*, works that were perilous ventures on the popular intelligence, big vessels to launch on streams running to shallows. The *Tartuffe* hove into view as an enemy's vessel; it offended, not '*Dieu, mais . . . les dévots,*' as the Prince de Condé explained the cabal raised against it to the King.

The *Femmes Savantes* is a capital instance of the uses of comedy in teaching the world to understand what ails it. The farce of the *Précieuses* ridiculed, and put a stop to, the monstrous romantic jargon made popular by certain famous novels. The comedy of the *Femmes Savantes* exposed the later and less apparent, but more finely comic, absurdity of an excessive purism in grammar and diction, and the tendency to be idiotic in precision. The French had felt the burden of this new nonsense; but they had to see the comedy several times before they were consoled in their suffering by seeing the cause of it exposed.

The *Misanthrope* was yet more frigidly received. Molière thought it dead. 'I can not improve on it, and assuredly never shall,' he said. It is one of the French titles to honor that this quintessential comedy of the opposition of Alceste and Célimène was ultimately understood and applauded. In all countries the middle class presents the public which, fighting the world, and with a good footing in the fight, knows the world best. It may be the most selfish, but that is a question leading us into sophistries. Cultivated men and women who do not skim the cream of life, and are attached to the duties, yet escape the harsher blows, make acute and balanced observers. Molière is their poet.

Of this class in England, a large body, neither Puritan nor Bacchanalian, have a sentimental objection to face the study of the actual world. They take up disdain of it, when its truths appear humiliating; when the facts are not immediately forced on them, they take up the pride of incredulity. They live in a hazy atmosphere that they suppose an ideal one. Humorous writing they will endure, perhaps approve, if it mingles with pathos to shake and elevate the feelings. They approve of satire, because, like the beak of the vulture, it smells of carrion, which they are not. But of comedy they have a shivering dread, for comedy enfolds them with the wretched host of the world, huddles them with us all in an ignoble assimilation, and cannot be used by any exalted variety as a scourge and a broom. Nay, to be an exalted variety is to come under the calm, curious eye of the Comic Spirit, and be probed for what you are. Men are seen among them, and very many cultivated women. You may distinguish them by a favorite phrase: 'Surely we are not so bad!' and the remark: 'If that is human nature, save us from it!'— as if it could be done; but in the peculiar paradise of the wilful people who will not see, the exclamation assumes the saving grace.

Yet, should you ask them whether they dislike sound sense, they vow they do not. And question cultivated women whether it pleases them to be shown moving on an intellectual level with men, they will answer that it does; numbers of them claim the situation. Now comedy is the fountain of sound sense; not the less perfectly sound on account of the sparkle; and comedy lifts women to a station offering them free play for their wit, as they usually show it, when they have it, on the side of sound sense. The higher the comedy, the more prominent the part they enjoy in it. Dorine in the *Tartuffe* is common sense incarnate, though palpably a waiting-maid. Célimène is undisputed mistress of the same attribute in the *Misanthrope;* wiser as a woman than Alceste as man. In Congreve's *Way of the*

World, Millamant overshadows Mirabell, the sprightliest male figure of English comedy.

But those two ravishing women, so copious and so choice of speech, who fence with men and pass their guard, are heartless! Is it not preferable to be the pretty idiot, the passive beauty, the adorable bundle of caprices, very feminine, very sympathetic, of romantic and sentimental fiction? Our women are taught to think so. The Agnès of the *École des Femmes* should be a lesson for men. The heroines of comedy are like women of the world, not necessarily heartless from being clear-sighted; they seem so to the sentimentally reared, only for the reason that they use their wits, and are not wandering vessels crying for a captain or a pilot. Comedy is an exhibition of their battle with men, and that of men with them; and as the two, however divergent, both look on one object, namely, life, the gradual similarity of their impressions must bring them to some resemblance. The comic poet dares to show us men and women coming to this mutual likeness; he is for saying that when they draw together in social life their minds grow liker; just as the philosopher discerns the similarity of boy and girl, until the girl is marched away to the nursery. Philosopher and comic poet are of a cousinship in the eye they cast on life; and they are equally unpopular with our wilful English of the hazy region and the ideal that is not to be disturbed.

Thus, for want of instruction in the comic idea, we lose a large audience among our cultivated middle class that we should expect to support comedy. The sentimentalist is as averse as the Puritan and as the Bacchanalian.

Our traditions are unfortunate. The public taste is with the idle laughers, and still inclines to follow them. It may be shown by an analysis of Wycherley's *Plain Dealer,* a coarse prose adaption of the *Misanthrope,* stuffed with lumps of realism in a vulgarized theme to hit the mark of English appetite, that we have in it the key-note of the comedy of our stage. It is Molière travestied, with the hoof to his foot, and hair on the pointed tip of his ear. And how difficult it is for writers to disentangle themselves from bad traditions is noticeable when we find Goldsmith, who had grave command of the comic in narrative, producing an elegant farce for a comedy; and Fielding, who was a master of the comic both in narrative and in dialogue, not even approaching to the presentable in farce.

These bad traditions of comedy affect us, not only on the stage, but in our literature, and may be tracked into our social life. They are the ground of the heavy moralizings by which we are outwearied, about life as a comedy, and comedy as a jade, when popular writers, conscious of fatigue in creativeness, desire to be cogent in a modish cynicism; perversions of the idea of life, and of the proper esteem for the society we have wrested from brutishness, and would carry higher. Stock images of this description are accepted by the timid and the sensitive, as well as by the saturnine, quite seriously; for not many look abroad with their own eyes—fewer still have the habit of thinking for themselves. Life, we know too well, is not a comedy, but something strangely mixed; nor is comedy a vile mask. The corrupted importation from France was noxious, a noble entertainment spoilt to suit the wretched taste of a villainous age; and the later imitations of it, partly drained of its poison and made decorous, became tiresome, notwithstanding their fun, in the perpetual recurring of the same situations, owing to the absence of original study and vigor of conception. Scene 5, Act 2, of the *Misanthrope,* owing, no doubt, to the fact of our not producing matter for original study, is repeated in succession by Wycherley, Congreve, and Sheridan, and, as it is at second hand, we have it done cynically—or such is the tone —in the manner of 'below stairs.' Comedy thus treated may be accepted as a version of the ordinary worldly understanding of our social life; at least, in accord with the current dicta concerning it. The epigrams can be made; but it is uninstructive, rather tending to do disservice. Comedy justly treated, as you find it in Molière, whom we so clownishly mishandled—the comedy of Molière throws no infamous reflection upon life. It is deeply conceived, in the first place, and therefore it cannot be impure. Meditate on that statement. Never did man wield so shrieking a scourge upon vice; but his consummate self-mastery is not shaken while administering it. Tartuffe and Harpagon, in fact, are made each to whip himself and his class—the false pietists, and the insanely covetous. Molière has only set them in motion. He strips Folly to the skin, displays the imposture of the creature, and is content to offer her better clothing, with the lesson Chrysale reads to Philaminte and Bélise. He conceives purely, and he writes purely, in the simplest language, the simplest of French verse. The source of his wit is clear reason; it is a fountain of that soil, and it springs to vindicate reason, common sense, rightness, and justice—for no vain purpose ever. The wit is of such pervading spirit that it inspires a pun with meaning and interest. His moral does not hang like a tail, or preach from one character incessantly cocking an eye at the audience, as in recent realistic French plays, but is in the heart of his work, throbbing with every pulsation of an organic structure. If life is likened to the comedy of Molière, there is no scandal in the comparison.

Congreve's *Way of the World* is an exception to our other comedies, his own among them, by virtue of the remarkable brilliancy of the writing, and the figure of Millamant. The comedy has no idea in it, beyond the stale one that so the world goes; and it concludes with the jaded discovery of a document at a convenient season for the descent of the curtain. A plot was an afterthought with Congreve. By the help of a wooden villain (Maskwell), marked gallows to the flattest eye, he gets a sort of plot in *The Double-Dealer*. His *Way of the World* might be called 'The Conquest of a Town Coquette'; and Millamant is a perfect portrait of a coquette, both in her resistance to Mirabell and the manner of her surrender, and also in her tongue. The wit here is not so salient as in certain passages of *Love for Love*, where Valentine feigns madness, or retorts on his father, or Mrs. Frail rejoices in the harmlessness of wounds to a woman's virtue, if she keeps them 'from air.' In *The Way of the World*, it appears less prepared in the smartness, and is more diffused in the more characteristic style of the speakers. Here, however, as elsewhere, his famous wit is like a bully-fencer, not ashamed to lay traps for its exhibition, transparently petulant for the train between certain ordinary words and the powder-magazine of the improprieties to be fired. Contrast the wit of Congreve with Molière's. That of the first is a Toledo blade, sharp, and wonderfully supple for steel; cast for dueling, restless in the scabbard, being so pretty when out of it. To shine, it must have an adversary. Molière's wit is like a running brook, with innumerable fresh lights on it at every turn of the wood through which its business is to find a way. It does not run in search of obstructions, to be noisy over them; but when dead leaves and viler substances are heaped along the course, its natural song is heightened. Without effort, and with no dazzling flashes of achievement, it is full of healing, the wit of good breeding, the wit of wisdom.

'Genuine humor and true wit,' says Landor, 'require a sound and capacious mind, which is always a grave one. . . . Rabelais and La Fontaine are recorded by their countrymen to have been *rêveurs*. Few men have been graver than Pascal; few have been wittier.' To apply the citation of so great a brain as Pascal's to our countryman would be unfair. Congreve had a certain soundness of mind; of capacity, in the sense intended by Landor, he had little. Judging him by his wit, he performed some happy thrusts; and, taking it for genuine, it is a surface wit, neither rising from a depth nor flowing from a spring:

On voit qu'il se travaille à dire de bons mots.

He drives the poor hack-word, 'fool,' as cruelly to the market for wit as any of his competitors. Here is an example, that has been held up for eulogy:

WITWOUD. He has brought me a letter from the fool my brother. . . .
MIRABELL. A fool, and your brother, Witwoud!
WITWOUD. Ay, ay, my half-brother. My half-brother he is; no nearer, upon honor.
MIRABELL. Then 'tis possible he may be but half a fool.

—By evident preparation. This is a sort of wit one remembers to have heard at school, of a brilliant outsider; perhaps to have been guilty of oneself a trifle later. It was, no doubt, a blaze of intellectual fireworks to the bumpkin squire who came to London to go to the theatre and learn manners.

Where Congreve excels all his English rivals is in his literary force, and a succinctness of style peculiar to him. He had correct judgment, a correct ear, readiness of illustration within a narrow range—in snap-shots of the obvious at the obvious—and copious language. He hits the mean of a fine style and a natural in dialogue. He is at once precise and voluble. If you have ever thought upon style, you will acknowledge it to be a signal accomplishment. In this he is a classic, and is worthy of treading a measure with Molière. *The Way of the World* may be read out currently at a first glance, so sure are the accents of the emphatic meaning to strike the eye, perforce of the crispness and cunning polish of the sentences. You have not to look over them before you confide yourself to him; he will carry you safe. Sheridan imitated, but was far from surpassing, him. The flow of boudoir billingsgate in Lady Wishfort is unmatched for the vigor and pointedness of the tongue. It spins along with a final ring, like the voice of Nature in a fury, and is, indeed, racy eloquence of the elevated fishwife.

Millamant is an admirable, almost a lovable, heroine. It is a piece of genius in a writer to make a woman's manner of speech portray her. You feel sensible of her presence in every line of her speaking. The stipulations with her lover in view of marriage, her fine lady's delicacy, and fine lady's easy evasions of indelicacy, coquettish airs, and playing with irresolution, which in a common maid would be bashfulness, until she submits to 'dwindle into a wife,' as she says, form a picture that lives in the frame, and is in harmony with Mirabell's description of her:

Here she comes, i' faith, full sail, with her fan spread
and her streamers out, and a shoal of fools for tenders.

And, after an interview:

Think of you? To think of a whirlwind, though 't were
in a whirlwind, were a case of more steady contempla-
tion; a very tranquillity of mind and mansion.

There is a picturesqueness, as of Millamant and no
other, in her voice, when she is encouraged to take
Mirabell by Mrs. Fainall, who is 'sure' she has 'a
mind to him':

MILLAMANT. Are you? I think I have—and the horrid
man looks as if he thought so too.—

One hears the tones, and sees the sketch and color
of the whole scene, in reading it.

Célimène is behind Millamant in vividness. An
air of bewitching whimsicality hovers over the
graces of this comic heroine, like the lively conversa-
tional play of a beautiful mouth. But in wit she is no
rival of Célimène. What she utters adds to her personal witchery, and is not further memorable. She is
a flashing portrait, and a type of the superior ladies
who do not think, not of those who do. In representing a class, therefore, it is a lower class, in the
proportion that one of Gainsborough's full-length
aristocratic women is below the permanent impres-
siveness of a fair Venetian head.

Millamant, side by side with Célimène, is an example of how far the realistic painting of a character
can be carried to win our favor, and of where it falls
short. Célimène is a woman's mind in movement,
armed with an ungovernable wit; with perspica-
cious, clear eyes for the world, and a very distinct
knowledge that she belongs to the world, and is most
at home in it. She is attracted to Alceste by her

esteem for his honesty; she cannot avoid seeing where the good sense of the man is diseased.

Rousseau, in his letter to D'Alembert on the subject of the *Misanthrope*, discusses the character of Alceste as though Molière had put him forth for an absolute example of misanthropy; whereas Alceste is only a misanthrope of the circle he finds himself placed in—he has a touching faith in the virtue residing in the country, and a critical love of sweet simpleness. Nor is he the principal person of the comedy to which he gives a name. He is only passively comic. Célimène is the active spirit. While he is denouncing and railing, the trial is imposed upon her to make the best of him, and control herself, as much as a witty woman, eagerly courted, can do. By appreciating him she practically confesses her faultiness, and she is better disposed to meet him half-way than he is to bend an inch; only she is *'une âme de vingt ans,'* the world is pleasant, and, if the gilded flies of the Court are silly, uncompromising fanatics have their ridiculous features as well. Can she abandon the life they make agreeable to her, for a man who will not be guided by the common sense of his class, and who insists on plunging into one extreme—equal to suicide in her eyes—to avoid another? That is the comic question of the *Misanthrope*. Why will he not continue to mix with the world smoothly, appeased by the flattery of her secret and really sincere preference of him, and taking his revenge in satire of it, as she does from her own not very loftly standard, and will by and by do from his more exalted one?

Célimène is worldliness; Alceste is unworldliness. It does not quite imply unselfishness; and that is perceived by her shrewd head. Still, he is a very uncommon figure in her circle, and she esteems him,

'*l'homme aux rubans verts*,' who 'sometimes diverts,'
but more often horribly vexes her—as she can say of
him when her satirical tongue is on the run. Unhap-
pily the soul of truth in him, which wins her esteem,
refuses to be tamed, or silent, or unsuspicious, and is
the perpetual obstacle to their good accord. He is
that melancholy person, the critic of everybody save
himself; intensely sensitive to the faults of others,
wounded by them; in love with his own indubitable
honesty, and with his ideal of the simpler form of
life befitting it—qualities which constitute the satirist. He is a Jean Jacques of the Court. His proposal
to Célimène, when he pardons her, that she should
follow him in flying humankind, and his frenzy of
detestation of her at her refusal, are thoroughly in
the mood of Jean Jacques. He is an impracticable
creature of a priceless virtue; but Célimène may
feel that to fly with him to the desert (that is, from
the Court to the country),

Où d'être homme d'honneur on ait la liberté,

she is likely to find herself the companion of a starv-
ing satirist, like that poor princess who ran away
with the waiting-man, and, when both were hungry
in the forest, was ordered to give him flesh. She is a
fieffée coquette, rejoicing in her wit and her attractions, and distinguished by her inclination for Alceste in the midst of her many other lovers; only she
finds it hard to cut them off—what woman with a
train does not?—and when the exposure of her
naughty wit has laid her under their rebuke, she will
do the utmost she can: she will give her hand to
honesty, but she cannot quite abandon worldliness.
She would be unwise if she did.

The fable is thin. Our pungent contrivers of plots
would see no indication of life in the outlines. The

life of the comedy is in the idea. As with the singing of the skylark out of sight, you must love the bird
to be attentive to the song, so in this highest flight o f
the comic Muse, you must love pure comedy warmly⁷
to understand the *Misanthrope;* you must be recep-·
tive of the idea of comedy. And to love comedy you
must know the real world, and know men and
women well enough not to expect too much of them,
though you may still hope for good.

Menander wrote a comedy called *Misogynes,*
said to have been the most celebrated of his works.
This misogynist is a married man, according to the
fragment surviving, and is a hater of women through
hatred of his wife. He generalizes upon them from
the example of this lamentable adjunct of his for-
tunes, and seems to have got the worst of it in the
contest with her, which is like the issue in reality in
the polite world. He seems also to have deserved it,
which may be as true to the copy. But we are unable
to say whether the wife was a good voice of her sex;
or how far Menander in this instance raised the idea
of woman from the mire it was plunged into by the
comic poets, or rather satiric dramatists, of the middle period of Greek comedy preceding him and the
New Comedy, who devoted their wit chiefly to the
abuse, and, for a diversity, to the eulogy of extra-
mural ladies of conspicuous fame. Menander idealized them, without purposely elevating. He satirized
a certain Thais, and his Thais of the *Eunuchus* of
Terence is neither professionally attractive nor re-
pulsive; his picture of the two Andrians, Chrysis and
her sister, is nowhere to be matched for tenderness.
But the condition of honest women in his day did
not permit of the freedom of action and fencing dia-
lectic of a Célimène, and consequently it is below
our mark of pure comedy.

Sainte-Beuve conjures up the ghost of Menander saying: 'For the love of me love Terence.' It is through love of Terence that moderns are able to love Menander; and what is preserved of Terence has not, apparently, given us the best of the friend of Epicurus. Μισούμενος, the lover taken in horror, and Περικειρομένη, the damsel shorn of her locks, have a promising sound for scenes of jealousy and a too masterful display of lordly authority, leading to regrets of the kind known to intemperate men who imagined they were fighting with the weaker, as the fragments indicate.

Of the six comedies of Terence, four are derived from Menander; two, the *Hecyra* and the *Phormio,* from Apollodorus. These two are inferior, in comic action and the peculiar sweetness of Menander, to the *Andria,* the *Adelphi,* the *Heauton Timorumenos,* and the *Eunuchus;* but Phormio is a more dashing and amusing convivial parasite than the Gnatho of the last-named comedy. There were numerous rivals of whom we know next to nothing (except by the quotations of Athenaeus and Plutarch, and the Greek grammarians who cited them to support a dictum) in this, as in the preceding periods of comedy in Athens; for Menander's plays are counted by many scores, and they were crowned by the prize only eight times. The favorite poet with critics, in Greece as in Rome, was Menander; and if some of his rivals here and there surpassed him in comic force, and outstripped him in competition by an appositeness to the occasion that had previously in the same way deprived the genius of Aristophanes of its due reward in *Clouds* and *Birds,* his position as chief of the comic poets of his age was unchallenged. Plutarch very unnecessarily drags Aristophanes into a comparison with him, to the confusion of the older poet. Their aims, the matter they dealt in, and the times, were quite dissimilar. But it is no wonder that Plutarch, writing when Athenian beauty of style was the delight of his patrons, should rank Menander at the highest. In what degree of faithfulness Terence copied Menander—whether, as he states of the passage in the *Adelphi* taken from Diphilus, *'verbum de verbo'* in the lovelier scenes (the description of the last words of the dying Andrian, and of her funeral, for instance)—remains conjectural. For us, Terence shares with his master the praise of an amenity that is like Elysian speech, equable and ever gracious; like the face of the Andrian's young sister:

> Adeo modesto, adeo venusto, ut nil supra.

The celebrated *'flens quam familiariter,'* of which the closest rendering grounds hopelessly on harsh prose, to express the sorrowful confidingness of a young girl who has lost her sister and dearest friend, and has but her lover left to her—'she turned and flung herself on his bosom, weeping as though at home there'—this our instinct tells us must be Greek, though hardly finer in Greek. Certain lines of Terence, compared with the original fragments, show that he embellished them; but his taste was too exquisite for him to do other than devote his genius to the honest translation of such pieces as the above. Menander, then; with him, through the affinity of sympathy, Terence; and Shakespeare and Molière, have this beautiful translucency of language. And the study of the comic poets might be recommended if for that only.

A singular ill fate befell the writings of Menander. What we have of him in Terence was chosen probably to please the cultivated Romans, and is a romantic play with a comic intrigue, obtained in two instances, the *Andria* and the *Eunuchus*, by rolling a couple of his originals into one. The titles of certain of the lost plays indicate the comic illumining character; a *Self-Pitier*, a *Self-Chastiser*, an *Ill-tempered Man*, a *Superstitious*, an *Incredulous*, etc., point to suggestive domestic themes. Terence forwarded manuscript translations from Greece that suffered shipwreck; he, who could have restored the treasure, died on the way home. The zealots of Byzantium completed the work of destruction. So we have the four comedies of Terence, numbering six of Menander, with a few sketches of plots (one of them, the *Thesaurus*, introduces a miser, whom we should have liked to contrast with Harpagon), and a multitude of small fragments of a sententious cast, fitted for quotation. Enough remains to make his greatness felt.

Without undervaluing other writers of comedy, I think it may be said that Menander and Molière stand alone specially as comic poets of the feelings and the idea. In each of them there is a conception of the comic that refines even to pain, as in the Menedemus of the *Heauton Timorumenos*, and in the Misanthrope. Menander and Molière have given the principal types to comedy hitherto. The Micio and Demea of the *Adelphi*, with their opposing views of the proper management of youth, are still alive; the Sganarelles and Arnolphes of the *École des Maris* and the *École des Femmes* are not all buried. Tartuffe is the father of the hypocrites; Orgon of the dupes; Thraso of the braggadocios; Alceste of the 'Manlys'; Davus and Syrus of the intriguing valets, the Scapins and Figaros. Ladies that soar in the realms of rose-pink, whose language wears the nodding plumes of intellectual conceit, are traceable to Philaminte and Bélise of the *Femmes Savantes;* and the mordant, witty women have the tongue of Célimène. The reason is that these two poets idealized upon life; the foundation of their types is real and in the quick, but they painted with spiritual strength, which is the solid in art.

The idealistic conception of comedy gives breadth and opportunities of daring to comic genius, and helps to solve the difficulties it creates. How, for example, shall an audience be assured that an evident and monstrous dupe is actually deceived without being an absolute fool? In *Le Tartuffe* the note of high comedy strikes when Orgon on his return home hears of his idol's excellent appetite. '*Le pauvre homme!*' he exclaims. He is told that the wife of his bosom has been unwell. '*Et Tartuffe?*' he asks, impatient to hear him spoken of, his mind suffused with the thought of Tartuffe, crazy with tenderness; and again he croons: '*Le pauvre homme!*' It is the mother's cry of pitying delight at a nurse's recital of the feats in young animal gluttony of her cherished infant. After this master-stroke of the comic, you not only put faith in Orgon's roseate prepossession, you share it with him by comic sympathy, and can listen with no more than a tremble of the laughing-muscles to the instance he gives of the sublime humanity of Tartuffe:

> Un rien presque suffit pour le scandaliser,
> Jusque-là qu'il se vint, l'autre jour, accuser
> D'avoir pris une puce en faisant sa prière,
> Et de l'avoir tuée avec trop de colère.

'And to have killed it too wrathfully'! Translating Molière is like humming an air one has heard performed by an accomplished violinist of the pure tones without flourish.

Orgon awakening to find another dupe in Madame Pernelle, incredulous of the revelations which have at last opened his own besotted eyes, is a scene of the double comic, vivified by the spell previously cast on the mind. There we feel the power of the poet's creation; and, in the sharp light of that sudden turn, the humanity is livelier than any realistic work can make it.

Italian comedy gives many hints for a Tartuffe; but they may be found in Boccaccio, as well as in Machiavelli's *Mandragola*. The Frate Timoteo of this piece is only a very oily friar, compliantly assisting an intrigue with ecclesiastical sophisms (to use the mildest word) for payment. Frate Timoteo has a fine Italian priestly pose:

DONNA. Credete voi, che 'l Turco passi questo anno in Italia?

FRATE TIMOTEO. Se voi non fate orazione, sì.

Priestly arrogance and unctuousness, and trickeries and casuistries, cannot be painted without our discovering a likeness in the long Italian gallery. Goldoni sketched the Venetian manners of the decadence of the Republic with a French pencil, and was an Italian scribe in style.

The Spanish stage is richer in such comedies as that which furnished the idea of the *Menteur* to Corneille. But you must force yourself to believe that this liar is not forcing his vein when he piles lie upon lie. There is no preceding touch to win the mind to credulity. Spanish comedy is generally in sharp outline, as of skeletons; in quick movement, as of marionettes. The comedy might be performed by a troop of the *corps de ballet;* and in the recollection of the reading it resolves to an animated shuffle of feet. It is, in fact, something other than the true idea of comedy. Where the sexes are separated, men and women grow, as the Portuguese call it, *afaimados* of one another, famine-stricken; and all the tragic elements are on the stage. Don Juan is a comic character that sends souls flying; nor does the humor of the breaking of a dozen women's hearts conciliate the comic Muse with the drawing of blood.

German attempts at comedy remind one vividly of Heine's image of his country in the dancing of Atta Troll. Lessing tried his hand at it, with a sobering effect upon readers. The intention to produce the reverse effect is just visible, and therein, like the portly graces of the poor old Pyrenean bear poising and twirling on his right hind-leg and his left, consists the fun. Jean Paul Richter gives the best edition of the German comic in the contrast of Siebenkäs with his Lenette. A light of the comic is in Goethe— enough to complete the splendid figure of the man, but no more.

The German literary laugh, like the timed awakenings of their Barbarossa in the hollows of the Untersberg, is infrequent, and rather monstrous—never a laugh of men and women in concert. It comes of unrefined, abstract fancy, grotesque or grim, or gross, like the peculiar humors of their little earthmen. Spiritual laughter they have not yet attained to; sentimentalism waylays them in the flight. Here and there a *volkslied* or *märchen* shows a national aptitude for stout animal laughter, and we see that the literature is built on it, which is hopeful so far; but to enjoy it, to enter into the philosophy of the broad grin that seems to hesitate between the skull and the embryo, and reaches its perfection in breadth from the pulling of two square fingers at the corners of the mouth, one must have aid of 'the good

Rhine wine,' and be of German blood unmixed besides. This treble-Dutch lumbersomeness of the Comic Spirit is of itself exclusive of the idea of comedy, and the poor voice allowed to women in German domestic life will account for the absence of comic dialogues reflecting upon life in that land. I shall speak of it again in the second section of this lecture.

Eastward you have total silence of comedy among a people intensely susceptible to laughter, as the *Arabian Nights* will testify. Where the veil is over women's faces, you cannot have society, without which the senses are barbarous and the Comic Spirit is driven to the gutters of grossness to slake its thirst. Arabs in this respect are worse than Italians—much worse than Germans—just in the degree that their system of treating women is worse.

M. Saint-Marc Girardin, the excellent French essayist and master of critical style, tells of a conversation he had once with an Arab gentleman on the topic of the different management of these difficult creatures in Orient and in Occident; and the Arab spoke in praise of many good results of the greater freedom enjoyed by Western ladies, and the charm of conversing with them. He was questioned why his countrymen took no measures to grant them something of that kind of liberty. He jumped out of his individuality in a twinkling, and entered into the sentiments of his race, replying, from the pinnacle of a splendid conceit, with affected humility of manner: '*You* can look on them without perturbation—but *we!* . . .' And, after this profoundly comic interjection, he added, in deep tones: 'The very face of a woman!' Our representative of temperate notions demurely consented that the Arab's pride of

inflammability should insist on the prudery of the
veil as the civilizing medium of his race.

There has been fun in Bagdad. But there never
will be civilization where comedy is not possible;
and that comes of some degree of social equality of
the sexes. I am not quoting the Arab to exhort and
disturb the somnolent East; rather for cultivated
women to recognize that the comic Muse is one of
their best friends. They are blind to their interests
in swelling the ranks of the sentimentalists. Let
them look with their clearest vision abroad and at
home. They will see that, where they have no social
freedom, comedy is absent; where they are household drudges, the form of comedy is primitive;
where they are tolerably independent, but unculti-
vated, exciting melodrama takes its place, and a
sentimental version of them. Yet the comic will out,
as they would know if they listened to some of the
private conversations of men whose minds are un-
directed by the comic Muse; as the sentimental man,
to his astonishment, would know likewise, if he in
similar fashion could receive a lesson. But where
women are on the road to an equal footing with men,
in attainments and in liberty—in what they have
won for themselves, and what has been granted
them by a fair civilization—there, and only waiting
to be transplanted from life to the stage, or the novel,
or the poem, pure comedy flourishes, and is, as it
would help them to be, the sweetest of diversions,
the wisest of delightful companions.

Now, to look about us in the present time, I think
it will be acknowledged that, in neglecting the cultivation of the comic idea, we are losing the aid of
a powerful auxiliar. You see Folly perpetually slid-
ing into new shapes in a society possessed of wealth

and leisure, with many whims, many strange ailments and strange doctors. Plenty of common sense is in the world to thrust her back when she pretends to empire. But the first-born of common sense, the vigilant Comic, which is the genius of thoughtful laughter, which would readily extinguish her at the outset, is not serving as a public advocate.

You will have noticed the disposition of common sense, under pressure of some pertinacious piece of light-headedness, to grow impatient and angry. That is a sign of the absence, or at least of the dormancy, of the comic idea. For Folly is the natural prey of the Comic, known to it in all her transformations, in every disguise; and it is with the springing delight of hawk over heron, hound after fox, that it gives her chase, never fretting, never tiring, sure of having her, allowing her no rest.

Contempt is a sentiment that cannot be entertained by comic intelligence. What is it but an excuse to be idly-minded, or personally lofty, or comfortably narrow, not perfectly humane? If we do not feign when we say that we despise Folly, we shut the brain. There is a disdainful attitude in the presence of Folly, partaking of the foolishness to comic perception; and anger is not much less foolish than disdain. The struggle we have to conduct is essence against essence. Let no one doubt of the sequel when this emanation of what is firmest in us is launched to strike down the daughter of Unreason and Sentimentalism—such being Folly's parentage, when it is respectable.

Our modern system of combating her is too long defensive, and carried on too ploddingly with concrete engines of war in the attack. She has time to get behind entrenchments. She is ready to stand a siege, before the heavily-armed man of science and the writer of the leading article or elaborate essay have primed their big guns. It should be remembered that she has charms for the multitude; and an English multitude, seeing her make a gallant fight of it, will be half in love with her, certainly willing to lend her a cheer. Benevolent subscriptions assist her to hire her own man of science, her own organ in the press. If ultimately she is cast out and overthrown, she can stretch a finger at gaps in our ranks. She can say that she commanded an army, and seduced men, whom we thought sober men and safe, to act as her lieutenants. We learn rather gloomily, after she has flashed her lantern, that we have in our midst able men, and men with minds, for whom there is no pole-star in intellectual navigation. Comedy, or the comic element, is the specific for the poison of delusion while Folly is passing from the state of vapor to substantial form.

O for a breath of Aristophanes, Rabelais, Voltaire, Cervantes, Fielding, Molière! These are spirits that, if you know them well, will come when you do call. You will find the very invocation of them act on you like a renovating air—the south-west coming off the sea, or a cry in the Alps.

No one would presume to say that we are deficient in jokers. They abound, and the organization directing their machinery to shoot them in the wake of the leading article and the popular sentiment is good. But the comic differs from them in addressing the wits for laughter; and the sluggish wits want some training to respond to it, whether in public life or private, and particularly when the feelings are excited. The sense of the comic is much blunted by habits of punning and of using humoristic phrase, the trick of employing Johnsonian polysyllables to treat of the infinitely little. And it really may be hu-

morous, of a kind; yet it will miss the point by going too much round about it.

A certain French Duc Pasquier died, some years
back, at a very advanced age. He had been the ven-
erable Duc Pasquier, in his later years, up to the period of his death. There was a report of Duc Pasquier that he was a man of profound egoism. Hence
an argument arose, and was warmly sustained, upon
the excessive selfishness of those who, in a world of
troubles, and calls to action, and innumerable duties,
husband their strength for the sake of living on. Can
it be possible, the argument ran, for a truly generous
heart to continue beating up to the age of a hundred? Duc Pasquier was not without his defenders,
who likened him to the oak of the forest—a venera-
ble comparison.

The argument was conducted on both sides with
spirit and earnestness, lightened here and there by
frisky touches of the polysyllabic playful, reminding
one of the serious pursuit of their fun by truant boys
that are assured they are out of the eye of their master, and now and then indulge in an imitation of him.
And well might it be supposed that the comic idea
was asleep, not overlooking them! It resolved at last
to this, that either Duc Pasquier was a scandal on
our humanity in clinging to life so long, or that he
honored it by so sturdy a resistance to the enemy.
As one who has entangled himself in a labyrinth is
glad to get out again at the entrance, the argument
ran about, to conclude with its commencement.

Now, imagine a master of the comic treating this
theme, and particularly the argument on it. Imagine
an Aristophanic comedy of the Centenarian, with
choric praises of heroical early death, and the same
of a stubborn vitality, and the poet laughing at the
Chorus; and the grand question for contention in

dialogue, as to the exact age when a man should die, to the identical minute, that he may preserve the respect of his fellows, followed by a systematic attempt to make an accurate measurement in parallel lines, with a tough rope-yarn by one party, and a string of yawns by the other, of the veteran's power of enduring life, and our capacity for enduring *him*, with tremendous pulling on both sides. Would not the comic view of the discussion illumine it and the disputants like very lightning? There are questions, as well as persons, that only the comic can fitly touch.

Aristophanes would probably have crowned the ancient tree with the consolatory observation to the haggard line of long-expectant heirs of the Centenarian, that they live to see the blessedness of coming of a strong stock. The shafts of his ridicule would mainly have been aimed at the disputants; for the sole ground of the argument was the old man's character, and sophists are not needed to demonstrate that we can very soon have too much of a bad thing. A centenarian does not necessarily provoke the comic idea, nor does the corpse of a duke. It is not provoked in the order of nature, until we draw its penetrating attentiveness to some circumstance with which we have been mixing our private interests, or our speculative obfuscation. Dulness, insensible to the comic, has the privilege of arousing it; and the laying of a dull finger on matters of human life is the surest method of establishing electrical communications with a battery of laughter—where the comic idea is prevalent.

But if the comic idea prevailed with us, and we had an Aristophanes to barb and wing it, we should be breathing air of Athens. Prosers now pouring forth on us like public fountains would be cut short in the street and left blinking, dumb as pillar-posts with letters thrust into their mouths. We should throw off incubus, our dreadful familiar—by some called boredom—whom it is our present humiliation to be just alive enough to loathe, never quick enough to foil. There would be a bright and positive, clear Hellenic perception of facts. The vapors of unreason and sentimentalism would be blown away before they were productive. Where would pessimist and optimist be? They would in any case have a diminished audience. Yet possibly the change of despots, from good-natured old obtuseness to keen-edged intelligence, which is by nature merciless, would be more than we could bear. The rupture of the link between dull people, consisting in the fraternal agreement that something is too clever for them, and a shot beyond them, is not to be thought of lightly; for, slender though the link may seem, it is equivalent to a cement forming a concrete of dense cohesion, very desirable in the estimation of the statesman.

A political Aristophanes, taking advantage of his lyrical Bacchic license, was found too much for political Athens. I would not ask to have him revived, but that the sharp light of such a spirit as his might be with us to strike now and then on public affairs, public themes, to make them spin along more briskly.

He hated with the politician's fervor the Sophist who corrupted simplicity of thought, the poet who destroyed purity of style, the demagogue, 'the saw-toothed monster,' who, as he conceived, chicaned the mob; and he held his own against them by strength of laughter, until fines, the curtailing of his comic license in the chorus, and ultimately the ruin of Athens, which could no longer support the expense of the chorus, threw him altogether on dialogue, and brought him under the law. After the catastrophe, the poet, who had ever been gazing back at the men of Marathon and Salamis, must have felt that he had foreseen it; and that he was wise when he pleaded for peace, and derided military coxcombry and the captious old creature Demus, we can admit. He had the comic poet's gift of common sense—which does not always include political intelligence; yet his political tendency raised him above the Old-Comedy turn for uproarious farce. He abused Socrates; but Xenophon, the disciple of Socrates, by his trained rhetoric saved the Ten Thousand. Aristophanes might say that, if his warnings had been followed, there would have been no such thing as a mercenary Greek expedition under Cyrus. Athens, however, was on a landslip, falling; none could arrest it. To gaze back, to uphold the old times, was a most natural conservatism, and fruitless. The aloe had bloomed. Whether right or wrong in his politics and his criticisms, and bearing in mind the instruments he played on and the audience he had to win, there is an idea in his comedies; it is the idea of good citizenship.

He is not likely to be revived. He stands, like Shakespeare, an unapproachable. Swift says of him, with a loving chuckle:

> But as to comic Aristophanes,
> The rogue too vicious and too profane is.

Aristophanes was 'prófane,' under satiric direction; unlike his rivals Cratinus, Phrynichus, Ameipsias, Eupolis, and others, if we are to believe him, who, in their extraordinary Donnybrook Fair of the day of comedy, thumped one another and everybody else with absolute heartiness, as he did, but aimed at small game, and dragged forth particular women, which he did not. He is an aggregate of many men, all of a certain greatness. We may build up a conception of his powers if we mount Rabelais upon *Hudibras*, lift him with the songfulness of Shelley, give him a vein of Heinrich Heine, and cover him with the mantle of the *Anti-Jacobin*, adding (that there may be some Irish in him) a dash of Grattan, before he is in motion.

But such efforts at conceiving one great one by incorporation of minors are vain, and cry for excuse. Supposing Wilkes for leading man in a country constantly plunging into war under some plumed Lamachus, with enemies periodically firing the land up to the gates of London, and a Samuel Foote, of prodigious genius, attacking him with ridicule: I think it gives a notion of the conflict engaged in by Aristophanes. This laughing bald-pate, as he calls himself, was a Titanic pamphleteer, using laughter for his political weapon; a laughter without scruple, the laughter of Hercules. He was primed with wit, as with the garlic he speaks of giving to the gamecocks to make them fight the better. And he was a lyric poet of aerial delicacy, with the homely song of a jolly national poet, and a poet of such feeling that the comic mask is at times no broader than a cloth on a face to show the serious features of our common likeness. He is not to be revived; but, if his method were studied, some of the fire in him would come to us, and *we* might be revived.

Taking them generally, the English public are most in sympathy with this primitive Aristophanic comedy, wherein the comic is capped by the grotesque, irony tips the wit, and satire is a naked sword. They have the basis of the comic in them— an esteem for common sense. They cordially dislike the reverse of it. They have a rich laugh, though it is not the *gros rire* of the Gaul tossing *gros sel,* nor the polished Frenchman's mentally digestive laugh. And if they have now, like a monarch with a troop of dwarfs, too many jesters kicking the dictionary about, to let them *reflect* that they are dull, occasionally (like the pensive monarch surprising himself with an idea of an idea of his own), they *look* so. And they are given to looking in the glass. They must see that something ails them. How much even the better order of them will endure, without a thought of the defensive, when the person afflicting them is protected from satire, we read in memoirs of a preceding age, where the vulgarly tyrannous hostess of a great house of reception shuffled the guests and played them like a pack of cards, with her exact estimate of the strength of each one printed on them; and still this house continued to be the most popular in England, nor did the lady ever appear in print or on the boards as the comic type that she was.

It has been suggested that they have not yet spiritually comprehended the signification of living in society; for who are cheerfuller, brisker of wit, in the fields, and as explorers, colonizers, backwoodsmen? They are happy in rough exercise, and also in complete repose. The intermediate condition, when they are called upon to talk to one another, upon other than affairs of business or their hobbies, reveals them wearing a curious look of vacancy, as it were the socket of an eye wanting. The comic is perpetually springing up in social life, and it oppresses them from not being perceived.

Thus, at a dinner-party, one of the guests, who happens to have enrolled himself in a burial-company, politely entreats the others to inscribe their

names as shareholders, expatiating on the advan-
tages accruing to them in the event of their very possible speedy death, the salubrity of the site, the aptitude of the soil for a quick consumption of their
remains, etc.; and they drink sadness from the incongruous man, and conceive indigestion not seeing
him in a sharply-defined light that would bid them
taste the comic of him. Or it is mentioned that a
newly-elected member of our Parliament celebrates
his arrival at eminence by the publication of a book
on cab-fares, dedicated to a beloved female relative
deceased, and the comment on it is the word 'Indeed.' But, merely for a contrast, turn to a not uncommon scene of yesterday in the hunting-field,
where a brilliant young rider, having broken his col-
lar-bone, trots away very soon after, against medical
interdict, half put together in splinters, to the most
distant meet of his neighborhood, sure of escaping
his doctor, who is the first person he encounters. 'I
came here purposely to avoid you,' says the patient.
'I came here purposely to take care of you,' says the
doctor. Off they go, and come to a swollen brook.
The patient clears it handsomely; the doctor tumbles in. All the field are alive with the heartiest relish
of every incident and every cross-light on it, and dull
would the man have been thought who had not his
word to say about it when riding home.

In our prose literature we have had delightful
comic writers. Besides Fielding and Goldsmith,
there is Miss Austen, whose Emma and Mr. Elton
might walk straight into a comedy, were the plot arranged for them. Galt's neglected novels have some
characters and strokes of shrewd comedy. In our
poetic literature the comic is delicate and graceful
above the touch of Italian and French. Generally,
however, the English elect excel in satire, and they

are noble humorists. The national disposition is for hard-hitting, with a moral purpose to sanction it; or for a rosy, sometimes a larmoyant, geniality, not unmanly in its verging upon tenderness, and with a singular attraction for thickheadedness, to decorate it with asses' ears and the most beautiful sylvan haloes. But the comic is a different spirit.

You may estimate your capacity for comic perception by being able to detect the ridicule of them you love without loving them less; and more by being able to see yourself somewhat ridiculous in dear eyes, and accepting the correction their image of you proposes.

Each one of an affectionate couple may be willing, as we say, to die for the other, yet unwilling to utter the agreeable word at the right moment; but if the wits were sufficiently quick for them to perceive that they are in a comic situation, as affectionate couples must be when they quarrel, they would not wait for the moon or the almanac, or a Dorine, to bring back the flood-tide of tender feelings, that they should join hands and lips.

If you detect the ridicule, and your kindliness is chilled by it, you are slipping into the grasp of Satire.

If, instead of falling foul of the ridiculous person with a satiric rod, to make him writhe and shriek aloud, you prefer to sting him under a semi-caress, by which he shall in his anguish be rendered dubious whether indeed anything has hurt him, you are an engine of Irony.

If you laugh all round him, tumble him, roll him about, deal him a smack, and drop a tear on him, own his likeness to you, and yours to your neighbor, spare him as little as you shun, pity him as much as you expose, it is a spirit of Humor that is moving you.

The comic, which is the perceptive, is the governing spirit, awakening and giving aim to these powers of laughter, but it is not to be confounded with them; it enfolds a thinner form of them, differing from satire in not sharply driving into the quivering sensibilities, and from humor in not comforting them and tucking them up, or indicating a broader than the range of this bustling world to them.

Fielding's Jonathan Wild presents a case of this peculiar distinction, when that man of eminent greatness remarks upon the unfairness of a trial in which the condemnation has been brought about by twelve men of the opposite party; for it is not satiric, it is not humorous; yet it is immensely comic to hear a guilty villain protesting that his own 'party' should have a voice in the law. It opens an avenue into villains' ratiocination. And the comic is not canceled though we should suppose Jonathan to be giving play to his humor. (I may have dreamed this, or had it suggested to me, for, on referring to *Jonathan Wild*, I do not find it.) Apply the case to the man of deep wit, who is ever certain of his condemnation by the opposite party, and then it ceases to be comic, and will be satiric.

The look of Fielding upon Richardson is essentially comic. His method of correcting the sentimental writer is a mixture of the comic and the humorous. Parson Adams is a creation of humor. But both the conception and the presentation of Alceste and of Tartuffe, of Célimène and Philaminte, are purely comic, addressed to the intellect; there is no humor in them, and they refresh the intellect they quicken to detect their comedy, by force of the contrast they offer between themselves and the wiser world about them—that is to say, society, or that assemblage of minds whereof the comic spirit has its origin.

Byron had splendid powers of humor, and the most poetic satire that we have example of, fusing at times to hard irony. He had no strong comic sense, or he would not have taken an anti-social position, which is directly opposed to the comic; and in his philosophy, judged by philosophers, he is a comic figure by reason of this deficiency. 'Sobald er reflectirt ist er ein Kind,' Goethe says of him. Carlyle sees him in this comic light, treats him in the humorous manner.

The satirist is a moral agent, often a social scavenger, working on a storage of bile.

The ironist is one thing or another, according to his caprice. Irony is the humor of satire; it may be savage, as in Swift, with a moral object, or sedate, as in Gibbon, with a malicious. The foppish irony fretting to be seen, and the irony which leers, that you shall not mistake its intention, are failures in satiric effort pretending to the treasures of ambiguity.

The humorist of mean order is a refreshing laugher, giving tone to the feelings, and sometimes allowing the feelings to be too much for him; but the humorist of high has an embrace of contrasts beyond the scope of the comic poet.

Heart and mind laugh out at Don Quixote, and still you brood on him. The juxtaposition of the knight and squire is a comic conception, the opposition of their natures most humorous. They are as different as the two hemispheres in the time of Columbus, yet they touch, and are bound in one, by laughter. The knight's great aims and constant mishaps, his chivalrous valiancy exercised on absurd objects, his good sense along the high road of the craziest of expeditions, the compassion he plucks out of derison, and the admirable figure he preserves while stalking through the frantically grotesque and burlesque assailing him, are in the loftiest moods of humor, fusing the tragic sentiment with the comic narrative. The stroke of the great humorist is world-wide, with lights of tragedy in his laughter.

Taking a living great, though not creative, humorist to guide our description: the skull of Yorick is in his hands in our seasons of festival; he sees visions of primitive man capering preposterously under the gorgeous robes of ceremonial. Our souls must be on fire when we wear solemnity, if we would not press upon his shrewdest nerve. Finite and infinite flash from one to the other with him, lending him a two-edged thought that peeps out of his peacefullest lines by fits, like the lantern of the fire-watcher at windows, going the rounds at night. The comportment and performances of men in society are to him, by the vivid comparison with their mortality, more grotesque than respectable. But ask yourself: 'Is he always to be relied on for justness?' He will fly straight as the emissary eagle back to Jove at the true Hero. He will also make as determined a swift descent upon the man of his wilful choice, whom we cannot distinguish as a true one. This vast power of his, built up of the feelings and the intellect in union, is often wanting in proportion and in discretion. Humorists touching upon history or society are given to be capricious. They are, as in the case of Sterne, given to be sentimental; for with them the feelings are primary, as with singers. Comedy, on the other hand, is an interpretation of the general mind, and is for that reason of necessity kept in restraint. The French lay marked stress on *mesure et goût*, and they own how much they owe to Molière for leading them in simple justness and taste. We can teach them many things; they can teach us in this.

The comic poet is in the narrow field, or enclosed square, of the society he depicts; and he addresses the still narrower enclosure of men's intellects, with reference to the operation of the social world upon their characters. He is not concerned with beginnings or endings or surroundings, but with what you are now weaving. To understand his work and value it, you must have a sober liking of your kind, and a sober estimate of our civilized qualities. The aim and business of the comic poet are misunderstood, his meaning is not seized nor his point of view taken, when he is accused of dishonoring our nature and being hostile to sentiment, tending to spitefulness and making an unfair use of laughter. Those who detect irony in comedy do so because they choose to see it in life. Poverty, says the satirist, 'has nothing harder in itself than that it makes men ridiculous.' But poverty is never ridiculous to comic perception until it attempts to make its rags conceal its bareness in a forlorn attempt at decency, or foolishly to rival ostentation. Caleb Balderstone, in his endeavor to keep up the honor of a noble household in a state of beggary, is an exquisitely comic character. In the case of 'poor relatives,' on the other hand, it is the rich, whom they perplex, that are really comic; and to laugh at the former, not seeing the comedy of the latter, is to betray dulness of vision. Humorist and satirist frequently hunt together as ironists in pursuit of the grotesque, to the exclusion of the comic. That was an affecting moment in the history of the Prince Regent, when the First Gentleman of Europe burst into tears at a sarcastic remark of Beau Brummell's on the cut of his coat. Humor, satire, irony, pounce on it altogether as their common prey.

The Comic Spirit eyes, but does not touch, it. Put into action, it would be farcical. It is too gross for comedy.

Incidents of a kind casting ridicule on our unfortunate nature, instead of our conventional life, provoke derisive laughter, which thwarts the comic idea. But derision is foiled by the play of the intellect. Most of doubtful causes in contest are open to comic interpretation, and any intellectual pleading of a doubtful cause contains germs of an idea of comedy.

The laughter of satire is a blow in the back or the face. The laughter of comedy is impersonal and of unrivaled politeness, nearer a smile—often no more than a smile. It laughs through the mind, for the mind directs it; and it might be called the humor of the mind.

One excellent test of the civilization of a country, as I have said, I take to be the flourishing of the comic idea and comedy; and the test of true comedy is that it shall awaken thoughtful laughter.

If you believe that our civilization is founded in common sense (and it is the first condition of sanity to believe it), you will, when contemplating men, discern a Spirit overhead; not more heavenly than the light flashed upward from glassy surfaces, but luminous and watchful; never shooting beyond them, nor lagging in the rear; so closely attached to them that it may be taken for a slavish reflex, until its features are studied. It has the sage's brows, and the sunny malice of a faun lurks at the corners of the half-closed lips drawn in an idle wariness of half-tension. That slim feasting smile, shaped like the long-bow, was once a big round satyr's laugh, that flung up the brows like a fortress lifted by gunpowder. The laugh will come again, but it will be of

the order of the smile, finely-tempered, showing sun-
light of the mind, mental richness rather than noisy
enormity. Its common aspect is one of unsolicitous
observation, as if surveying a full field and having
leisure to dart on its chosen morsels, without any
fluttering eagerness. Men's future upon earth does
not attract it; their honesty and shapeliness in the
present does; and whenever they wax out of proportion, overblown, affected, pretentious, bombastical,
hypocritical, pedantic, fantastically delicate; whenever it sees them self-deceived or hoodwinked, given
to run riot in idolatries, drifting into vanities, con-
gregating in absurdities, planning short-sightedly,
plotting dementedly; whenever they are at variance
with their professions, and violate the unwritten but
perceptible laws binding them in consideration one
to another; whenever they offend sound reason, fair
justice; are false in humility or mined with conceit,
individually, or in the bulk; the Spirit overhead will
look humanely malign, and cast an oblique light on
them, followed by volleys of silvery laughter. That is
the Comic Spirit.

Not to distinguish it is to be bull-blind to the
spiritual, and to deny the existence of a mind of man
where minds of men are in working conjunction.

You must, as I have said, believe that our state of
society is founded in common sense, otherwise you
will not be struck by the contrasts the Comic Spirit
perceives, or have it to look to for your consolation.
You will, in fact, be standing in that peculiar oblique
beam of light, yourself illuminated to the general eye
as the very object of chase and doomed quarry of
the thing obscure to you. But to feel its presence,
and to see it, is your assurance that many sane and
solid minds are with you in what you are experienc-
ing; and this of itself spares you the pain of satirical

heat, and the bitter craving to strike heavy blows. You share the sublime of wrath, that would not have hurt the foolish, but merely demonstrate their foolishness. Molière was contented to revenge himself on the critics of the *École des Femmes* by writing the *Critique de l'École des Femmes,* one of the wisest as well as the playfullest of studies in criticism. A perception of the Comic Spirit gives high fellowship. You become a citizen of the selecter world, the highest we know of in connection with our old world, which is not supermundane. Look there for your unchallengeable upper class! You feel that you are one of this our civilized community, that you cannot escape from it, and would not if you could. Good hope sustains you; weariness does not overwhelm you; in isolation you see no charms for vanity; personal pride is greatly moderated. Nor shall your title of citizenship exclude you from worlds of imagination or of devotion. The Comic Spirit is not hostile to the sweetest songfully poetic. Chaucer bubbles with it; Shakespeare overflows; there is a mild moon's ray of it (pale with super-refinement through distance from our flesh and blood planet) in *Comus.* Pope has it, and it is the daylight side of the night half-obscuring Cowper. It is only hostile to the priestly element when that, by baleful swelling, transcends and overlaps the bounds of its office; and then, in extreme cases, it is too true to itself to speak, and veils the lamp—as, for example, the spectacle of Bossuet over the dead body of Molière, at which the dark angels may, but men do not, laugh.

We have had comic pulpits, for a sign that the laughter-moving and the worshipful may be in alliance; I know not how far comic, or how much assisted in seeming so by the unexpectedness and the

relief of its appearance; at least they are popular—
they are said to win the ear. Laughter is open to
perversion, like other good things; the scornful and
the brutal sorts are not unknown to us; but the laughter directed by the Comic Spirit is a harmless wine,
conducing to sobriety in the degree that it enlivens.
It enters you like fresh air into a study, as when one
of the sudden contrasts of the comic idea floods the
brain like reassuring daylight. You are cognizant of
the true kind by feeling that you take it in, savor it,
and have what flowers live on, natural air for food.
That which you give out—the joyful roar—is not the
better part; let that go to good-fellowship and the
benefit of the lungs. Aristophanes promises his audi-
tors that, if they will retain the ideas of the comic
poet carefully, as they keep dried fruits in boxes,
their garments shall smell odoriferous of wisdom
throughout the year. The boast will not be thought
an empty one by those who have choice friends that
have stocked themselves according to his directions.
Such treasuries of sparkling laughter are wells in
our desert. Sensitiveness to the comic laugh is a step
in civilization. To shrink from being an object of it
is a step in cultivation. We know the degree of re-
finement in men by the matter they will laugh at,
and the ring of the laugh; but we know likewise that
the larger natures are distinguished by the great
breadth of their power of laughter, and no one really
loving Molière is refined by that love to despise or
be dense to Aristophanes, though it may be that the
lover of Aristophanes will not have risen to the
height of Molière. Embrace them both, and you
have the whole scale of laughter in your breast.
Nothing in the world surpasses in stormy fun the
scene in the *Frogs*, when Bacchus and Xanthias receive their thrashings from the hands of business-

like Aeacus, to discover which is the divinity of the
two by his imperviousness to the mortal condition
of pain, and each, under the obligation of not crying
out, makes believe that his horrible bellow—the god's
'*iou! iou!*' being the lustier—means only the stopping
of a sneeze, or horsemen sighted, or the prelude to
an invocation to some deity, and the slave contrives
that the god shall get the bigger lot of blows. Passages of Rabelais, one or two in *Don Quixote,* and
the supper 'in the manner of the ancients' in *Pere-
grine Pickle,* are of a similar cataract of laughter.
But it is not illuminating; it is not the laughter of
the mind. Molière's laughter, in his purest comedies,
is ethereal—as light to our nature, as color to our
thoughts. The *Misanthrope* and the *Tartuffe* have no
audible laughter, but the characters are steeped in
the comic spirit. They quicken the mind through
laughter, from coming out of the mind; and the mind
accepts them because they are clear interpretations
of certain chapters of the Book lying open before us
all. Between these two stand Shakespeare and Cervantes, with the richer laugh of heart and mind
in one; with much of the Aristophanic robustness,
something of Molière's delicacy.

The laughter heard in circles not pervaded by the
comic idea will sound harsh and soulless, like versi-
fied prose, if you step into them with a sense of the
distinction. You will fancy you have changed your
habitation to a planet remoter from the sun. You may
be among powerful brains, too. You will not find
poets—or but a stray one, overworshiped. You will
find learned men undoubtedly, professors, reputed
philosophers, and illustrious dilettanti. They have in
them, perhaps, every element composing light, except the comic. They read verse, they discourse of
art; but their eminent faculties are not under that

vigilant sense of a collective supervision, spiritual and present, which we have taken note of. They build a temple of arrogance; they speak much in the voice of oracles; their hilarity, if it does not dip in grossness, is usually a form of pugnacity.

Insufficiency of sight in the eye looking outward has deprived them of the eye that should look inward. They have never weighed themselves in the delicate balance of the comic idea, so as to obtain a suspicion of the rights and dues of the world; and they have, in consequence, an irritable personality. A very learned English professor crushed an argument in a political discussion by asking his adversary angrily: 'Are you aware, Sir, that I am a philologer?'

The practice of polite society will help in training them, and the professor on a sofa, with beautiful ladies on each side of him, may become their pupil and a scholar in manners without knowing it; he is at least a fair and pleasing spectacle to the comic Muse. But the society named polite is volatile in its adorations, and to-morrow will be petting a bronzed soldier, or a black African, or a prince, or a spiritualist; ideas cannot take root in its ever-shifting soil. It is besides addicted in self-defence to gabble exclusively of the affairs of its rapidly revolving world, as children on a whirli-go-round bestow their attention on the wooden horse or cradle ahead of them, to escape from giddiness and preserve a notion of identity. The professor is better out of a circle that often confounds by lionizing, sometimes annoys by abandoning, and always confuses. The school that teaches gently what peril there is lest a cultivated head should still be coxcomb's, and the collisions which may befall high-soaring minds, empty or full, is more to be recommended than the sphere of incessant motion supplying it with material.

Lands where the Comic Spirit is obscure over-head are rank with raw crops of matter. The traveler accustomed to smooth highways and people not covered with burrs and prickles is amazed, amid so much that is fair and cherishable, to come upon such curious barbarism. An Englishman paid a visit of admiration to a professor in the land of culture, and was introduced by him to another distinguished pro-fessor, to whom he took so cordially as to walk out with him alone one afternoon. The first professor, an erudite entirely worthy of the sentiment of schol-arly esteem prompting the visit, behaved (if we exclude the dagger) with the vindictive jealousy of an injured Spanish beauty. After a short prelude of gloom and obscure explosions, he discharged upon his faithless admirer the bolts of passionate logic familiar to the ears of flighty caballeros: 'Either I am a fit object of your admiration, or I am not. Of these things, one: either you are competent to judge, in which case I stand condemned by you; or you are incompetent, and therefore impertinent, and you may betake yourself to your country again, hypo-crite!' The admirer was for persuading the wounded scholar that it is given to us to be able to admire two professors at a time. He was driven forth.

Perhaps this might have occurred in any country, and a comedy of The Pedant, discovering the greedy humanity within the dusty scholar, would not bring it home to one in particular. I am mindful that it was in Germany, when I observe that the Germans have gone through no comic training to warn them of the sly, wise emanation eyeing them from aloft, nor much of satirical. Heinrich Heine has not been enough to cause them to smart and meditate. Na-tionally, as well as individually, when they are ex-cited they are in danger of the grotesque; as when, for instance, they decline to listen to evidence, and raise a national outcry because one of German blood had been convicted of crime in a foreign country. They are acute critics, yet they still wield clubs in controversy. Compare them in this respect with the people schooled in La Bruyère, La Fontaine, Molière; with the people who have the figures of a Trissotin and a Vadius before them for a comic warning of the personal vanities of the caressed professor. It is more than difference of race. It is the difference of traditions, temper, and style, which comes of schooling.

The French controversialist is a polished swordsman, to be dreaded in his graces and courtesies. The German is Orson, or the mob, or a marching army, in defence of a good case or a bad—a big or a little. His irony is a missile of terrific tonnage; sarcasm he emits like a blast from a dragon's mouth. He must and will be Titan. He stamps his foe underfoot, and is astonished that the creature is not dead, but stinging; for, in truth, the Titan is contending, by comparison, with a god.

When the Germans lie on their arms, looking across the Alsatian frontier at the crowds of Frenchmen rushing to applaud *L'Ami Fritz* at the Théâtre Français, looking and considering the meaning of that applause, which is grimly comic in its political response to the domestic moral of the play—when the Germans watch and are silent, their force of character tells. They are kings in music, we may say princes in poetry, good speculators in philosophy, and our leaders in scholarship. That so gifted a race, possessed, moreover, of the stern good sense which collects the waters of laughter to make the wells, should show at a disadvantage, I hold for a proof, instructive to us, that the discipline of the Comic

Spirit is needful to their growth. We see what they can reach to in that great figure of modern manhood, Goethe. They are a growing people; they are conversable as well; and when their men, as in France, and at intervals at Berlin tea-tables, consent to talk on equal terms with their women, and to listen to them, their growth will be accelerated and be shapelier. Comedy, or, in any form, the Comic Spirit, will then come to them to cut some figures out of the block, show them the mirror, enliven and irradiate the social intelligence.

Modern French comedy is commendable for the directness of the study of actual life, as far as that (which is but the early step in such a scholarship) can be of service in composing and coloring the picture. A consequence of this crude, though well-meant, realism is the collision of the writers in their scenes and incidents, and in their characters. The Muse of most of them is an *Aventurière*. She is clever, and a certain diversion exists in the united scheme for confounding her. The object of this person is to reinstate herself in the decorous world; and either, having accomplished this purpose through deceit, she has a *nostalgie de la boue* that eventually casts her back into it, or she is exposed in her course of deception when she is about to gain her end. A very good, innocent young man is her victim, or a very astute, goodish young man obstructs her path. This latter is enabled to be the champion of the decorous world by knowing the indecorous well. He has assisted in the progress of *aventurières* downward; he will not help them to ascend. The world is with him; and certainly it is not much of an ascension they aspire to; but what sort of a figure is he? The triumph of a candid realism is to show him no hero. You are to admire him (for it must be supposed that

realism pretends to waken some admiration) as a
credibly living young man; no better, only a little
firmer and shrewder, than the rest. If, however, you
think at all, after the curtain has fallen, you are
likely to think that the *aventurières* have a case to
plead against him. True, and the author has not said
anything to the contrary; he has but painted from
the life; he leaves his audience to the reflections of
unphilosophic minds upon life, from the specimen
he has presented in the bright and narrow circle of
a spy-glass.

I do not know that the fly in amber is of any particular use, but the comic idea enclosed in a comedy
makes it more generally perceptible and portable,
and that is an advantage. There is a benefit to men
in taking the lessons of comedy in congregations, for
it enlivens the wits; and to writers it is beneficial,
for they must have a clear scheme, and even if they
have no idea to present, they must prove that they
have made the public sit to them before the sitting,
to see the picture. And writing for the stage would
be a corrective of a too-incrusted scholarly style, into
which some great ones fall at times. It keeps minor
writers to a definite plan, and to English. Many of
them now swelling a plethoric market in the composition of novels, in pun-manufactories, and in
journalism—attached to the machinery forcing per-
ishable matter on a public that swallows voraciously
and groans—might, with encouragement, be attend-
ing to the study of art in literature. Our critics appear
to be fascinated by the quaintness of our public, as
the world is when our beast-garden has a new importation of magnitude, and the creature's appetite
is reverently consulted. They stipulate for a writer's
popularity before they will do much more than take
the position of umpires to record his failure or

success. Now the pig supplies the most popular of dishes, but it is not accounted the most honored of animals, unless it be by the cottager. Our public might surely be led to try other, perhaps finer, meat. It has good taste in song. It might be taught as justly, on the whole (and the sooner when the cottager's view of the feast shall cease to be the humble one of our literary critics), to extend this capacity for delicate choosing in the direction of the matter arousing laughter.

LAUGHTER

Henri Bergson

Chapter I

What does laughter mean? What is the basal element in the laughable? What common ground can we find between the grimace of a merry-andrew, a play upon words, an equivocal situation in a burlesque and a scene of high comedy? What method of distillation will yield us invariably the same essence from which so many different products borrow either their obtrusive odour or their delicate perfume? The greatest of thinkers, from Aristotle downwards, have tackled this little problem, which has a knack of baffling every effort, of slipping away and escaping only to bob up again, a pert challenge flung at philosophic speculation.

Our excuse for attacking the problem in our turn must lie in the fact that we shall not aim at imprisoning the comic spirit within a definition. We regard it, above all, as a living thing. However trivial it may be, we shall treat it with the respect due to life. We shall confine ourselves to watching it grow and expand. Passing by imperceptible gradations from one form to another, it will be seen to achieve the strangest metamorphoses. We shall disdain nothing we have seen. Maybe we may gain from this prolonged contact, for the matter of that, something more flexible than an abstract definition,—a practical, intimate acquaintance, such as springs from a long companionship. And maybe we may also find that, unintentionally, we have made an acquaintance that is useful. For the comic spirit has a logic of its own, even in its wildest eccentricities. It has a method in its madness. It dreams, I admit, but it conjures up in its dreams visions that are at once accepted and understood by the whole of a social group. Can it then fail to throw light for us on the way that human imagination works, and more particularly social, collective, and popular imagination? Begotten of real life and akin to art, should it not also have something of its own to tell us about art and life?

At the outset we shall put forward three observations which we look upon as fundamental. They have less bearing on the actually comic than on the field within which it must be sought.

I

The first point to which attention should be called is that the comic does not exist outside the pale of what is strictly *human*. A landscape may be beautiful, charming and sublime, or insignificant and ugly; it will never be laughable. You may laugh at an animal, but only because you have detected in it some human attitude or expression. You may laugh at a hat, but what you are making fun of, in this case, is not the piece of felt or straw, but the shape that men have given it,—the human caprice whose mould it has assumed. It is strange that so important a fact, and such a simple one too, has not attracted to a greater degree the attention of philosophers. Several have defined man as "an animal which laughs." They might equally well have defined him as an animal which is laughed at; for if any other animal, or some lifeless object, produces the same effect, it is always because of some resemblance to man, of the stamp he gives it or the use he puts it to.

Here I would point out, as a symptom equally worthy of notice, the *absence of feeling* which usually accompanies laughter. It seems as though the comic could not produce its disturbing effect unless it fell, so to say, on the surface of a soul that is thoroughly calm and unruffled. Indifference is its natural environment, for laughter has no greater foe than emotion. I do not mean that we could not laugh at a person who inspires us with pity, for instance, or even with affection, but in such a case we must, for the moment, put our affection out of court and impose silence upon our pity. In a society composed of pure intelligences there would probably be no more tears, though perhaps there would still be laughter; whereas highly emotional souls, in tune and unison with life, in whom every event would be sentimentally prolonged and re-echoed, would neither know nor understand laughter. Try, for a moment, to become interested in everything that is being said and done; act, in imagination, with those who act, and feel with those who feel; in a word, give your sympathy its widest expansion: as though at the touch of a fairy wand you will see the flimsiest of objects assume importance, and a gloomy hue spread over everything. Now step aside, look upon life as a disinterested spectator: many a drama will turn into a comedy. It is enough for us to stop our ears to the sound of music in a room, where dancing is going on, for the dancers at once to appear ridiculous. How many human actions would stand a similar test? Should we not see many of them suddenly pass from grave to gay, on isolating them from the accompanying music of sentiment? To produce the whole of its effect, then, the comic demands something like a momentary anesthesia of the heart. Its appeal is to intelligence, pure and simple.

This intelligence, however, must always remain in touch with other intelligences. And here is the third fact to which attention should be drawn. You would hardly appreciate the comic if you felt yourself isolated from others. Laughter appears to stand in need of an echo. Listen to it carefully: it is not an articulate, clear, well-defined sound; it is something which would fain be prolonged by reverberating from one to another, something beginning with a crash, to continue in successive rumblings, like thunder in a mountain. Still, this reverberation cannot go on for ever. It can travel within as wide a circle as you please: the circle remains, none the less, a closed one. Our laughter is always the laughter of a group. It may, perchance, have happened to you, when seated in a railway carriage or at *table d'hôte*, to hear travellers relating to one another stories which must have been comic to them, for they laughed heartily. Had you been one of their company, you would have laughed like them, but, as you were not, you had no desire whatever to do so. A man who was once asked why he did not weep at a sermon when everybody else was shedding tears replied: "I don't belong to the parish!" What that man thought of tears would be still more true of laughter. However spontaneous it seems, laughter always implies a kind of secret freemasonry, or even complicity, with other laughers, real or imaginary. How often has it been said that the fuller the theatre, the more uncontrolled the laughter of the audience! On the other hand, how often has the remark been made that many comic effects are incapable of translation from one language to another, because they refer to the customs and ideas of a particular social group! It is through not understanding the importance of this double fact that the comic has been looked upon as a mere curiosity in which the mind finds amusement, and laughter itself as a strange, isolated phenomenon, without any bearing on the rest of human activity. Hence those definitions which tend to make the comic into an abstract relation between ideas: "an intellectual contrast," "a patent absurdity," etc., definitions which, even were they really suitable to every form of the comic, would not in the least explain why the comic makes us laugh. How, indeed, should it come about that this particular logical relation, as soon as it is perceived, contracts, expands and shakes our limbs, whilst all other relations leave the body unaffected? It is not from this point of view that we shall approach the problem. To understand laughter, we must put it back into its natural environment, which is society, and above all must we determine the utility of its function, which is a social one. Such, let us say at once, will be the leading idea of all our investigations. Laughter must answer to certain requirements of life in common. It must have a *social* signification.

Let us clearly mark the point towards which our three preliminary observations are converging. The comic will come into being, it appears, whenever a group of men concentrate their attention on one of their number, imposing silence on their emotions and calling into play nothing but their intelligence. What, now, is the particular point on which their attention will have to be concentrated, and what will here be the function of intelligence? To reply to these questions will be at once to come to closer grips with the problem. But here a few examples have become indispensable.

II

A man, running along the street, stumbles and falls; the passers-by burst out laughing. They would not laugh at him, I imagine, could they suppose that the whim had suddenly seized him to sit down on the ground. They laugh because his sitting down is involuntary. Consequently, it is not his sudden change of attitude that raises a laugh, but rather the involuntary element in this change,—his clumsiness, in fact. Perhaps there was a stone on the road. He should have altered his pace or avoided the obstacle. Instead of that, through lack of elasticity, through absentmindedness and a kind of physical obstinacy, *as a result, in fact, of rigidity or of momentum,* the muscles continued to perform the same movement when the circumstances of the case called for something else. That is the reason of the man's fall, and also of the people's laughter.

Now, take the case of a person who attends to the petty occupations of his everyday life with mathematical precision. The objects around him, however, have all been tampered with by a mischievous wag, the result being that when he dips his pen into the inkstand he draws it out all covered with mud, when he fancies he is sitting down on a solid chair he finds himself sprawling on the floor, in a word his actions are all topsy-turvy or mere beating the air, while in every case the effect is invariably one of momentum. Habit has given the impulse: what was wanted was to check the movement or deflect it. He did nothing of the sort, but continued like a machine in the same straight line. The victim, then, of a practical joke is in a position similar to that of a runner who falls,—he is comic for the same reason. The laughable element in both cases consists of a certain *mechanical inelasticity*, just where one would expect to find the wideawake adaptability and the living pliableness of a human being. The only difference in the two cases is that the former happened of itself, whilst the latter was obtained artificially. In the first instance, the passer-by does nothing but look on, but in the second the mischievous wag intervenes.

All the same, in both cases the result has been brought about by an external circumstance. The comic is therefore accidental: it remains, so to speak, in superficial contact with the person. How is it to penetrate within? The necessary conditions will be fulfilled when mechanical rigidity no longer requires for its manifestation a stumbling-block which either the hazard of circumstance or human knavery has set in its way, but extracts by natural processes, from its own store, an inexhaustible series of opportunities for externally revealing its presence. Suppose, then, we imagine a mind always thinking of what it has just done and never of what it is doing, like a song which lags behind its accompaniment. Let us try to picture to ourselves a certain inborn lack of elasticity of both senses and intelligence, which brings it to pass that we continue to see what is no longer visible, to hear what is no longer audible, to say what is no longer to the point: in short, to adapt ourselves to a past and therefore imaginary situation, when we ought to be shaping our conduct in accordance with the reality which is present. This time the comic will take up its abode in the person himself; it is the person who will supply it with everything—matter and form, cause and opportunity. Is it then surprising that the absent-minded individual—for this is the character we have just been describing—has usually fired the imagination of comic authors? When La Bruyère came across this particular type, he realised, on analysing it, that he had got hold of a recipe for the wholesale manufacture of comic effects. As a matter of fact he overdid it, and gave us far too lengthy and detailed a description of *Ménalque,* coming back to his subject, dwelling and expatiating on it beyond all bounds. The very facility of the subject fascinated him. Absentmindedness, indeed, is not perhaps the actual fountain-head of the comic, but surely it is contiguous to a certain stream of facts and fancies which flows straight from the fountain-head. It is situated, so to say, on one of the great natural watersheds of laughter.

Now, the effect of absentmindedness may gather strength in its turn. There is a general law, the first example of which we have just encountered, and which we will formulate in the following terms: when a certain comic effect has its origin in a certain cause, the more natural we regard the cause to be, the more comic shall we find the effect. Even now we laugh at absentmindedness when presented to us as a simple fact. Still more laughable will be the absentmindedness we have seen springing up and growing before our very eyes, with whose origin we are acquainted and whose life-history we can reconstruct. To choose a definite example: suppose a man has taken to reading nothing but romances of love and chivalry. Attracted and fascinated by his heroes, his thoughts and intentions gradually turn more and more towards them, till one fine day we find him walking among us like a somnambulist. His actions are distractions. But then his distractions can be traced back to a definite, positive cause. They are no longer cases of *absence* of mind, pure and simple; they find their explanation in the *presence* of the individual in quite definite, though imaginary, surroundings. Doubtless a fall is always a fall, but it is one thing to tumble into a well because you were looking anywhere but in front of you, it is quite another thing to fall into it because you were intent upon a star. It was certainly a star at which Don Quixote was gazing. How profound is the comic element in the over-romantic, Utopian bent of mind! And yet, if you reintroduce the idea of absentmindedness, which acts as a go-between you will see this profound comic element uniting with the most superficial type. Yes, indeed, these whimsical wild enthusiasts, these madmen who are yet so strangely reasonable, excite us to laughter by playing on the same chords within ourselves, by setting in motion the same inner mechanism, as does the victim of a practical joke or the passer-by who slips down in the street. They, too, are runners who fall and simple souls who are being hoaxed—runners after the ideal who stumble over realities, child-like dreamers for whom life delights to lie in wait. But, above all, they are past-masters in absentmindedness, with this superiority over their fellows that their absentmindedness is systematic and organised around one central idea, and that their mishaps are also quite coherent, thanks to the inexorable logic which reality applies to the correction of dreams, so that they kindle in those around them, by a series of cumulative effects, a hilarity capable of unlimited expansion.

Now, let us go a little further. Might not certain vices have the same relation to character that the rigidity of a fixed idea has to intellect? Whether as a moral kink or a crooked twist given to the will, vice has often the appearance of a curvature of the soul. Doubtless there are vices into which the soul plunges deeply with all its pregnant potency, which it rejuvenates and drags along with it into a moving circle of reincarnations. Those are tragic vices. But the vice capable of making us comic is, on the contrary, that which is brought from without, like a ready-made frame into which we are to step. It lends us its own rigidity instead of borrowing from us our flexibility. We do not render it more complicated; on the contrary, it simplifies us. Here, as we shall see later on in the concluding section of this study, lies the essential difference between comedy and drama. A drama, even when portraying passions or vices that bear a name, so completely incorporates them in the person that their names are forgotten, their general characteristics effaced, and we no longer think of them at all, but rather of the person in whom they are assimilated; hence, the title of a drama can seldom be anything else than a proper noun. On the other hand, many comedies have a common noun as their title: *l'Avare, le Joueur,* etc. Were you asked to think of a play capable of being called *le Jaloux,* for instance, you would find that *Sganarelle* or *George Dandin* would occur to your mind, but not *Othello: le Jaloux* could only be the title of a comedy. The reason is that, however intimately vice, when comic, is associated with persons, it none the less retains its simple, independent existence, it remains the central character, present though invisible, to which the characters in flesh and blood on the stage are attached. At times it delights in dragging them down with its own weight and making them share in its tumbles. More frequently, however, it plays on them as on an instrument or pulls the strings as though they were puppets. Look closely: you will find that the art of the comic poet consists in making us so well acquainted with the particular vice, in introducing us, the spectators, to such a degree of intimacy with it, that in the end we get hold of some of the strings of the marionette with which he is playing, and actually work them ourselves; this it is that explains part of the pleasure we feel. Here, too, it is really a kind of automatism that makes us laugh—an automatism, as we have already remarked, closely akin to mere absentmindedness. To realise this more fully, it need only be noted that a comic character is generally comic in proportion to his ignorance of himself. The comic person is unconscious. As though wearing the ring of Gyges with reverse effect, he becomes invisible to himself while remaining visible to all the world. A character in a tragedy will make no change in his conduct because he will know how it is judged by us; he may continue therein even though fully conscious of what he is and feeling keenly the horror he inspires in us. But a defect that is ridiculous, as soon as it feels itself to be so, endeavours to modify itself or at least to appear as though it did. Were Harpagon to see us laugh at his miserliness, I do not say that he would get rid of it, but he would either show it less or show it differently. Indeed, it is in this sense only that laughter "corrects men's manners." It makes us at once endeavour to appear what we ought to be, what some day we shall perhaps end in being.

It is unnecessary to carry this analysis any further. From the runner who falls to the simpleton who is hoaxed, from a state of being hoaxed to one of absentmindedness, from absentmindedness to wild enthusiasm, from wild enthusiasm to various distortions of character and will, we have followed the line of progress along which the comic becomes more and more deeply imbedded in the person, yet without ceasing, in its subtler manifestations, to recall to us some trace of what we noticed in its grosser forms, an effect of automatism and of inelasticity. Now we can obtain a first glimpse—a distant one, it is true, and still hazy and confused—of the laughable side of human nature and of the ordinary function of laughter.

What life and society require of each of us is a constantly alert attention that discerns the outlines of the present situation, together with a certain elasticity of mind and body to enable us to adapt ourselves in consequence. *Tension* and *elasticity* are two forces, mutually complementary, which life brings into play. If these two forces are lacking in the body to any considerable extent, we have sickness and infirmity and accidents of every kind. If they are lacking in the mind, we find every degree of mental deficiency, every variety of insanity. Finally, if they are lacking in the character, we have cases of the gravest inadaptibility to social life, which are the sources of misery and at times the causes of crime. Once these elements of inferiority that affect the serious side of existence are removed —and they tend to eliminate themselves in what has been called the struggle for life—the person can live, and that in common with other persons. But society asks for something more; it is not satisfied with simply living, it insists on living well. What it now has to dread is that each one of us, content with paying attention to what affects the essentials of life, will, so far as the rest is concerned, give way to the easy automatism of acquired habits. Another thing it must fear is that the members of whom it is made up, instead of aiming after an increasingly delicate adjustment of wills which will fit more and more perfectly into one another, will confine themselves to respecting simply the fundamental conditions of this adjustment: a cut-and-dried agreement among the persons will not satisfy it, it insists on a constant striving after reciprocal adaptation. Society will therefore be suspicious of all *inelasticity* of character, of mind and even of body, because it is the possible sign of a slumbering activity as well as of an activity with separatist tendencies, that inclines to swerve from the common centre round which society gravitates: in short, because it is the sign of an eccentricity. And yet, society cannot intervene at this stage by material repression, since it is not affected in a material fashion. It is confronted with something that makes it uneasy, but only as a symptom—scarcely a threat, at the very most a gesture. A gesture, therefore, will be its reply. Laughter must be something of this kind, a sort of *social gesture*. By the fear which it inspires, it restrains eccentricity, keeps constantly awake and in mutual contact certain activities of a secondary order which might retire into their shell and go to sleep, and in short, softens down whatever the surface of the social body may retain of mechanical inelasticity. Laughter, then, does not belong to the province of esthetics alone, since unconsciously (and even immorally in many particular instances) it pursues a utilitarian aim of general improvement. And yet there is something esthetic about it, since the comic comes into being just when society and the individual, freed from the worry of self-preservation, begin to regard themselves as works of art. In a word, if a circle be drawn round those actions and dispositions—implied in individual or social life—to which their natural consequences bring their own penalties, there remains outside this sphere of emotion and struggle—and within a neutral zone in which man simply exposes himself to man's curiosity—a certain rigidity of

body, mind and character that society would still
like to get rid of in order to obtain from its members
the greatest possible degree of elasticity and sociability. This rigidity is the comic, and laughter is its
corrective.

Still, we must not accept this formula as a definition of the comic. It is suitable only for cases that
are elementary, theoretical and perfect, in which the
comic is free from all adulteration. Nor do we offer
it, either, as an explanation. We prefer to make it, if
you will, the *leitmotiv* which is to accompany all
our explanations. We must ever keep it in mind,
though without dwelling on it too much, somewhat
as a skilful fencer must think of the discontinuous
movements of the lesson whilst his body is given up
to the continuity of the fencing-match. We will now
endeavour to reconstruct the sequence of comic
forms, taking up again the thread that leads from
the horseplay of a clown up to the most refined
effects of comedy, following this thread in its often
unforeseen windings, halting at intervals to look
around, and finally getting back, if possible, to the
point at which the thread is dangling and where we
shall perhaps find—since the comic oscillates between life and art—the general relation that art bears
to life.

III

Let us begin at the simplest point. What is a comic
physiognomy? Where does a ridiculous expression
of the face come from? And what is, in this case, the
distinction between the comic and the ugly? Thus
stated, the question could scarcely be answered in
any other than an arbitrary fashion. Simple though
it may appear, it is, even now, too subtle to allow of
a direct attack. We should have to begin with a

definition of ugliness, and then discover what addition the comic makes to it; now, ugliness is not much easier to analyse than is beauty. However, we will employ an artifice which will often stand us in good stead. We will exaggerate the problem, so to speak, by magnifying the effect to the point of making the cause visible. Suppose, then, we intensify ugliness to the point of deformity, and study the transition from the deformed to the ridiculous.

Now, certain deformities undoubtedly possess over others the sorry privilege of causing some persons to laugh; some hunchbacks, for instance, will excite laughter. Without at this point entering into useless details, we will simply ask the reader to think of a number of deformities, and then to divide them into two groups: on the one hand, those which nature has directed towards the ridiculous; and on the other, those which absolutely diverge from it. No doubt he will hit upon the following law: *A deformity that may become comic is a deformity that a normally built person could successfully imitate.*

Is it not, then, the case that the hunchback suggests the appearance of a person who holds himself badly? His back seems to have contracted an ugly stoop. By a kind of physical obstinacy, by *rigidity*, in a word, it persists in the habit it has contracted. Try to see with your eyes alone. Avoid reflection, and above all, do not reason. Abandon all your prepossessions; seek to recapture a fresh, direct and primitive impression. The vision you will reacquire will be one of this kind. You will have before you a man bent on cultivating a certain rigid attitude whose body, if one may use the expression, is one vast grin.

Now, let us go back to the point we wished to clear up. By toning down a deformity that is laughable, we ought to obtain an ugliness that is comic. A laughable expression of the face, then, is one that will make us think of something rigid and, so to speak, coagulated, in the wonted mobility of the face. What we shall see will be an ingrained twitching or a fixed grimace. It may be objected that every habitual expression of the face, even when graceful and beautiful, gives us this same impression of something stereotyped? Here an important distinction must be drawn. When we speak of expressive beauty or even expressive ugliness, when we say that a face possesses expression, we mean expression that may be stable, but which we conjecture to be mobile. It maintains, in the midst of its fixity, a certain indecision in which are obscurely portrayed all possible shades of the state of mind it expresses, just as the sunny promise of a warm day manifests itself in the haze of a spring morning. But a comic expression of the face is one that promises nothing more than it gives. It is a unique and permanent grimace. One would say that the person's whole moral life has crystallised into this particular cast of features. This is the reason why a face is all the more comic, the more nearly it suggests to us the idea of some simple mechanical action in which its personality would for ever be absorbed. Some faces seem to be always engaged in weeping, others in laughing or whistling, others, again, in eternally blowing an imaginary trumpet, and these are the most comic faces of all. Here again is exemplified the law according to which the more natural the explanation of the cause, the more comic is the effect. Automatism, *inelasticity*, habit that has been contracted and maintained, are clearly the causes why a face makes us laugh. But this effect gains in intensity when we are able to connect these characteristics with some deep-seated cause, a certain *fundamental absentmind-edness,* as though the soul had allowed itself to be fascinated and hypnotised by the materiality of a simple action.

We shall now understand the comic element in caricature. However regular we may imagine a face to be, however harmonious its lines and supple its movements, their adjustment is never altogether perfect: there will always be discoverable the signs of some impending bias, the vague suggestion of a possible grimace, in short, some favourite distortion towards which nature seems to be particularly inclined. The art of the caricaturist consists in detecting this, at times, imperceptible tendency, and in rendering it visible to all eyes by magnifying it. He makes his models grimace, as they would do themselves if they went to the end of their tether. Beneath the skin-deep harmony of form, he divines the deep-seated recalcitrance of matter. He realises disproportions and deformations which must have existed in nature as mere inclinations, but which have not succeeded in coming to a head, being held in check by a higher force. His art, which has a touch of the diabolical, raises up the demon who had been overthrown by the angel. Certainly, it is an art that exaggerates, and yet the definition would be very far from complete were exaggeration alone alleged to be its aim and object, for there exist caricatures that are more lifelike than portraits, caricatures in which the exaggeration is scarcely noticeable, whilst, inversely, it is quite possible to exaggerate to excess without obtaining a real caricature. For exaggeration to be comic, it must not appear as an aim, but rather as a means that the artist is using in order to make manifest to our eyes the distortions which he sees in embryo. It is this process of distortion that is of

Caricature

moment and interest. And that is precisely why we shall look for it even in those elements of the face that are incapable of movement, in the curve of a nose or the shape of an ear. For, in our eyes, form is always the outline of a movement. The caricaturist who alters the size of a nose, but respects its ground plan, lengthening it, for instance, in the very direction in which it was being lengthened by nature, is really making the nose indulge in a grin. Henceforth we shall always look upon the original as having determined to lengthen itself and start grinning. In this sense, one might say that Nature herself often meets with the successes of a caricaturist. In the movement through which she has slit that mouth, curtailed that chin and bulged out that cheek, she would appear to have succeeded in completing the intended grimace, thus outwitting the restraining supervision of a more reasonable force. In that case, the face we laugh at is, so to speak, its own caricature.

To sum up, whatever be the doctrine to which our reason assents, our imagination has a very clear-cut philosophy of its own: in every human form it sees the effort of a soul which is shaping matter, a soul which is infinitely supple and perpetually in motion, subject to no law of gravitation, for it is not the earth that attracts it. This soul imparts a portion of its winged lightness to the body it animates: the immateriality which thus passes into matter is what is called gracefulness. Matter, however, is obstinate and resists. It draws to itself the ever-alert activity of this higher principle, would fain convert it to its own inertia and cause it to revert to mere automatism. It would fain immobilise the intelligently varied movements of the body in stupidly contracted grooves, stereotype in permanent grimaces the fleeting expressions of the face, in short imprint on the whole person such an attitude as to make it appear immersed and absorbed in the materiality of some mechanical occupation instead of ceaselessly renewing its vitality by keeping in touch with a living ideal. Where matter thus succeeds in dulling the outward life of the soul, in petrifying its movements and thwarting its gracefulness, it achieves, at the expense of a body, an effect that is comic. If, then, at this point we wish to define the comic by comparing it with its contrary, we should have to contrast it with gracefulness even more than with beauty. It partakes rather of the unsprightly than of the unsightly, of *rigidness* rather than of *ugliness*.

IV

We will now pass from the comic element in *forms* to that in *gestures* and *movements*. Let us at once state the law which seems to govern all the phenomena of this kind. It may indeed be deduced without any difficulty from the considerations stated above.

The attitudes, gestures and movements of the human body are laughable in exact proportion as that body reminds us of a mere machine.

There is no need to follow this law through the details of its immediate applications, which are innumerable. To verify it directly, it would be sufficient to study closely the work of comic artists, eliminating entirely the element of caricature, and omitting that portion of the comic which is not inherent in the drawing itself. For, obviously, the comic element in a drawing is often a borrowed one, for which the text supplies all the stock-in-trade. I mean that the artist may be his own understudy in the shape of a satirist, or even a playwright, and that then we laugh far less at the drawings themselves than at the satire or comic incident they represent. But if we devote our whole attention to the drawing with the firm resolve to think of nothing else, we shall probably find that it is generally comic in proportion to the clearness, as well as the subtleness, with which it enables us to see a man as a jointed puppet. The suggestion must be a clear one, for inside the person we must distinctly perceive, as though through a glass, a set-up mechanism. But the suggestion must also be a subtle one, for the general appearance of the person, whose every limb has been made rigid as a machine, must continue to give us the impression of a living being. The more exactly these two images, that of a person and that of a machine, fit into each other, the more striking is the comic effect, and the more consummate the art of the draughtsman. The originality of a comic artist is thus expressed in the special kind of life he imparts to a mere puppet.

We will, however, leave on one side the immediate application of the principle, and at this point insist only on the more remote consequences. The illusion of a machine working in the inside of the person is a thing that only crops up amid a host of amusing effects; but for the most part it is a fleeting glimpse, that is immediately lost in the laughter it provokes. To render it permanent, analysis and reflection must be called into play.

In a public speaker, for instance, we find that gesture vies with speech. Jealous of the latter, gesture closely dogs the speaker's thought, demanding also to act as interpreter. Well and good; but then it must pledge itself to follow thought through all the phases of its development. An idea is something that grows, buds, blossoms and ripens from the beginning to the end of a speech. It never halts, never repeats itself. It must be changing every moment, for to cease to change would be to cease to live. Then let gesture display a like animation! Let it accept the fundamental law of life, which is the complete negation of repetition! But I find that a certain movement of head or arm, a movement always the same, seems to return at regular intervals. If I notice it and it succeeds in diverting my attention, if I wait for it to occur and it occurs when I expect it, then involuntarily I laugh. Why? Because I now have before me a machine that works automatically. This is no longer life, it is automatism established in life and imitating it. It belongs to the comic.

This is also the reason why gestures, at which we never dreamt of laughing, become laughable when imitated by another individual. The most elaborate explanations have been offered for this extremely simple fact. A little reflection, however, will show that our mental state is ever changing, and that if our gestures faithfully followed these inner movements, if they were as fully alive as we, they would never repeat themselves, and so would keep imitation at bay. We begin, then, to become imitable only when we cease to be ourselves. I mean our gestures can only be imitated in their mechanical uniformity, and therefore exactly in what is alien to our living personality. To imitate any one is to bring out the element of automatism he has allowed to creep into his person. And as this is the very essence of the ludicrous, it is no wonder that imitation gives rise to laughter.

Still, if the imitation of gestures is intrinsically laughable, it will become even more so when it busies itself in deflecting them, though without altering their form, towards some mechanical occupation, such as sawing wood, striking on an anvil, or tugging away at an imaginary bell-rope. Not that vulgarity is the essence of the comic,—although certainly it is to some extent an ingredient,—but rather that the incriminated gesture seems more frankly mechanical when it can be connected with a simple operation, as though it were intentionally mechanical. To suggest this mechanical interpretation ought to be one of the favourite devices of parody. We have reached this result through deduction, but I imagine clowns have long had an intuition of the fact.

This seems to me the solution of the little riddle propounded by Pascal in one passage of his *Thoughts*: "Two faces that are alike, although neither of them excites laughter by itself, make us laugh when together, on account of their likeness." It might just as well be said: "The gestures of a public speaker, no one of which is laughable by itself, excite laughter by their repetition." The truth is that a really living life should never repeat itself. Wherever there is repetition or complete similarity, we always suspect some mechanism at work behind the living. Analyse the impression you get from two faces that are too much alike, and you will find that you are thinking of two copies cast in the same mould, or two impressions of the same seal, or two reproductions of the same negative,—in a word, of some manufacturing process or other. This deflection of life towards the mechanical is here the real cause of laughter.

And laughter will be more pronounced still, if we find on the stage not merely two characters, as in the example from Pascal, but several, nay, as great a number as possible, the image of one another, who

come and go, dance and gesticulate together, simultaneously striking the same attitudes and tossing
their arms about in the same manner. This time, we
distinctly think of marionettes. Invisible threads
seem to us to be joining arms to arms, legs to legs,
each muscle in one face to its fellow-muscle in the
other: by reason of the absolute uniformity which
prevails, the very litheness of the bodies seems to
stiffen as we gaze, and the actors themselves seem
transformed into lifeless automata. Such, at least,
appears to be the artifice underlying this somewhat
obvious form of amusement. I daresay the perform-
ers have never read Pascal, but what they do is
merely to realise to the full the suggestions contained in Pascal's words. If, as is undoubtedly the
case, laughter is caused in the second instance by
the hallucination of a mechanical effect, it must already have been so, though in more subtle fashion,
in the first.

Continuing along this path, we dimly perceive the
increasingly important and far-reaching consequences of the law we have just stated. We faintly
catch still more fugitive glimpses of the mechanical
effects, glimpses suggested by man's complex actions, no longer merely by his gestures. We instinctively feel that the usual devices of comedy, the
periodical repetition of a word or a scene, the systematic inversion of the parts, the geometrical development of a farcical misunderstanding and many
other stage contrivances must derive their comic
force from the same source,—the art of the playwright probably consisting in setting before us an
obvious clockwork arrangement of human events,
while carefully preserving an outward aspect of
probability and thereby retaining something of the
suppleness of life. But we must not forestall results

which will be duly disclosed in the course of our analysis.

v

Before going further, let us halt a moment and glance around. As we hinted at the outset of this study, it would be idle to attempt to derive every comic effect from one simple formula. The formula exists well enough in a certain sense, but its development does not follow a straightforward course. What I mean is that the process of deduction ought from time to time to stop and study certain culminating effects, and that these effects each appear as models round which new effects resembling them take their places in a circle. These latter are not deductions from the formula, but are comic through their relationship with those that are. To quote Pascal again, I see no objection, at this stage, to defining the process by the curve which that geometrician studied under the name of *roulette* or cycloid—the curve traced by a point in the circumference of a wheel when the carriage is advancing in a straight line: this point turns like the wheel, though it advances like the carriage. Or else we might think of an immense avenue such as are to be seen in the forest of Fontainebleau, with *crosses* at intervals to indicate the crossways: at each of these we shall walk round the cross, explore for a while the paths that open out before us, and then return to our original course. Now, we have just reached one of these mental crossways. *Something mechanical encrusted on the living* will represent a cross at which we must halt, a central image from which the imagination branches off in different directions. What are these directions? There appear to be three main ones. We will follow them one after the other, and then continue our onward course.

1. In the first place, this view of the mechanical and the living dovetailed into each other makes us incline towards the vaguer image of *some rigidity or other* applied to the mobility of life, in an awkward attempt to follow its lines and counterfeit its suppleness. Here we perceive how easy it is for a garment to become ridiculous. It might almost be said that every fashion is laughable in some respect. Only, when we are dealing with the fashion of the day, we are so accustomed to it that the garment seems, in our mind, to form one with the individual wearing it. We do not separate them in imagination. The idea no longer occurs to us to contrast the inert rigidity of the covering with the living suppleness of the object covered: consequently, the comic here remains in a latent condition. It will only succeed in emerging when the natural incompatibility is so deep-seated between the covering and the covered that even an immemorial association fails to cement this union: a case in point is our head and top hat. Suppose, however, some eccentric individual dresses himself in the fashion of former times our attention is immediately drawn to the clothes themselves; we absolutely distinguish them from the individual, we say that the latter *is disguising himself,* —as though every article of clothing were not a disguise!—and the laughable aspect of fashion comes out of the shadow into the light.

Here we are beginning to catch a faint glimpse of the highly intricate difficulties raised by this problem of the comic. One of the reasons that must have given rise to many erroneous or unsatisfactory theories of laughter is that many things are comic *de jure* without being comic *de facto,* the continuity of custom having deadened within them the comic quality. A sudden dissolution of continuity is needed, a break with fashion, for this quality to revive. Hence the impression that this dissolution of continuity is the parent of the comic, whereas all it does is to bring it to our notice. Hence, again, the explanation of laughter by *surprise, contrast,* etc., definitions which would equally apply to a host of cases in which we have no inclination whatever to laugh. The truth of the matter is far from being so simple.

But to return to our idea of disguise, which, as we have just shown, has been entrusted with the special mandate of arousing laughter. It will not be out of place to investigate the uses it makes of this power.

Why do we laugh at a head of hair which has changed from dark to blond? What is there comic about a rubicund nose? And why does one laugh at a negro? The question would appear to be an embarrassing one, for it has been asked by successive psychologists such as Hecker, Kraepelin and Lipps, and all have given different replies. And yet I rather fancy the correct answer was suggested to me one day in the street by an ordinary cabby, who applied the expression "unwashed" to the negro fare he was driving. Unwashed! Does not this mean that a black face, in our imagination, is one daubed over with ink or soot? If so, then a red nose can only be one which has received a coating of vermilion. And so we see that the notion of disguise has passed on something of its comic quality to instances in which there is actually no disguise, though there might be. In the former set of examples, although his usual dress was distinct from the individual, it appeared in our mind to form one with him, because we had become accustomed to the sight. In the latter, although the black or red colour is indeed inherent in the skin, we look upon it as artificially laid on, because it surprises us.

But here we meet with a fresh crop of difficulties in the theory of the comic. Such a proposition as the following: "My usual dress forms part of my body" is absurd in the eyes of reason. Yet imagination looks upon it as true. "A red nose is a painted nose," "A negro is a white man in disguise," are also absurd to the reason which rationalises; but they are gospel truths to pure imagination. So there is a logic of the imagination which is not the logic of reason, one which at times is even opposed to the latter, with which, however, philosophy must reckon, not only in the study of the comic, but in every other investigation of the same kind. It is something like the logic of dreams, though of dreams that have not been left to the whim of individual fancy, being the dreams dreamt by the whole of society. In order to reconstruct this hidden logic, a special kind of effort is needed, by which the outer crust of carefully stratified judgments and firmly established ideas will be lifted, and we shall behold in the depths of our mind, like a sheet of subterranean water, the flow of an unbroken stream of images which pass from one into another. This interpenetration of images does not come about by chance. It obeys laws, or rather habits, which hold the same relation to imagination that logic does to thought.

Let us then follow this logic of the imagination in the special case in hand. A man in disguise is comic. A man we regard as disguised is also comic. So, by analogy, any disguise is seen to become comic, not only that of a man, but that of society also, and even the disguise of nature.

Let us start with nature. You laugh at a dog that is half-clipped, at a bed of artificially coloured flowers, at a wood in which the trees are plastered over with election addresses, etc. Look for the reason, and you will see that you are once more thinking of a masquerade. Here, however, the comic element is very faint; it is too far from its source. If you wish to strengthen it, you must go back to the source itself and contrast the derived image, that of a masquerade, with the original one, which, be it remembered, was that of a mechanical tampering with life. In "a nature that is mechanically tampered with" we possess a thoroughly comic theme, on which fancy will be able to play ever so many variations with the certainty of successfully provoking the heartiest hilarity. You may call to mind that amusing passage in *Tartarin sur les Alpes*, in which Bompard makes Tartarin—and therefore also the reader to some slight extent—accept the idea of a Switzerland choke-full of machinery like the basement of the *Opéra*, and run by a company which maintains a series of waterfalls, glaciers and artificial crevasses. The same theme reappears, though transposed in quite another key, in the *Novel Notes* of the English humorist, Jerome K. Jerome. An elderly Lady Bountiful, who does not want her deeds of charity to take up too much of her time, provides homes within easy hail of her mansion for the conversion of atheists who have been specially manufactured for her, so to speak, and for a number of honest folk who have been made into drunkards so that she may cure them of their failing, etc. There are comic phrases in which this theme is audible, like a distant echo, coupled with an ingenuousness, whether sincere or affected, which acts as accompaniment. Take, as an instance, the remark made by a lady whom Cassini, the astronomer, had invited to see an eclipse of the moon. Arriving too late, she said, "M. de Cassini, I know, will have the goodness to begin it all over again, to please me." Or, take again the exclamation of one of Gondinet's characters on arriving in a town and learning that there is an extinct volcano in the neighbourhood, "They had a volcano, and they have let it go out!"

Let us go on to society. As we are both in and of it, we cannot help treating it as a living being. Any image, then, suggestive of the notion of a society disguising itself, or of a social masquerade, so to speak, will be laughable. Now, such a notion is formed when we perceive anything inert or stereotyped, or simply ready-made, on the surface of living society. There we have rigidity over again, clashing with the inner suppleness of life. The ceremonial side of social life must, therefore, always include a latent comic element, which is only waiting for an opportunity to burst into full view. It might be said that ceremonies are to the social body what clothing is to the individual body: they owe their seriousness to the fact that they are identified, in our minds, with the serious object with which custom associates them, and when we isolate them in imagination, they forthwith lose their seriousness. For any ceremony, then, to become comic, it is enough that our attention be fixed on the ceremonial element in it, and that we neglect its matter, as philosophers say, and think only of its form. Every one knows how easily the comic spirit exercises its ingenuity on social actions of a stereotyped nature, from an ordinary prize-distribution to the solemn sitting of a court of justice. Any form or formula is a ready-made frame into which the comic element may be fitted.

Here, again, the comic will be emphasised by bringing it nearer to its source. From the idea of travesty, a derived one, we must go back to the original idea, that of a mechanism superposed upon life. Already, the stiff and starched formality of any ceremonial suggests to us an image of this kind. For, as soon as we forget the serious object of a solemnity or a ceremony, those taking part in it give us the impression of puppets in motion. Their mobility seems to adopt as a model the immobility of a formula. It becomes automatism. But complete automatism is only reached in the official, for instance, who performs his duty like a mere machine, or again in the unconsciousness that marks an administrative regulation working with inexorable fatality, and setting itself up for a law of nature. Quite by chance, when reading the newspaper, I came across a specimen of the comic of this type. Twenty years ago, a large steamer was wrecked off the coast at Dieppe. With considerable difficulty some of the passengers were rescued in a boat. A few custom-house officers, who had courageously rushed to their assistance, began by asking them "if they had anything to declare." We find something similar, though the idea is a more subtle one, in the remark of an M.P. when questioning the Home Secretary on the morrow of a terrible murder which took place in a railway carriage: "The assassin, after despatching his victim, must have got out the wrong side of the train, thereby infringing the Company's rules."

A mechanical element introduced into nature and an automatic regulation of society, such, then, are the two types of laughable effects at which we have arrived. It remains for us, in conclusion, to combine them and see what the result will be.

The result of the combination will evidently be a

human regulation of affairs usurping the place of the laws of nature. We may call to mind the answer Sganarelle gave Géronte when the latter remarked that the heart was on the left side and the liver on the right: "Yes, it was so formerly, but we have altered all that; now, we practise medicine in quite a new way." We may also recall the consultation between M. de Pourceaugnac's two doctors: "The arguments you have used are so erudite and elegant that it is impossible for the patient not to be hypochondriacally melancholic; or, even if he were not, he must surely become so because of the elegance of the things you have said and the accuracy of your reasoning." We might multiply examples, for all we need do would be to call up Molière's doctors, one after the other. However far, moreover, comic fancy may seem to go, reality at times undertakes to improve upon it. It was suggested to a contemporary philosopher, an out-and-out arguer, that his arguments, though irreproachable in their deductions, had experience against them. He put an end to the discussion by merely remarking, "Experience is in the wrong." The truth is, this idea of regulating life as a matter of business routine is more widespread than might be imagined; it is natural in its way, although we have just obtained it by an artificial process of reconstruction. One might say that it gives us the very quintessence of pedantry, which, at bottom, is nothing else than art pretending to outdo nature.

To sum up, then, we have one and the same effect, which assumes ever subtler forms as it passes from the idea of an artificial *mechanisation* of the human body, if such an expression is permissible, to that of any substitution whatsoever of the artificial for the natural. A less and less rigorous logic, that more and more resembles the logic of dreamland, transfers the same relationship into higher and higher spheres, between increasingly immaterial terms, till in the end we find a mere administrative enactment occupying the same relation to a natural or moral law that a ready-made garment, for instance, does to the living body. We have now gone right to the end of the first of the three directions we had to follow. Let us turn to the second and see where it will lead us.

2. Our starting-point is again "something mechanical encrusted upon the living." Where did the comic come from in this case? It came from the fact that the living body became rigid, like a machine. Accordingly, it seemed to us that the living body ought to be the perfection of suppleness, the ever-alert activity of a principle always at work. But this activity would really belong to the soul rather than to the body. It would be the very flame of life, kindled within us by a higher principle and perceived through the body, as though through a glass. When we see only gracefulness and suppleness in the living body, it is because we disregard in it the elements of weight, of resistance, and, in a word, of matter; we forget its materiality and think only of its vitality, a vitality which we regard as derived from the very principle of intellectual and moral life. Let us suppose, however, that our attention is drawn to this material side of the body; that, so far from sharing in the lightness and subtlety of the principle with which it is animated, the body is no more in our eyes than a heavy and cumbersome vesture, a kind of irksome ballast which holds down to earth a soul eager to rise aloft. Then the body will become to the soul what, as we have just seen, the garment was to the body itself—inert matter dumped down

upon living energy. The impression of the comic will be produced as soon as we have a clear apprehension of this putting the one on the other. And we shall experience it most strongly when we are shown the soul *tantalised* by the needs of the body: on the one hand, the moral personality with its intelligently varied energy, and, on the other, the stupidly monotonous body, perpetually obstructing everything with its machine-like obstinacy. The more paltry and uniformly repeated these claims of the body, the more striking will be the result. But that is only a matter of degree, and the general law of these phenomena may be formulated as follows: *Any incident is comic that calls our attention to the physical in a person, when it is the moral side that is concerned.*

Why do we laugh at a public speaker who sneezes just at the most pathetic moment of his speech? Where lies the comic element in this sentence, taken from a funeral speech and quoted by a German philosopher: "He was virtuous and plump"? It lies in the fact that our attention is suddenly recalled from the soul to the body. Similar instances abound in daily life, but if you do not care to take the trouble to look for them, you have only to open at random a volume of Labiche, you will be almost certain to light upon an effect of this kind. Now, we have a speaker whose most eloquent sentences are cut short by the twinges of a bad tooth; now, one of the characters who never begins to speak without stopping in the middle to complain of his shoes being too small, or his belt too tight, etc. *A person embarrassed by his body* is the image suggested to us in all these examples. The reason that excessive stoutness is laughable is probably because it calls up an image of the same kind. I almost think that this too is what sometimes makes bashfulness somewhat ridiculous. The bashful man rather gives the impression of a person embarrassed by his body, looking round for some convenient cloak-room in which to deposit it.

This is just why the tragic poet is so careful to avoid anything calculated to attract attention to the material side of his heroes. No sooner does anxiety about the body manifest itself than the intrusion of a comic element is to be feared. On this account, the hero in a tragedy does not eat or drink or warm himself. He does not even sit down any more than can be helped. To sit down in the middle of a fine speech would imply that you remembered you had a body. Napoleon, who was a psychologist when he wished to be so, had noticed that the transition from tragedy to comedy is effected simply by sitting down. In the *Journal inédit* of Baron Gourgaud— when speaking of an interview with the Queen of Prussia after the battle of Iéna—he expresses him- self in the following terms: "She received me in tragic fashion like Chimène: Justice! Sire, Justice! Magdeburg! Thus she continued in a way most em- barrassing to me. Finally, to make her change her style, I requested her to take a seat. This is the best method for cutting short a tragic scene, for as soon as you are seated it all becomes comedy."

Let us now give a wider scope to this image of *the body taking precedence of the soul.* We shall obtain something more general—*the manner seeking to outdo the matter, the letter aiming at ousting the spirit.* Is it not perchance this idea that comedy is trying to suggest to us when holding up a profession to ridicule? It makes the lawyer, the magistrate and the doctor speak as though health and justice were of little moment, the main point being that we should have lawyers, magistrates and doctors, and that all outward formalities pertaining to these professions should be scrupulously respected. And so we find the means substituted for the end, the manner for the matter; no longer is it the profession that is made for the public, but rather the public for the profession. Constant attention to form and the mechanical application of rules here bring about a kind of professional automatism analogous to that imposed upon the soul by the habits of the body, and equally laughable. Numerous are the examples of this on the stage. Without entering into details of the variations executed on this theme, let us quote two or three passages in which the theme itself is set forth in all its simplicity. "You are only bound to treat people according to form," says Doctor Diafoirus in the *Malade Imaginaire*. Again, says Doctor Bahis, in *L'Amour médecin:* "It is better to die through following the rules than to recover through violating them." In the same play, Desfonandrès had previously said: "We must always observe the formalities of professional etiquette, whatever may happen." And the reason is given by Tomès, his colleague: "A dead man is but a dead man, but the non-observance of a formality causes a notable prejudice to the whole faculty." Brid'oison's words, though embodying a rather different idea, are none the less significant: "F-form, mind you, f-form. A man laughs at a judge in a morning coat, and yet he would quake with dread at the mere sight of an attorney in his gown. F-form, all a matter of f-form."

Here we have the first illustration of a law which will appear with increasing distinctness as we proceed with our task. When a musician strikes a note on an instrument, other notes start up of themselves, not so loud as the first, yet connected with it by certain definite relations, which coalesce with it and determine its quality. These are what are called in physics the overtones of the fundamental note. It would seem that comic fancy, even in its most far-fetched inventions, obeys a similar law. For instance, consider this comic note: appearance seeking to triumph over reality. If our analysis is correct, this note must have as its overtones the body tantalizing the mind, the body taking precedence of the mind. No sooner, then, does the comic poet strike the first note than he will add the second on to it, involuntarily and instinctively. In other words, *he will duplicate what is ridiculous professionally with something that is ridiculous physically.*

When Brid'oison the judge comes stammering on to the stage, is he not actually preparing us, by this very stammering, to understand the phenomenon of intellectual ossification we are about to witness? What bond of secret relationship can there be between the physical defect and the moral infirmity? It is difficult to say; yet we feel that the relationship is there, though we cannot express it in words. Perhaps the situation required that this judging machine should also appear before us as a talking machine. However it may be, no other overtone could more perfectly have completed the fundamental note.

When Molière introduces to us the two ridiculous doctors, Bahis and Macroton, in *L'Amour médecin,* he makes one of them speak very slowly, as though scanning his words syllable by syllable, whilst the other stutters. We find the same contrast between the two lawyers in *Monsieur de Pourceaugnac.* In the rhythm of speech is generally to be found the physical peculiarity that is destined to complete the element of professional ridicule. When the author has failed to suggest a defect of this kind, it is seldom the case that the actor does not instinctively invent one.

Consequently, there is a natural relationship, which we equally naturally recognise, between the two images we have been comparing with each other, the mind crystallising in certain grooves, and the body losing its elasticity through the influence of certain defects. Whether or not our attention be diverted from the matter to the manner, or from the moral to the physical, in both cases the same sort of impression is conveyed to our imagination; in both, then, the comic is of the same kind. Here, once more, it has been our aim to follow the natural trend of the movement of the imagination. This trend or direction, it may be remembered, was the second of those offered to us, starting from a central image. A third and final path remains unexplored, along which we will now proceed.

3. Let us then return, for the last time, to our central image—something mechanical encrusted on something living. Here, the living being under discussion was a human being, a person. A mechanical arrangement, on the other hand, is a thing. What, therefore, incited laughter, was the momentary transformation of a person into a thing, if one considers the image from this standpoint. Let us then pass from the exact idea of a machine to the vaguer one of a thing in general. We shall have a fresh series of laughable images which will be obtained by taking a blurred impression, so to speak, of the outlines of the former and will bring us to this new law: *We laugh every time a person gives us the impression of being a thing.*

We laugh at Sancho Panza tumbled into a bedquilt and tossed into the air like a football. We laugh at Baron Munchausen turned into a cannon-ball and travelling through space. But certain tricks of circus clowns might afford a still more precise exemplification of the same law. True, we should have to eliminate the jokes, mere interpolations by the clown in his main theme, and keep in mind only the theme itself, that is to say, the divers attitudes, capers and movements which form the strictly "clownish" element in the clown's art. On two occasions only have I been able to observe this style of the comic in its unadulterated state, and in both I received the same impression. The first time, the clowns came and went, collided, fell and jumped up again in a uniformly accelerated rhythm, visibly intent upon effecting a *crescendo*. And it was more and more to the jumping up again, the *rebound*, that the attention of the public was attracted. Gradually, one lost sight of the fact that they were men of flesh and blood like ourselves; one began to think of bundles of all sorts, falling and knocking against each other. Then the vision assumed a more definite aspect. The forms grew rounder, the bodies rolled together and seemed to pick themselves up like balls. Then at last appeared the image towards which the whole of this scene had doubtless been unconsciously evolving,—large rubber balls hurled against one another in every direction. The second scene, though even coarser than the first, was no less instructive. There came on the stage two men, each with an enormous head, bald as a billiard ball. In their hands they carried large sticks which each, in turn, brought down on to the other's cranium. Here, again, a certain gradation was observable. After each blow, the bodies seemed to grow heavier and more unyielding, overpowered by an increasing degree of rigidity. Then came the return blow, in each case heavier and more resounding than the last, coming, too, after a longer interval. The skulls gave forth a formidable ring throughout the silent house. At last the two bodies, each quite rigid and as straight as an arrow, slowly bent over towards each other, the sticks came crashing down for the last time on to the two heads with a thud as of enormous mallets falling upon oaken beams, and the pair lay prone upon the ground. At that instant appeared in all its vividness the suggestion that the two artists had gradually driven into the imagination of the spectators: "We are about to become . . . we have now become solid wooden dummies."

A kind of dim, vague instinct may enable even an uncultured mind to get an inkling here of the subtler results of psychological science. We know that it is possible to call up hallucinatory visions in a hypnotised subject by simple suggestion. If he be told that a bird is perched on his hand, he will see the bird and watch it fly away. The idea suggested, however, is far from being always accepted with like docility. Not infrequently, the mesmeriser only succeeds in getting an idea into his subject's head by slow degrees through a carefully graduated series of hints. He will then start with objects really perceived by the subject, and will endeavour to make the perception of these objects more and more indefinite; then, step by step, he will bring out of this state of mental chaos the precise form of the object of which he wishes to create an hallucination. Something of the kind happens to many people when dropping off to sleep; they see those coloured, fluid, shapeless masses, which occupy the field of vision, insensibly solidifying into distinct objects. Consequently, the gradual passing from the dim and vague to the clear and distinct is the method of sug-

gestion *par excellence*. I fancy it might be found to
be at the root of a good many comic suggestions,
especially in the coarser forms of the comic, in
which the transformation of a person into a thing
seems to be taking place before our eyes. But there
are other and more subtle methods in use, among
poets, for instance, which perhaps unconsciously
lead to the same end. By a certain arrangement of
rhythm, rhyme and assonance, it is possible to lull
the imagination, to rock it to and fro between like
and like with a regular see-saw motion, and thus
prepare it submissively to accept the vision suggested. Listen to these few lines of Régnard, and
see whether something like the fleeting image of a
doll does not cross the field of your imagination:

> . . . Plus, il doit à maints particuliers
> La somme de dix mil une livre une obole,
> Pour l'avoir sans relâche un an sur sa parole
> Habillé, voituré, chauffé, chaussé, ganté,
> Alimenté, rasé, désaltéré, porté.[1]

Is not something of the same kind found in the
following sally of Figaro's (though here an attempt
is perhaps made to suggest the image of an animal
rather than that of a thing): "Quel homme est-ce?
—C'est un beau, gros, court, jeune vieillard, gris
pommelé, rusé, rasé, blasé, qui guette et furette, et
gronde et geint tout à la fois."[2]

---

[1] Further, he owes to many an honest wight
   Item—the sum two thousand pounds, one farthing,
   For having on his simple word of honour
   Sans intermission for an entire year
   Clothed him, conveyed him, warmed him, shod him,
      gloved him,
   Fed him and shaved him, quenched his thirst and borne
      him.
[2] "What sort of man is here?—He is a handsome, stout,
short, youthful old gentleman, iron-grey, an artful knave,

Now, between these coarse scenes and these subtle suggestions there is room for a countless number of amusing effects, for all those that can be obtained by talking about persons as one would do about mere things. We will only select one or two instances from the plays of Labiche, in which they are legion.

Just as M. Perrichon is getting into the railway carriage, he makes certain of not forgetting any of his parcels: "Four, five, six, my wife seven, my daughter eight, and myself nine." In another play, a fond father is boasting of his daughter's learning in the following terms: "She will tell you, without faltering, all the kings of France that have occurred." This phrase, "that have occurred," though not exactly transforming the kings into mere things, likens them, all the same, to events of an impersonal nature.

As regards this latter example, note that it is unnecessary to complete the identification of the person with the thing to ensure a comic effect. It is sufficient for us to start in this direction by feigning, for instance, to confuse the person with the function he exercises. I will only quote a sentence spoken by a village mayor in one of About's novels: "The prefect, who has always shown us the same kindness, though he has been changed several times since 1847 . . ."

All these witticisms are constructed on the same model. We might make up any number of them, when once we are in possession of the recipe. But the art of the story-teller or the playwright does not merely consist in concocting jokes. The difficulty lies

clean shaved, clean 'used up,' who spies and pries and growls and groans all in the same breath."

in giving to a joke its power of suggestion, *i.e.* in making it acceptable. And we only do accept it either because it seems to be the natural product of a particular state of mind or because it is in keeping with the circumstances of the case. For instance, we are aware that M. Perrichon is greatly excited on the occasion of his first railway journey. The expression "to occur" is one that must have cropped up a good many times in the lessons repeated by the girl before her father; it makes us think of such a repetition. Lastly, admiration of the governmental machine might, at a pinch, be extended to the point of making us believe that no change takes place in the prefect when he changes his name, and that the function gets carried on independently of the functionary.

We have now reached a point very far from the original cause of laughter. Many a comic form, that cannot be explained by itself, can indeed only be understood from its resemblance to another, which only makes us laugh by reason of its relationship with a third, and so on indefinitely, so that psychological analysis, however luminous and searching, will go astray unless it holds the thread along which the comic impression has travelled from one end of the series to the other. Where does this progressive continuity come from? What can be the driving force, the strange impulse which causes the comic to glide thus from image to image, farther and farther away from the starting-point, until it is broken up and lost in infinitely remote analogies? But what is that force which divides and subdivides the branches of a tree into smaller boughs and its roots into radicles? An inexorable law dooms every living energy, during the brief interval allotted to it in time, to cover the widest possible extent in space. Now, comic fancy is indeed a living energy, a

strange plant that has flourished on the stony portions of the social soil, until such time as culture
should allow it to vie with the most refined products of art. True, we are far from great art in the
examples of the comic we have just been reviewing.
But we shall draw nearer to it, though without
attaining to it completely, in the following chapter.
Below art, we find artifice, and it is this zone of
artifice, midway between nature and art, that we
are now about to enter. We are going to deal with
the comic playwright and the wit.

repetition
inversion
reciprocity p 123

THE COMIC ELEMENT IN SITUATIONS AND THE COMIC ELEMENT IN WORDS

I

We have studied the comic element in forms, in attitudes, and in movements generally; now let us look for it in actions and in situations. We encounter, indeed, this kind of comic readily enough in everyday life. It is not here, however, that it best lends itself to analysis. Assuming that the stage is both a magnified and a simplified view of life, we shall find that comedy is capable of furnishing us with more information than real life on this particular part of our subject. Perhaps we ought even to carry simplification still farther, and, going back to our earliest recollections, try to discover, in the games that amused us as children, the first faint traces of the combinations that make us laugh as grown-up persons. We are too apt to speak of our feelings of pleasure and of pain as though full grown at birth, as though each one of them had not a history of its own. Above all, we are too apt to ignore the childish element, so to speak, latent in most of our joyful emotions. And yet, how many of our present pleasures, were we to examine them closely, would shrink into nothing more than memories of past ones! What would there be left of many of our emotions, were we to reduce them to the exact quantum of pure feeling they contain by subtracting from them all that is merely reminiscence? Indeed, it seems possible that, after a certain age, we become impervious to all fresh or novel forms of joy, and

pleasure and reaction based on reminiscence a previous experience

the sweetest pleasures of the middle-aged man are perhaps nothing more than a revival of the sensations of childhood, a balmy zephyr wafted in fainter and fainter breaths by a past that is ever receding. In any case, whatever reply we give to this broad question, one thing is certain: there can be no break in continuity between the child's delight in games and that of the grown-up person. Now, comedy is a game, a game that imitates life. And since, in the games of the child when working its dolls and puppets, many of the movements are produced by strings, ought we not to find those same strings, somewhat frayed by wear, reappearing as the threads that knot together the situations in a comedy? Let us, then, start with the games of a child, and follow the imperceptible process by which, as he grows himself, he makes his puppets grow, inspires them with life, and finally brings them to an ambiguous state in which, without ceasing to be puppets, they have yet become human beings. We thus obtain characters of a comedy type. And upon them we can test the truth of the law of which all our preceding analyses gave an inkling, a law in accordance with which we will define all broadly comic situations in general. *Any arrangement of acts and events is comic which gives us, in a single combination, the illusion of life and the distinct impression of a mechanical arrangement.*

1. *The Jack-in-the-box.*—As children we have all played with the little man who springs out of his box. You squeeze him flat, he jumps up again. Push him lower, and he shoots up still higher. Crush him down beneath the lid, and often he will send everything flying. It is hard to tell whether or not the toy itself is very ancient, but the kind of amusement it affords

repetition

belongs to all time. It is a struggle between two
stubborn elements, one of which, being simply mechanical, generally ends by giving in to the other,
which treats it as a plaything. A cat playing with a
mouse, which from time to time she releases like a
spring, only to pull it up short with a stroke of her
paw, indulges in the same kind of amusement.

We will now pass on to the theatre, beginning
with a Punch and Judy show. No sooner does the
policeman put in an appearance on the stage than,
naturally enough, he receives a blow which fells him.
He springs to his feet, a second blow lays him flat.
A repetition of the offence is followed by a repetition of the punishment. Up and down the constable
flops and hops with the uniform rhythm of the bend-
ing and release of a spring, whilst the spectators
laugh louder and louder.

Now, let us think of a spring that is rather of a
moral type, an idea that is first expressed, then repressed, and then expressed again; a stream of words
that bursts forth, is checked, and keeps on starting
afresh. Once more we have the vision of one stubborn force, counteracted by another, equally pertinacious. This vision, however, will have discarded a
portion of its materiality. No longer is it Punch and
Judy that we are watching, but rather a real comedy.

Many a comic scene may indeed be referred to
this simple type. For instance, in the scene of the
Mariage forcé between Sganarelle and Pancrace,
the entire *vis comica* lies in the conflict set up between the idea of Sganarelle, who wishes to make
the philosopher listen to him, and the obstinacy of
the philosopher, a regular talking-machine, working
automatically. As the scene progresses, the image of
the Jack-in-the-box becomes more apparent, so that
at last the characters themselves adopt its move-

ments—Sganarelle pushing Pancrace, each time he shows himself, back into the wings, Pancrace returning to the stage after each repulse, to continue his patter. And when Sganarelle finally drives Pancrace back and shuts him up inside the house—inside the box, one is tempted to say—a window suddenly flies open, and the head of the philosopher again appears, as though it had burst open the lid of a box.

The same by-play occurs in the *Malade Imaginaire*. Through the mouth of Monsieur Purgon the outraged medical profession pours out its vials of wrath upon Argan, threatening him with every disease that flesh is heir to. And every time Argan rises from his seat, as though to silence Purgon, the latter disappears for a moment, being, as it were, thrust back into the wings; then, as though impelled by a spring, he rebounds on to the stage with a fresh curse on his lips. The self-same exclamation: "Monsieur Purgon!" recurs at regular beats, and, as it were, marks the *tempo* of this little scene.

Let us scrutinise more closely the image of the spring which is bent, released, and bent again. Let us disentangle its central element, and we shall hit upon one of the usual processes of classic comedy, —*repetition*.

Why is it there is something comic in the repetition of a word on the stage? No theory of the ludicrous seems to offer a satisfactory answer to this very simple question. Nor can an answer be found, so long as we look for the explanation of an amusing word or phrase in the phrase or word itself, apart from all it suggests to us. Nowhere will the usual method prove to be so inadequate as here. With the exception, however, of a few special instances to which we shall recur later, the repetition of a word is never laughable in itself. It makes us laugh only because it symbolises a special play of moral elements, this play itself being the symbol of an altogether material diversion. It is the diversion of the cat with the mouse, the diversion of the child pushing back the Jack-in-the-box, time after time, to the bottom of his box—but in a refined and spiritualised form, transferred to the realm of feelings and ideas. Let us then state the law which we think defines the main comic varieties of word-repetition on the stage: *In a comic repetition of words we generally find two terms: a repressed feeling which goes off like a spring, and an idea that delights in repressing the feeling anew.*

When Dorine is telling Orgon of his wife's illness, and the latter continually interrupts him with inquiries as to the health of Tartuffe, the question: "Et Tartuffe?" repeated every few moments, affords us the distinct sensation of a spring being released. This spring Dorine delights in pushing back, each time she resumes her account of Elmire's illness. And when Scapin informs old Géronte that his son has been taken prisoner on the famous galley, and that a ransom must be paid without delay, he is playing with the avarice of Géronte exactly as Dorine does with the infatuation of Orgon. The old man's avarice is no sooner repressed than up it springs again automatically, and it is this automatism that Molière tries to indicate by the mechanical repetition of a sentence expressing regret at the money that would have to be forthcoming: "What the deuce did he want in that galley?" The same criticism is applicable to the scene in which Valère points out to Harpagon the wrong he would be doing in marrying his daughter to a man she did not love. "No dowry wanted!" interrupts the miserly Harpagon every few moments. Behind this exclamation, which recurs

automatically we faintly discern a complete repeat-
ing-machine set going by a fixed idea.

At times this mechanism is less easy to detect, and
here we encounter a fresh difficulty in the theory of
the comic. Sometimes the whole interest of a scene
lies in one character playing a double part, the
intervening speaker acting as a mere prism, so to
speak, through which the dual personality is developed. We run the risk, then, of going astray, if we
look for the secret of the effect in what we see and
hear,—in the external scene played by the characters,—and not in the altogether inner comedy of
which this scene is no more than the outer refraction.
For instance, when Alceste stubbornly repeats the
words, "I don't say that!" on Oronte asking him if
he thinks his poetry bad, the repetition is laughable,
though evidently Oronte is not now playing with
Alceste at the game we have just described. We
must be careful, however, for, in reality, we have
two men in Alceste: on the one hand, the "misan-
thropist" who has vowed henceforth to call a spade
a spade, and on the other the gentleman who cannot
unlearn, in a trice, the usual forms of politeness, or
even, it may be, just the honest fellow who, when
called upon to put his words into practice, shrinks
from wounding another's self-esteem or hurting his
feelings. Accordingly, the real scene is not between
Alceste and Oronte, it is between Alceste and himself. The one Alceste would fain blurt out the truth,
and the other stops his mouth just as he is on the
point of telling everything. Each "I don't say that!"
reveals a growing effort to repress something that
strives and struggles to get out. And so the tone in
which the phrase is uttered gets more and more
violent, Alceste becoming more and more angry—
not with Oronte, as he thinks—but with himself. The

tension of the spring is continually being renewed and reinforced, until it at last goes off with a bang. Here, as elsewhere, we have the same identical mechanism of repetition.

For a man to make a resolution never henceforth to say what he does not think, even though he "openly defy the whole human race," is not necessarily laughable; it is a phase of life at its highest and best. For another man, through amiability, selfishness or disdain, to prefer to flatter people, is only another phase of life; there is nothing in it to make us laugh. You may even combine these two men into one, and arrange that the individual waver between offensive frankness and delusive politeness, this duel between two opposing feelings will not even then be comic, rather it will appear the essence of seriousness if these two feelings through their very distinctness complete each other, develop side by side, and make up between them a composite mental condition, adopting, in short, a *modus vivendi* which merely gives us the complex impression of life. But imagine these two feelings as *inelastic* and unvarying elements in a really living man, make him oscillate from one to the other; above all, arrange that this oscillation becomes entirely mechanical by adopting the well-known form of some habitual, simple, childish contrivance: then you will get the image we have so far found in all laughable objects, *something mechanical in something living;* in fact, something comic.

We have dwelt on this first image, the Jack-in-the-box, sufficiently to show how comic fancy gradually converts a material mechanism into a moral one. Now we will consider one or two other games, confining ourselves to their most striking aspects.

Control of freedom

2. *The Dancing-jack.*—There are innumerable comedies in which one of the characters thinks he is speaking and acting freely, and consequently, retains all the essentials of life, whereas, viewed from a certain standpoint, he appears as a mere toy in the hands of another, who is playing with him. The transition is easily made, from the dancing-jack which a child works with a string, to Géronte and Argante manipulated by Scapin. Listen to Scapin himself: "The *machine* is all there," and again: "Providence has brought them into my net," etc. Instinctively, and because one would rather be a cheat than be cheated, in imagination at all events, the spectator sides with the knaves; and for the rest of the time, like a child who has persuaded his play-mate to lend him his doll, he takes hold of the strings himself and makes the marionette come and go on the stage as he pleases. But this latter condition is not indispensable; we can remain outside the pale of what is taking place if only we retain the distinct impression of a mechanical arrangement. This is what happens whenever one of the characters vacillates between two contrary opinions, each in turn appealing to him, as when Panurge asks Tom, Dick and Harry whether or not he ought to get married. Note that, in such a case, a comic author is always careful to *personify* the two opposing decisions. For, if there is no spectator, there must at all events be actors to hold the strings.

All that is serious in life comes from our freedom. The feelings we have matured, the passions we have brooded over, the actions we have weighed, decided upon and carried through, in short, all that comes from us and is our very own, these are the things that give life its ofttimes dramatic and generally grave aspect. What, then, is requisite to transform all this into a comedy? Merely to fancy that our seeming freedom conceals the strings of a dancing-jack, and that we are, as the poet says,

> . . . humble marionettes
> The wires of which are pulled by Fate.[1]

So there is not a real, a serious, or even a dramatic scene that fancy cannot render comic by simply calling forth this image. Nor is there a game for which a wider field lies open.

snowballing

3. *The Snow-ball.*—The farther we proceed in this investigation into the methods of comedy, the more clearly we see the part played by childhood's memories. These memories refer, perhaps, less to any special game than to the mechanical device of which that game is a particular instance. The same general device, moreover, may be met with in widely different games, just as the same operatic air is found in many different arrangements and variations. What is here of importance and is retained in the mind, what passes by imperceptible stages from the games of a child to those of a man, is the mental diagram, the skeleton outline of the combination, or, if you like, the abstract formula of which these games are particular illustrations. Take, for instance, the rolling snow-ball, which increases in size as it moves along. We might just as well think of toy soldiers standing behind one another. Push the first and it tumbles down on the second, this latter knocks down the third, and the state of things goes from bad to worse until they all lie prone on the floor. Or again,

---

[1] . . . d'humbles marionnettes
Dont le fil est aux mains de la Nécessité.
SULLY-PRUDHOMME.

take a house of cards that has been built up with
infinite care: the first you touch seems uncertain
whether to move or not, its tottering neighbour
comes to a quicker decision, and the work of destruction, gathering momentum as it goes on, rushes
headlong to the final collapse. These instances are
all different, but they suggest the same abstract
vision, that of an effect which grows by arithmetical
progression, so that the cause, insignificant at the
outset, culminates by a necessary evolution in a
result as important as it is unexpected. Now let us
open a children's picture-book; we shall find this
arrangement already on the high road to becoming
comic. Here, for instance,—in one of the comic chap-
books picked up by chance,—we have a caller rushing violently into a drawing-room; he knocks against
a lady, who upsets her cup of tea over an old gentleman, who slips against a glass window which falls
in the street on to the head of a constable, who sets
the whole police force agog, etc. The same arrangement reappears in many a picture intended
for grown-up persons. In the "stories without words"
sketched by humorous artists we are often shown an
object which moves from place to place, and persons
who are closely connected with it, so that through
a series of scenes a change in the position of the
object mechanically brings about increasingly serious changes in the situation of the persons. Let us
now turn to comedy. Many a droll scene, many a
comedy even, may be referred to this simple type.
Read the speech of Chicanneau in the *Plaideurs;*
here we find lawsuits within lawsuits, and the mechanism works faster and faster—Racine produces in
us this feeling of increasing acceleration by crowding
his law terms ever closer together—until the lawsuit
over a truss of hay costs the plaintiff the best part

of his fortune. And again the same arrangement occurs in certain scenes of Don Quixote; for instance, in the inn scene, where, by an extraordinary concatenation of circumstances, the mule-driver strikes Sancho, who belabours Maritornes, upon whom the innkeeper falls, etc. Finally, let us pass to the light comedy of to-day. Need we call to mind all the forms in which this same combination appears? There is one that is employed rather frequently. For instance a certain thing, say a letter, happens to be of supreme importance to a certain person and must be recovered at all costs. This thing, which always vanishes just when you think you have caught it, pervades the entire play, "rolling up" increasingly serious and unexpected incidents as it proceeds. All this is far more like a child's game than appears at first blush. Once more the effect produced is that of the snow-ball.

It is the characteristic of a mechanical combination to be generally *reversible.* A child is delighted when he sees the ball in a game of ninepins knocking down everything in its way and spreading havoc in all directions; he laughs louder than ever when the ball returns to its starting-point after twists and turns and waverings of every kind. In other words, the mechanism just described is laughable even when rectilinear, it is much more so on becoming circular and when every effort the player makes, by a fatal interaction of cause and effect, merely results in bringing it back to the same spot. Now, a considerable number of light comedies revolve round this idea. An Italian straw hat has been eaten up by a horse.[2] There is only one other hat like it in the whole of Paris; it *must* be secured regardless of cost.

[2] *Un chapeau de paille d'Italie* (Labiche).

This hat, which always slips away at the moment
its capture seems inevitable, keeps the principal
character on the run, and through him all the others
who hang, so to say, on to his coat tails, like a magnet
which, by a successive series of attractions, draws
along in its train the grains of iron filings that hang
on to each other. And when at last, after all sorts of
difficulties, the goal seems in sight, it is found that
the hat so ardently sought is precisely the one that
has been eaten. The same voyage of discovery is
depicted in another equally well-known comedy of
Labiche.[3] The curtain rises on an old bachelor and
an old maid, acquaintances of long standing, at the
moment of enjoying their daily rubber. Each of them,
unknown to the other, has applied to the same
matrimonial agency. Through innumerable difficulties, one mishap following on the heels of another,
they hurry along, side by side, right through the
play, to the interview which brings them back,
purely and simply, into each other's presence. We
have the same circular effect, the same return to
the starting-point, in a more recent play.[4] A hen-
pecked husband imagines he has escaped by divorce
from the clutches of his wife and his mother-in-law.
He marries again, when, lo and behold, the double
combination of marriage and divorce brings back
to him his former wife in the aggravated form of a
second mother-in-law!

When we think how intense and how common is
this type of the comic, we understand why it has
fascinated the imagination of certain philosophers.
To cover a good deal of ground only to come back
unwittingly to the starting-point, is to make a great

[3] *La Cagnotte.*
[4] *Les surprises du divorce.*

effort for a result that is nil. So we might be tempted to define the comic in this latter fashion. And such, indeed, seems to be the idea of Herbert Spencer: according to him, laughter is the indication of an effort which suddenly encounters a void. Kant had already said something of the kind: "Laughter is the result of an expectation which, of a sudden, ends in nothing." No doubt these definitions would apply to the last few examples given, although, even then, the formula needs the addition of sundry limitations, for we often make an ineffectual effort which is in no way provocative of laughter. While, however, the last few examples are illustrations of a great cause resulting in a small effect, we quoted others, immediately before, which might be defined inversely as a great effect springing from a small cause. The truth is, this second definition has scarcely more validity than the first. Lack of proportion between cause and effect, whether appearing in one or in the other, is never the direct source of laughter. What we do laugh at is something that this lack of proportion may in certain cases disclose, namely, a particular mechanical arrangement which it reveals to us, as through a glass, at the back of the series of effects and causes. Disregard this arrangement, and you let go the only clue capable of guiding you through the labyrinth of the comic. Any hypothesis you otherwise would select, while possibly applicable to a few carefully chosen cases, is liable at any moment to be met and overthrown by the first unsuitable instance that comes along.

But why is it we laugh at this mechanical arrangement? It is doubtless strange that the history of a person or of a group should sometimes appear like a game worked by strings, or gearings, or springs; but from what source does the special character of this strangeness arise? What is it that makes it laughable? To this question, which we have already propounded in various forms, our answer must always be the same. The rigid mechanism which we occasionally detect, as a foreign body, in the living continuity of human affairs is of peculiar interest to us as being a kind of *absentmindedness* on the part of life. Were events unceasingly mindful of their own course, there would be no coincidences, no conjunctures and no circular series; everything would evolve and progress continuously. And were all men always attentive to life, were we constantly keeping in touch with others as well as with ourselves, nothing within us would ever appear as due to the working of strings or springs. The comic is that side of a person which reveals his likeness to a thing, that aspect of human events which, through its peculiar inelasticity, conveys the impression of pure mechanism, of automatism, of movement without life. Consequently it expresses an individual or collective imperfection which calls for an immediate corrective. This corrective is laughter, a social gesture that singles out and represses a special kind of absentmindedness in men and in events.

But this in turn tempts us to make further investigations. So far, we have spent our time in rediscovering, in the diversions of the grown-up man, those mechanical combinations which amused him as a child. Our methods, in fact, have been entirely empirical. Let us now attempt to frame a full and methodical theory, by seeking, as it were, at the fountain-head, the changeless and simple archetypes of the manifold and transient practices of the comic stage. Comedy, we said, combines events so as to introduce mechanism into the outer forms of life. Let us now ascertain in what essential characteristics life, when viewed from without, seems to contrast with mere mechanism. We shall only have, then, to turn to the opposite characteristics, in order to discover the abstract formula, this time a general and complete one, for every real and possible method of comedy.

Life presents itself to us as evolution in time and complexity in space. Regarded in time, it is the continuous evolution of a being ever growing older; it never goes backwards and never repeats itself. Considered in space, it exhibits certain coexisting elements so closely interdependent, so exclusively made for one another, that not one of them could, at the same time, belong to two different organisms: each living being is a closed system of phenomena, incapable of interfering with other systems. A continual change of aspect, the irreversibility of the order of phenomena, the perfect individuality of a perfectly self-contained series: such, then, are the outward characteristics—whether real or apparent is of little moment—which distinguish the living from the merely mechanical. Let us take the counterpart of each of these: we shall obtain three processes which might be called *repetition, inversion,* and *reciprocal interference of series*. Now, it is easy to see that these are also the methods of light comedy, and that no others are possible.

As a matter of fact, we could discover them, as ingredients of varying importance, in the composition of all the scenes we have just been considering, and, *a fortiori,* in the children's games, the mechanism of which they reproduce. The requisite analysis would, however, delay us too long, and it is more profitable to study them in their purity by taking fresh examples. Nothing could be easier, for it is in their pure state that they are found, both in classic comedy and in contemporary plays.

1. *Repetition.*—Our present problem no longer deals, like the preceding one, with a word or a sentence repeated by an individual, but rather with a situation, that is, a combination of circumstances, which recurs several times in its original form and thus contrasts with the changing stream of life. Everyday experience supplies us with this type of the comic, though only in a rudimentary state. Thus, you meet a friend in the street whom you have not seen for an age; there is nothing comic in the situation. If, however, you meet him again the same day, and then a third and a fourth time, you may laugh at the "coincidence." Now, picture to yourself a series of imaginary events which affords a tolerably fair illusion of life, and within this ever-moving series imagine one and the same scene reproduced either by the same characters or by different ones: again you will have a coincidence, though a far more extraordinary one. Such are the repetitions produced on the stage. They are the more laughable in proportion as the scene repeated is more complex and more naturally introduced—two conditions which seem mutually exclusive, and which the playwriter must be clever enough to reconcile.

Contemporary light comedy employs this method in every shape and form. One of the best-known examples consists in bringing a group of characters, act after act, into the most varied surroundings, so as to reproduce, under ever fresh circumstances, one and the same series of incidents or accidents more or less symmetrically identical.

In several of Molière's plays we find one and the same arrangement of events repeated right through the comedy from beginning to end. Thus, the *École des Femmes* does nothing more than reproduce and repeat a single incident in three *tempi:* first *tempo,* Horace tells Arnolphe of the plan he has devised to deceive Agnès's guardian, who turns out to be Arnolphe himself; second *tempo,* Arnolphe thinks he has checkmated the move; third *tempo,* Agnès contrives that Horace gets all the benefit of Arnolphe's precautionary measures. There is the same symmetrical repetition in the *École des Maris,* in *L'Étourdi,* and above all in *George Dandin,* where the same effect in three *tempi* is again met with: first *tempo,* George Dandin discovers that his wife is unfaithful; second *tempo,* he summons his father- and mother-in-law to his assistance; third *tempo,* it is George Dandin himself, after all, who has to apologise.

At times the same scene is reproduced with groups of different characters. Then it not infrequently happens that the first group consists of masters and the second of servants. The latter repeat in another key a scene already played by the former, though the rendering is naturally less refined. A part of the *Dépit amoureux* is constructed on this plan, as is also *Amphitryon.* In an amusing little comedy of Benedix, *Der Eigensinn,* the order is inverted: we have the masters reproducing a scene of stubbornness in which their servants have set the example.

But, quite irrespective of the characters who serve as pegs for the arrangement of symmetrical situations, there seems to be a wide gulf between classic comedy and the theatre of to-day. Both aim at introducing a certain mathematical order into events, while none the less maintaining their aspect of likelihood, that is to say, of life. But the means

they employ are different. The majority of light
comedies of our day seek to mesmerise directly the
mind of the spectator. For, however extraordinary
the coincidence, it becomes acceptable from the
very fact that it is accepted; and we do accept it, if
we have been gradually prepared for its reception.
Such is often the procedure adopted by contemporary authors. In Molière's plays, on the contrary, it is
the moods of the persons on the stage, not of the
audience, that make repetition seem natural. Each
of the characters represents a certain force applied
in a certain direction, and it is because these forces,
constant in direction, necessarily combine together
in the same way, that the same situation is reproduced. Thus interpreted, the comedy of situation is akin to the comedy of character. It deserves
to be called classic, if classic art is indeed that which
does not claim to derive from the effect more than it
has put into the cause.

2. *Inversion.*—This second method has so much
analogy with the first that we will merely define it
without insisting on illustrations. Picture to yourself
certain characters in a certain situation: if you reverse the situation and invert the *rôles,* you obtain
a comic scene. The double rescue scene in *Le Voyage de M. Perrichon* belongs to this class.[5] There is
no necessity, however, for both the identical scenes
to be played before us. We may be shown only one,
provided the other is really in our minds. Thus, we
laugh at the prisoner at the bar lecturing the magistrate; at a child presuming to teach its parents; in
a word, at everything that comes under the heading
of "topsyturvydom."

[5] Labiche, *Le Voyage de M. Perrichon.*

Not infrequently comedy sets before us a character who lays a trap in which he is the first to be
caught. The plot of the villain who is the victim of
his own villainy, or the cheat cheated, forms the
stock-in-trade of a good many plays. We find this
even in primitive farce. Lawyer Pathelin tells his
client of a trick to outwit the magistrate; the client
employs the self-same trick to avoid paying the
lawyer. A termagant of a wife insists upon her
husband doing all the housework; she has put down
each separate item on a 'rota.' Now let her fall into
a copper, her husband will refuse to drag her out,
for "that is not down on his 'rota.'" In modern literature we meet with hundreds of variations on the
theme of the robber robbed. In every case the root
idea involves an inversion of *rôles,* and a situation
which recoils on the head of its author.

Here we apparently find the confirmation of a
law, some illustrations of which we have already
pointed out. When a comic scene has been reproduced a number of times, it reaches the stage of
being a classical type or model. It becomes amusing
in itself, quite apart from the causes which render
it amusing. Henceforth, new scenes, which are not
comic *de jure,* may become amusing *de facto,* on
account of their partial resemblance to this model.
They call up in our mind a more or less confused
image which we know to be comical. They range
themselves in a category representing an officially
recognised type of the comic. The scene of the
"robber robbed" belongs to this class. It casts over a
host of other scenes a reflection of the comic element
it contains. In the end it renders comic any mishap
that befalls one through one's own fault, no matter
what the fault or mishap may be,—nay, an allusion
to this mishap, a single word that recalls it, is suffi-

cient. There would be nothing amusing in the saying, "It serves you right, George Dandin," were it
not for the comic overtones that take up and re-echo
it.

3. We have dwelt at considerable length on repetition and inversion; we now come to the *reciprocal
interference*[6] *of series.* This is a comic effect, the
precise formula of which is very difficult to disentangle, by reason of the extraordinary variety of
forms in which it appears on the stage. Perhaps it
might be defined as follows: *A situation is invariably
comic when it belongs simultaneously to two altogether independent series of events and is capable
of being interpreted in two entirely different meanings at the same time.*
You will at once think of an *equivocal situation.*
And the equivocal situation is indeed one which
permits of two different meanings at the same time,
the one merely plausible, which is put forward by
the actors; the other a real one, which is given by
the public. We see the real meaning of the situation,
because care has been taken to show us every aspect
of it, but each of the actors knows only one of these
aspects; hence the mistakes they make and the erroneous judgments they pass both on what is going
on around them and on what they are doing themselves. We proceed from this erroneous judgment to
the correct one, we waver between the possible
meaning and the real, and it is this mental see-saw
between two contrary interpretations which is at
first apparent in the enjoyment we derive from an
equivocal situation. It is natural that certain philos-

[6] The word "interference" has here the meaning given to
it in Optics, where it indicates the partial superposition and
neutralisation, by each other, of two series of light-waves.

ophers should have been specially struck by this
mental instability, and that some of them should regard the very essence of the ludicrous as consisting
in the collision or coincidence of two judgments that
contradict each other. Their definition, however, is
far from meeting every case, and even when it does,
it defines—not the principle of the ludicrous, but
only one of its more or less distant consequences. Indeed, it is easy to see that the stage-made misunderstanding is nothing but a particular instance of a far
more general phenomenon,—the reciprocal interference of independent series, and that, moreover,
it is not laughable in itself, but only as a *sign* of such
an interference.

As a matter of fact, each of the characters in every
stage-made misunderstanding has his setting in an
appropriate series of events which he correctly interprets as far as he is concerned, and which give
the key-note to his words and actions. Each of the
series peculiar to the several characters develop
independently, but at a certain moment they meet
under such conditions that the actions and words
that belong to one might just as well belong to another. Hence arise the misunderstandings and the
equivocal nature of the situation. But this latter is
not laughable in itself, it is so only because it reveals
the coincidence of the two independent series. The
proof of this lies in the fact that the author must be
continually taxing his ingenuity to recall our attention to the double fact of independence and coincidence. This he generally succeeds in doing by constantly renewing the vain threat of dissolving part-
nership between the two coinciding series. Every
moment the whole thing threatens to break down,
but manages to get patched up again; it is this
diversion that excites laughter, far more than the

oscillation of the mind between two contradictory ideas. It makes us laugh because it reveals to us the reciprocal interference of two independent series, the real source of the comic effect.

And so the stage-made misunderstanding is nothing more than one particular instance, one means—perhaps the most artificial—of illustrating the reciprocal interferences of series, but it is not the only one. Instead of two contemporary series, you might take one series of events belonging to the past and another belonging to the present: if the two series happen to coincide in our imagination, there will be no resulting cross-purposes, and yet the same comic effect will continue to take place. Think of Bonivard, captive in the Castle of Chillon: one series of facts. Now picture to yourself Tartarin, travelling in Switzerland, arrested and imprisoned: second series, independent of the former. Now let Tartarin be manacled to Bonivard's chain, thus making the two stories seem for a moment to coincide, and you will get a very amusing scene, one of the most amusing that Daudet's imagination has pictured.[7] Numerous incidents of the mock-heroic style, if analysed, would reveal the same elements. The transposition from the ancient to the modern—always a laughable one—draws its inspiration from the same idea.

Labiche has made use of this method in every shape and form. Sometimes he begins by building up the series separately, and then delights in making them interfere with one another: he takes an independent group—a wedding-party, for instance —and throws them into altogether unconnected surroundings, into which certain coincidences allow of their being foisted for the time being. Sometimes he

[7] *Tartarin sur les Alpes,* by Daudet.

keeps one and the same set of characters right
through the play, but contrives that certain of these
characters have something to conceal—have in fact,
a secret understanding on the point—in short, play
a smaller comedy within the principal one: at one
moment, one of the two comedies is on the point of
upsetting the other; the next, everything comes
right and the coincidence between the two series is
restored. Sometimes, even, he introduces into the
actual series a purely immaterial series of events, an
inconvenient past, for instance, that some one has
an interest in concealing, but which is continually
cropping up in the present, and on each occasion is
successfully brought into line with situations with
which it seemed destined to play havoc. But in every case we find the two independent series, and
also their partial coincidence.

We will not carry any further this analysis of the
methods of light comedy. Whether we find reciprocal interference of series, inversion, or repetition, we
see that the objective is always the same—to obtain
what we have called a *mechanisation* of life. You
take a set of actions and relations and repeat it as it
is, or turn it upside down, or transfer it bodily to
another set with which it partially coincides—all
these being processes that consist in looking upon
life as a repeating mechanism, with reversible action
and interchangeable parts. Actual life is comedy just
so far as it produces, in a natural fashion, actions of
the same kind; consequently, just so far as it forgets
itself, for were it always on the alert, it would be
ever-changing continuity, irreversible progress, un-
divided unity. And so the ludicrous in events may
be defined as absentmindedness in things, just as
the ludicrous in an individual character always results from some fundamental absentmindedness in

the person, as we have already intimated and shall prove later on. This absentmindedness in events, however, is exceptional. Its results are slight. At any rate it is incurable, so that it is useless to laugh at it. Therefore the idea would never have occurred to any one of exaggerating absentmindedness, of converting it into a system, and creating an art for it, if laughter were not always a pleasure, and mankind did not pounce upon the slightest excuse for indulging in it. This is the real explanation of light comedy, which holds the same relation to actual life as does a jointed dancing-doll to a man walking,—being, as it is, an artificial exaggeration of a natural rigidity in things. The thread that binds it to actual life is a very fragile one. It is scarcely more than a game which, like all games, depends on a previously accepted convention. Comedy in character strikes far deeper roots into life. With that kind of comedy we shall deal more particularly in the final portion of our investigation. But we must first analyse a certain type of the comic, in many respects similar to that of light comedy: the comic in words.

II

There may be something artificial in making a special category for the comic in words, since most of the varieties of the comic that we have examined so far were produced through the medium of language. We must make a distinction, however, between the comic *expressed* and the comic *created* by language. The former could, if necessary, be translated from one language into another, though at the cost of losing the greater portion of its significance when introduced into a fresh society different in manners, in literature, and above all in association of ideas. But it is generally impossible to translate the latter. It owes its entire being to the structure of the sentence or to the choice of the words. It does not set forth, by means of language, special cases of absentmindedness in man or in events. It lays stress on lapses of attention in language itself. In this case, it is language itself that becomes comic.

Comic sayings, however, are not a matter of spontaneous generation; if we laugh at them, we are equally entitled to laugh at their author. This latter condition, however, is not indispensable, since the saying or expression has a comic virtue of its own. This is proved by the fact that we find it very difficult, in the majority of these cases, to say whom we are laughing at, although at times we have a dim, vague feeling that there is some one in the background.

Moreover, the person implicated is not always the speaker. Here it seems as though we should draw an important distinction between the *witty* (*spirituel*) and the *comic*. A word is said to be comic when it makes us laugh at the person who utters it, and witty when it makes us laugh either at a third party or at ourselves. But in most cases we can hardly make up our minds whether the word is comic or witty. All that we can say is that it is laughable.

Before proceeding, it might be well to examine more closely what is meant by wit (*esprit*). A witty saying makes us at least smile; consequently, no investigation into laughter would be complete did it not get to the bottom of the nature of wit and throw light on the underlying idea. It is to be feared, however, that this extremely subtle essence is one that evaporates when exposed to the light.

Let us first make a distinction between the two meanings of the word "wit" (*esprit*), the broader one and the more restricted. In the broader meaning of the word, it would seem that what is called wit is a certain *dramatic* way of thinking. Instead of treating his ideas as mere symbols, the wit sees them, he hears them and, above all, makes them converse with one another like persons. He puts them on the stage, and himself, to some extent, into the bargain. A witty nation is, of necessity, a nation enamoured of the theatre. In every wit there is something of a poet—just as in every good reader there is the making of an actor. This comparison is made purposely, because a proportion might easily be established between the four terms. In order to read well we need only the intellectual side of the actor's art; but in order to act well one must be an actor in all one's soul and body. In just the same way, poetic creation calls for some degree of self-forgetfulness, whilst the wit does not usually err in this respect. We always get a glimpse of the latter behind what he says and does. He is not wholly engrossed in the business, because he only brings his intelligence into play.

So any poet may reveal himself as a wit when he pleases. To do this there will be no need for him to acquire anything; it seems rather as though he would have to give up something. He would simply have to let his ideas hold converse with one another "for nothing, for the mere joy of the thing!"[8] He would only have to unfasten the double bond which keeps his ideas in touch with his feelings and his soul in touch with life. In short, he would turn into a wit by simply resolving to be no longer a poet in feeling, but only in intelligence.

But if wit consists, for the most part, in seeing

[8] "Pour rien, pour le plaisir," is a quotation from Victor Hugo's *Marion Delorme*.

things *sub specie theatri,* it is evidently capable of being specially directed to one variety of dramatic art, namely, comedy. Here we have a more restricted meaning of the term, and, moreover, the only one that interests us from the point of view of the theory of laughter. What is here called *wit* is a gift for dashing off comic scenes in a few strokes —dashing them off, however, so subtly, delicately and rapidly, that all is over as soon as we begin to notice them.

Who are the actors in these scenes? With whom has the wit to deal? First of all, with his interlocutors themselves, when his witticism is a direct retort to one of them. Often with an absent person whom he supposes to have spoken and to whom he is replying. Still oftener, with the whole world,—in the ordinary meaning of the term,—which he takes to task, twisting a current idea into a paradox, or making use of a hackneyed phrase, or parodying some quotation or proverb. If we compare these scenes in miniature with one another, we find they are almost always variations of a comic theme with which we are well acquainted, that of the "robber robbed." You take up a metaphor, a phrase, an argument, and turn it against the man who is, or might be, its author, so that he is made to say what he did not mean to say and lets himself be caught, to some extent, in the toils of language. But the theme of the "robber robbed" is not the only possible one. We have gone over many varieties of the comic, and there is not one of them that is incapable of being volatilised into a witticism.

Every witty remark, then, lends itself to an analysis, whose chemical formula, so to say, we are now in a position to state. It runs as follows: Take the remark, first enlarge it into a regular scene, then find out the category of the comic to which the scene evidently belongs: by this means you reduce the witty remark to its simplest elements and obtain a full explanation of it.

Let us apply this method to a classic example. "Your chest hurts me" (*J'ai mal à votre poitrine*), wrote Mme. de Sévigné to her ailing daughter—clearly a witty saying. If our theory is correct, we need only lay stress upon the saying, enlarge and magnify it, and we shall see it expand into a comic scene. Now, we find this very scene, ready made, in the *Amour médicin* of Molière. The sham doctor, Clitandre, who has been summoned to attend Sganarelle's daughter, contents himself with feeling Sganarelle's own pulse, whereupon, relying on the sympathy there must be between father and daughter, he unhesitatingly concludes: "Your daughter is very ill!" Here we have the transition from the witty to the comical. To complete our analysis, then, all we have to do is to discover what there is comical in the idea of giving a diagnosis of the child after sounding the father or the mother. Well, we know that one essential form of comic fancy lies in picturing to ourselves a living person as a kind of jointed dancing-doll, and that frequently, with the object of inducing us to form this mental picture, we are shown two or more persons speaking and acting as though attached to one another by invisible strings. Is not this the idea here suggested when we are led to materialise, so to speak, the sympathy we postulate as existing between father and daughter?

We now see how it is that writers on wit have perforce confined themselves to commenting on the extraordinary complexity of the things denoted by the term without ever succeeding in defining it. There are many ways of being witty, almost as many

as there are of being the reverse. How can we detect what they have in common with one another,
unless we first determine the general relationship
between the witty and the comic? Once, however,
this relationship is cleared up, everything is plain
sailing. We then find the same connection between
the comic and the witty as exists between a regular
scene and the fugitive suggestion of a possible one.
Hence, however numerous the forms assumed by the
comic, wit will possess an equal number of corresponding varieties. So that the comic, in all its forms,
is what should be defined first, by discovering (a
task which is already quite difficult enough) the
clue that leads from one form to the other. By that
very operation wit will have been analysed, and
will then appear as nothing more than the comic in
a highly volatile state. To follow the opposite plan,
however, and attempt directly to evolve a formula
for wit, would be courting certain failure. What
should we think of a chemist who, having ever so
many jars of a certain substance in his laboratory,
would prefer getting that substance from the atmosphere, in which merely infinitesimal traces of its
vapour are to be found?

But this comparison between the witty and the
comic is also indicative of the line we must take in
studying the comic in words. On the one hand, indeed, we find there is no essential difference between a word that is comic and one that is witty;
on the other hand, the latter, although connected
with a figure of speech, invariably calls up the
image, dim or distinct, of a comic scene. This
amounts to saying that the comic in speech should
correspond, point by point, with the comic in actions and in situations, and is nothing more, if one
may so express oneself, than their projection on to

the plane of words. So let us return to the comic in actions and in situations, consider the chief methods by which it is obtained, and apply them to the choice of words and the building up of sentences. We shall thus have every possible form of the comic in words as well as every variety of wit.

1. Inadvertently to say or do what we have no intention of saying or doing, as a result of inelasticity or momentum, is, as we are aware, one of the main sources of the comic. Thus, absentmindedness is essentially laughable, and so we laugh at anything rigid, ready-made, mechanical in gesture, attitude and even facial expression. Do we find this kind of rigidity in language also? No doubt we do, since language contains ready-made formulas and stereotyped phrases. The man who always expressed himself in such terms would invariably be comic. But if an isolated phrase is to be comic in itself, when once separated from the person who utters it, it must be something more than ready-made, it must bear within itself some sign which tells us, beyond the possibility of doubt, that it was uttered automatically. This can only happen when the phrase embodies some evident absurdity, either a palpable error or a contradiction in terms. Hence the following general rule: *A comic meaning is invariably obtained when an absurd idea is fitted into a well-established phrase-form.*

"Ce sabre est le plus beau jour de ma vie," said M. Prudhomme. Translate the phrase into English or German and it becomes purely absurd, though it is comic enough in French. The reason is that "le plus beau jour de ma vie" is one of those ready-made phrase-endings to which a Frenchman's ear is accustomed. To make it comic, then, we need only clearly indicate the automatism of the person who utters it. This is what we get when we introduce an absurdity into the phrase. Here the absurdity is by no means the source of the comic, it is only a very simple and effective means of making it obvious.

We have quoted only one saying of M. Prudhomme, but the majority of those attributed to him belong to the same class. M. Prudhomme is a man of ready-made phrases. And as there are ready-made phrases in all languages, M. Prudhomme is always capable of being transposed, though seldom of being translated.

At times the commonplace phrase, under cover of which the absurdity slips in, is not so readily noticeable. "I don't like working between meals," said a lazy lout. There would be nothing amusing in the saying did there not exist that salutary precept in the realm of hygiene: "One should not eat between meals."

Sometimes too the effect is a complicated one. Instead of one commonplace phrase-form, there are two or three which are dovetailed into each other. Take, for instance, the remark of one of the characters in a play by Labiche: "Only God has the right to kill His fellow-creature." It would seem that advantage is here taken of two separate familiar sayings: "It is God who disposes of the lives of men," and, "It is criminal for a man to kill his fellow-creature." But the two sayings are combined so as to deceive the ear and leave the impression of being one of those hackneyed sentences that are accepted as a matter of course. Hence our attention nods, until we are suddenly aroused by the absurdity of the meaning.

These examples suffice to show how one of the most important types of the comic can be projected

not by design,
maybe, but
by

Molière, unwittingly,
X - xi   by using stereotypes,
          makes
          his char.
          like   ⊶ instinct
(gnd)   modern   or natural
          comic   genius
          types : automated
                  professionally callous
                  ready-made
                  standardized
                  lives by formulas
                  life a series of repetitions
          [that which]
          "what is mechanical suffers
                  a death of the heart

          "a comic impasse occurs
          wherever a human being
          ceases to behave like a
          human ... resembles a
          piece of clockwork ... " (xii)

Bergson
(63)   laughter has no
        greater foe than emotion"

                to laugh "we must
m's   impose silence on our pity"
        "have invoke
        no pity,
        + little
          emotion

Berg's view "mechan-
                    encrusted on
                              living"
formulated in machine
age might seem
to apply to comic
as perceived in
past-index. Centuries
only ——— yet it
applies equally as
well to Molière

2/

(63) when we "look upon life
as a disinterested spectator,*
many a drama will
turn into a comedy"

comedy demands a
"momentary anesthesia
of the heart. Its appeal
is to intelligence ..." (64)

laughter needs an echo —
a group (64)

the comic comes from a
mechanical inelasticity
where we expect a human
pliableness (67)

ex. Harpagon's rigidity

* "something mechanical
encrusted on the living" [84]

"Any incident is comic that calls
our attention to the physical in   over
a person, when it is the
moral side that is concerned" (93)

N. in serious drama, a
char. does not even sit down
~~in it~~ during an important,
revealing ~~speech~~. To do
so would ~~even~~ call attention
to him/her physicality.

So, note ~~how~~ M's char.
are continually interrupted,
called aside, never
alone.
        Surrounded by events
that point to their physicality.

...mic,
...ituations'
reproducing a scene
between the same
char under the same
circum., 3

repetition
ie. jack-in-the-box

ex'. The Miser "my box"

Tartuffe "et Tartuffe?"
when Dorine tells
Orgon his wife has been ill

Control of freedom
i.e. dancing-jack

snowballing

In M. "each char represents
a certain force (applied.)
in a certain direction;
consistently, thus creating
reproduction of same
situation

reversal — a "robber-robbed"
ex'. The Miser

Exaggeration

Comedy in Char:

a comic char" goes his
own way w/out troubling
himself about getting
in touch w/ the rest
of his fellow beings " (147)

ingredients:
rigidity
automatism
absentmindedness
unsociability
" professional callousness " (175)

Comedy takes note of
similarities — it depicts
char. we have already
come across + shall
meet with again.
" It aims at placing
types before our eyes " (16 6)

—in a simplified form—on the plane of speech. We will now proceed to a form which is not so general.

2. "We laugh if our attention is diverted to the physical in a person when it is the moral that is in question," is a law we laid down in the first part of this work. Let us apply it to language. Most words might be said to have a *physical* and a *moral* meaning, according as they are interpreted literally or figuratively. Every word, indeed, begins by denoting a concrete object or a material action; but by degrees the meaning of the word is refined into an abstract relation or a pure idea. If then the above law holds good here, it should be stated as follows: "*A comic effect is obtained whenever we pretend to take literally an expression which was used figuratively*"; or, "*Once our attention is fixed on the material aspect of a metaphor the idea expressed becomes comic.*"

In the phrase, "Tous les arts sont frères" (all the arts are brothers), the word "frère" (brother) is used metaphorically to indicate a more or less striking resemblance. The word is so often used in this way, that when we hear it we do not think of the concrete, the material connection implied in every relationship. We should notice it more if we were told that "Tous les arts sont cousins," for the word "cousin" is not so often employed in a figurative sense; that is why the word here already assumes a slight tinge of the comic. But let us go further still, and suppose that our attention is attracted to the material side of the metaphor by the choice of a relationship which is incompatible with the gender of the two words composing the metaphorical expression, we get a laughable result. Such is the well-known saying, also attributed to M. Prudhomme, "Tous les arts (masculine) sont sœurs (feminine)."

"He is always running after a joke," was said in Boufflers' presence regarding a very conceited fellow. Had Boufflers replied, "He won't catch it," that would have been the beginning of a witty saying, though nothing more than the beginning, for the word "catch" is interpreted figuratively almost as often as the word "run"; nor does it compel us more strongly than the latter to materialise the image of two runners, the one at the heels of the other. In order that the rejoinder may appear to be a thoroughly witty one, we must borrow from the language of sport an expression so vivid and concrete that we cannot refrain from witnessing the race in good earnest. This is what Boufflers does when he retorts, "I'll back the joke!"

We said that wit often consists in extending the idea of one's interlocutor to the point of making him express the opposite of what he thinks and getting him, so to say, entrapt by his own words. We must now add that this trap is almost always some metaphor or comparison the concrete aspect of which is turned against him. You may remember the dialogue between a mother and her son in the *Faux Bonhommes*: "My dear boy, gambling on 'Change is very risky. You win one day and lose the next."—"Well, then, I will gamble only every other day." In the same play too we find the following edifying conversation between two company-promoters: "Is this a very honourable thing we are doing? These unfortunate shareholders, you see, we are taking the money out of their very pockets. . . ."—"Well, out of what do you expect us to take it?"

An amusing result is likewise obtainable whenever a symbol or an emblem is expanded on its concrete side, and a pretence is made of retaining the same symbolical value for this expansion as for the emblem itself. In a very lively comedy we are introduced to a Monte Carlo official whose uniform is covered with medals, although he has only received a single decoration. "You see, I staked my medal on a number at roulette," he said, "and as the number turned up, I was entitled to thirty-six times my stake." This reasoning is very similar to that offered by Giboyer in the *Effrontés*. Criticism is made of a bride of forty summers who is wearing orange-blossoms with her wedding costume: "Why, she was entitled to oranges, let alone orange-blossoms!" remarked Giboyer.

But we should never cease were we to take one by one all the laws we have stated, and try to prove them on what we have called the plane of language. We had better confine ourselves to the three general propositions of the preceding section. We have shown that "series of events" may become comic either by *repetition*, by *inversion* or by *reciprocal interference*. Now we shall see that this is also the case with series of words.

To take series of events and repeat them in another key or another environment, or to invert them whilst still leaving them a certain meaning, or mix them up so that their respective meanings jostle one another, is invariably comic, as we have already said, for it is getting life to submit to be treated as a machine. But thought too is a living thing. And language, the translation of thought, should be just as living. We may thus surmise that a phrase is likely to become comic, if, though reversed, it still makes sense, or if it expresses equally well two quite independent sets of ideas, or, finally, if it has been obtained by transposing an idea into some key other than its own. Such, indeed, are the three fundamental laws of what might be called *the comic transformation of sentences,* as we shall show by a few examples.

Let it first be said that these three laws are far from being of equal importance as regards the theory of the ludicrous. *Inversion* is the least interesting of the three. It must be easy of application, however, for it is noticeable that, no sooner do professional wits hear a sentence spoken than they experiment to see if a meaning cannot be obtained by reversing it, by putting, for instance, the subject in place of the object, and the object in place of the subject. It is not unusual for this device to be employed for refuting an idea in more or less humorous terms. One of the characters in a comedy of Labiche shouts out to his neighbour on the floor above, who is in the habit of dirtying his balcony, "What do you mean by emptying your pipe on to my terrace?" The neighbour retorts, "What do you mean by putting your terrace under my pipe?" There is no necessity to dwell upon this kind of wit, instances of which could easily be multiplied.

The *reciprocal interference* of two sets of ideas in the same sentence is an inexhaustible source of amusing varieties. There are many ways of bringing about this interference, I mean of bracketing in the same expression two independent meanings that apparently tally. The least reputable of these ways is the pun. In the pun, the same sentence appears to offer two independent meanings, but it is only an appearance; in reality there are two different sentences made up of different words, but claiming to be one and the same because both have the same sound. We pass from the pun, by imperceptible stages, to the true play upon words. Here there is really one and the same sentence through which two different sets of ideas are expressed, and we are confronted with only one series of words; but advantage is taken of the different meanings a word may have, especially when used figuratively instead of literally. So that in fact there is often only a slight difference between the play upon words on the one hand, and a poetic metaphor or an illuminating comparison on the other. Whereas an illuminating comparison and a striking image always seem to reveal the close harmony that exists between language and nature, regarded as two parallel forms of life, the play upon words makes us think somehow of a negligence on the part of language, which, for the time being, seems to have forgotten its real function and now claims to accommodate things to itself instead of accommodating itself to things. And so the play upon words always betrays a momentary *lapse of attention* in language, and it is precisely on that account that it is amusing.

Inversion and *reciprocal interference*, after all, are only a certain playfulness of the mind which ends at playing upon words. The comic in *transposition* is much more far-reaching. Indeed, transposition is to ordinary language what repetition is to comedy.

We said that repetition is the favourite method of classic comedy. It consists in so arranging events that a scene is reproduced either between the same characters under fresh circumstances or between fresh characters under the same circumstances. Thus we have, repeated by lackeys in less dignified language, a scene already played by their masters. Now, imagine ideas expressed in suitable style and thus placed in the setting of their natural environment. If you think of some arrangement whereby they are transferred to fresh surroundings, while maintaining their mutual relations, or, in other words, if you can induce them to express themselves in an altogether different style and to transpose themselves into another key,—you will have language itself playing a comedy—language itself made comic. There will be no need, moreover, actually to set before us both expressions of the same ideas, the transposed expression and the natural one. For we are acquainted with the natural one—the one which we should have chosen instinctively. So it will be enough if the effort of comic invention bears on the other, and on the other alone. No sooner is the second set before us than we spontaneously supply the first. Hence the following general rule: *A comic effect is always obtainable by transposing the natural expression of an idea into another key.*

The means of transposition are so many and varied, language affords so rich a continuity of themes and the comic is here capable of passing through so great a number of stages, from the most insipid buffoonery up to the loftiest forms of humour and irony, that we shall forego the attempt to make out a complete list. Having stated the rule, we will simply, here and there, verify its main applications.

In the first place, we may distinguish two keys at the extreme ends of the scale, the solemn and the familiar. The most obvious effects are obtained by merely transposing the one into the other, which thus provides us with two opposite currents of comic fancy.

Transpose the solemn into the familiar and the result is *parody*. The effect of parody, thus defined, extends to instances in which the idea expressed in familiar terms is one that, if only in deference to custom, ought to be pitched in another key. Take as an example the following description of the dawn, quoted by Jean Paul Richter: "The sky was beginning to change from black to red, like a lobster being boiled." Note that the expression of old-world matters in terms of modern life produces the same effect, by reason of the halo of poetry which surrounds classical antiquity.

It is doubtless the comic in parody that has suggested to some philosophers, and in particular to Alexander Bain, the idea of defining the comic, in general, as a species of *degradation*. They describe the laughable as causing something to appear mean that was formerly dignified. But if our analysis is correct, degradation is only one form of transposition, and transposition itself only one of the means of obtaining laughter. There is a host of others, and the source of laughter must be sought for much further back. Moreover, without going so far, we see that while the transposition from solemn to trivial, from better to worse, is comic, the inverse transposition may be even more so.

It is met with as often as the other, and, apparently, we may distinguish two main forms of it, according as it refers to the *physical dimensions* of an object or to its *moral value*.

To speak of small things as though they were large is, in a general way, *to exaggerate*. Exaggeration is always comic when prolonged, and especially when systematic; then, indeed, it appears as one method of transposition. It excites so much laughter that some writers have been led to define the comic as exaggeration, just as others have defined it as degradation. As a matter of fact, exaggeration, like degradation, is only one form of one kind of the comic. Still, it is a very striking form. It has given

birth to the mock-heroic poem, a rather old-fash-
ioned device, I admit, though traces of it are still to
be found in persons inclined to exaggerate method-
ically. It might often be said of braggadocio that it
is its mock-heroic aspect which makes us laugh.

Far more artificial, but also far more refined, is
the transposition upwards from below when applied to the moral value of things, not to their physical dimensions. To express in reputable language
some disreputable idea, to take some scandalous
situation, some low-class calling or disgraceful behaviour, and describe them in terms of the utmost
"respectability," is generally comic. The English
word is here purposely employed, as the practice
itself is characteristically English. Many instances of
it may be found in Dickens and Thackeray, and in
English literature generally. Let us remark, in passing, that the intensity of the effect does not here
depend on its length. A word is sometimes sufficient,
provided it gives us a glimpse of an entire system
of transposition accepted in certain social circles and
reveals, as it were, a moral organisation of immorality. Take the following remark made by an official
to one of his subordinates in a novel of Gogol's,
"Your peculations are too extensive for an official of
your rank."

Summing up the foregoing, then, there are two
extreme terms of comparison, the very large and the
very small, the best and the worst, between which
transposition may be effected in one direction or the
other. Now, if the interval be gradually narrowed,
the contrast between the terms obtained will be less
and less violent, and the varieties of comic transposition more and more subtle.

The most common of these contrasts is perhaps
that between the real and the ideal, between what

is and what ought to be. Here again transposition
may take place in either direction. Sometimes we
state what ought to be done, and pretend to believe
that this is just what is actually being done; then we
have *irony*. Sometimes, on the contrary, we describe
with scrupulous minuteness what is being done, and
pretend to believe that this is just what ought to be
done; such is often the method of *humour*. Humour,
thus defined, is the counterpart of irony. Both are
forms of satire, but irony is oratorical in its nature,
whilst humour partakes of the scientific. Irony is
emphasised the higher we allow ourselves to be up-
lifted by the idea of the good that ought to be: thus
irony may grow so hot within us that it becomes a
kind of high-pressure eloquence. On the other hand,
humour is the more emphasised the deeper we go
down into an evil that actually is, in order to set
down its details in the most cold-blooded indifference. Several authors, Jean Paul amongst them, have
noticed that humour delights in concrete terms,
technical details, definite facts. If our analysis is correct, this is not an accidental trait of humour, it is
its very essence. A humourist is a moralist disguised
as a scientist, something like an anatomist who
practises dissection with the sole object of filling us
with disgust; so that humour, in the restricted sense
in which we are here regarding the word, is really
a transposition from the moral to the scientific.

By still further curtailing the interval between the
terms transposed, we may now obtain more and
more specialised types of comic transpositions. Thus,
certain professions have a technical vocabulary:
what a wealth of laughable results have been obtained by transposing the ideas of everyday life into
this professional jargon! Equally comic is the exten-
sion of business phraseology to the social relations

of life,—for instance, the phrase of one of Labiche's characters in allusion to an invitation he has received, "Your kindness of the third ult.," thus transposing the commercial formula, "Your favour of the third instant." This class of the comic, moreover, may attain a special profundity of its own when it discloses not merely a professional practice, but a fault in character. Recall to mind the scenes in the *Faux Bonhommes* and the *Famille Benoiton,* where marriage is dealt with as a business affair, and matters of sentiment are set down in strictly commercial language.

Here, however, we reach the point at which peculiarities of language really express peculiarities of character, a closer investigation of which we must hold over to the next chapter. Thus, as might have been expected and may be seen from the foregoing, the comic in words follows closely on the comic in situation and is finally merged, along with the latter, in the comic in character. Language only attains laughable results because it is a human product, modelled as exactly as possible on the forms of the human mind. We feel it contains some living element of our own life; and if this life of language were complete and perfect, if there were nothing stereotype in it, if, in short, language were an absolutely unified organism incapable of being split up into independent organisms, it would evade the comic as would a soul whose life was one harmonious whole, unruffled as the calm surface of a peaceful lake. There is no pool, however, which has not some dead leaves floating on its surface, no human soul upon which there do not settle habits that make it rigid against itself by making it rigid against others, no language, in short, so subtle and instinct with life, so fully alert in each of its parts as to

eliminate the ready-made and oppose the mechanical operations of inversion, transposition, etc.,
which one would fain perform upon it as on some
lifeless thing. The rigid, the ready-made the mechanical, in contrast with the supple, the ever-
changing and the living, absentmindedness in contrast with attention, in a word, automatism in
contrast with free activity, such are the defects that
laughter singles out and would fain correct. We appealed to this idea to give us light at the outset,
when starting upon the analysis of the ludicrous. We
have seen it shining at every decisive turning in our
road. With its help, we shall now enter upon a more
important investigation, one that will, we hope, be
more instructive. We purpose, in short, studying
comic characters, or rather determining the essential
conditions of comedy in character, while endeavour-
ing to bring it about that this study may contribute
to a better understanding of the real nature of art
and the general relation between art and life.

Chapter III

THE COMIC IN CHARACTER

I

We have followed the comic along many of its winding channels in an endeavour to discover how it percolates into a form, an attitude, or a gesture; a situation, an action, or an expression. The analysis of comic *characters* has now brought us to the most important part of our task. It would also be the most difficult, had we yielded to the temptation of defining the laughable by a few striking—and consequently obvious—examples; for then, in proportion as we advanced towards the loftiest manifestations of the comic, we should have found the facts slipping between the over-wide meshes of the definition intended to retain them. But, as a matter of fact, we have followed the opposite plan, by throwing light on the subject from above. Convinced that laughter has a social meaning and import, that the comic expresses, above all else, a special lack of adaptability to society, and that, in short, there is nothing comic apart from man, we have made man and character generally our main objective. Our chief difficulty, therefore, has lain in explaining how we come to laugh at anything else than character, and by what subtle processes of fertilisation, combination, or amalgamation the comic can worm its way into a mere movement, an impersonal situation, or an independent phrase. This is what we have done so far. We started with the pure metal, and all our endeavours have been directed solely towards reconstructing the ore. It is the metal itself we are now about to study. Nothing could be easier, for this time we have a simple element to deal with. Let us examine it closely and see how it reacts upon everything else.

There are moods, we said, which move us as soon as we perceive them, joys and sorrows with which we sympathise, passions and vices which call forth painful astonishment, terror, or pity, in the beholder; in short, sentiments that are prolonged in sentimental overtones from mind to mind. All this concerns the essentials of life. All this is serious, at times even tragic. Comedy can only begin at the point where our neighbour's personality ceases to affect us. It begins, in fact, with what might be called *a growing callousness to social life*. Any individual is comic who automatically goes his own way without troubling himself about getting into touch with the rest of his fellow-beings. It is the part of laughter to reprove his absentmindedness and wake him out of his dream. If it is permissible to compare important things with trivial ones, we would call to mind what happens when a youth enters one of our military academies. After getting through the dreaded ordeal of the examination, he finds he has other ordeals to face, which his seniors have arranged with the object of fitting him for the new life he is entering upon, or, as they say, of "breaking him into harness." Every small society that forms within the larger is thus impelled, by a vague kind of instinct, to devise some method of discipline or "breaking in," so as to deal with the rigidity of habits that have been formed elsewhere and have now to undergo a partial modification. Society, properly so called, proceeds in exactly the same way. Each member must be ever attentive to his social surroundings; he must model himself on his environment; in short, he must avoid shutting himself up in his own peculiar character as a philosopher in his ivory tower. Therefore society holds suspended over each individual member, if not the threat of correction, at all events the prospect of a snubbing, which, although it is slight, is none the less dreaded. Such must be the function of laughter. Always rather humiliating for the one against whom it is directed, laughter is really and truly a kind of social "ragging."

Hence the equivocal nature of the comic. It belongs neither altogether to art nor altogether to life. On the one hand, characters in real life would never make us laugh were we not capable of watching their vagaries in the same way as we look down at a play from our seat in a box; they are only comic in our eyes because they perform a kind of comedy before us. But, on the other hand, the pleasure caused by laughter, even on the stage, is not an unadulterated enjoyment; it is not a pleasure that is exclusively esthetic or altogether disinterested. It always implies a secret or unconscious intent, if not of each one of us, at all events of society as a whole. In laughter we always find an unavowed intention to humiliate, and consequently to correct our neighbour, if not in his will, at least in his deed. This is the reason a comedy is far more like real life than a drama is. The more sublime the drama, the more profound the analysis to which the poet has had to subject the raw materials of daily life in order to obtain the tragic element in its unadulterated form. On the contrary, it is only in its lower aspects, in light comedy and farce, that comedy is in striking contrast to reality: the higher it rises, the more it approximates to life; in fact, there are scenes in real life so closely bordering on high-class comedy that the stage might adopt them without changing a single word.

Hence it follows that the elements of comic character on the stage and in actual life will be the same. What are these elements? We shall find no difficulty in deducing them.

It has often been said that it is the *trifling* faults of our fellow-men that make us laugh. Evidently there is a considerable amount of truth in this opinion; still, it cannot be regarded as altogether correct. First, as regards faults, it is no easy matter to draw the line between the trifling and the serious; maybe it is not because a fault is trifling, that it makes us laugh, but rather because it makes us laugh that we regard it as trifling; for there is nothing disarms us like laughter. But we may go even farther, and maintain that there are faults at which we laugh, even though fully aware that they are serious,—Harpagon's avarice, for instance. And then, we may as well confess—though somewhat reluctantly—that we laugh not only at the faults of our fellow-men, but also, at times, at their good qualities. We laugh at Alceste. The objection may be urged that it is not the earnestness of Alceste that is ludicrous, but rather the special aspect which earnestness assumes in his case; and, in short, a certain eccentricity that mars it in our eyes. Agreed; but it is none the less true that this eccentricity in Alceste, at which we laugh, *makes his earnestness laughable,* and that is the main point. So we may conclude that the comic is not always an indication of a fault, in the moral meaning of the word, and if critics insist on seeing a fault, even though a trifling one, in the ludicrous, they must point out what it is here that exactly distinguishes the trifling from the serious.

The truth is, the comic character may, strictly speaking, be quite in accord with stern morality. All it has to do is to bring itself into accord with society. The character of Alceste is that of a thoroughly honest man. But then he is unsociable, and, on that very account, ludicrous. A flexible vice may not be so easy to ridicule as a rigid virtue. It is *rigidity* that society eyes with suspicion. Consequently, it is the rigidity of Alceste that makes us laugh, though here rigidity stands for honesty. The man who withdraws into himself is liable to ridicule, because the comic is largely made up of this very withdrawal. This accounts for the comic being so frequently dependent on the manners or ideas, or, to put it bluntly, on the prejudices, of a society.

It must be acknowledged, however, to the credit of mankind, that there is no essential difference between the social ideal and the moral. We may therefore admit, as a general rule, that it is the faults of others that make us laugh, provided we add that they make us laugh by reason of their *unsociability* rather than of their *immorality*. What, then, are the faults capable of becoming ludicrous, and in what circumstances do we regard them as being too serious to be laughed at?

We have already given an implicit answer to this question. The comic, we said, appeals to the intelligence pure and simple; laughter is incompatible with emotion. Depict some fault, however trifling, in such a way as to arouse sympathy, fear, or pity; the mischief is done, it is impossible for us to laugh. On the other hand, take a downright vice,—even one that is, generally speaking, of an odious nature,—you may make it ludicrous if, by some suitable contrivance, you arrange so that it leaves our emotions unaffected Not that the vice *must* then be ludicrous, but it *may*, from that time forth, become so. *It must not arouse our feelings;* that is the sole condition really necessary, though assuredly it is not sufficient.

But, then, how will the comic poet set to work to prevent our feelings being moved? The question is an embarrassing one. To clear it up thoroughly, we should have to enter upon a rather novel line of investigation, to analyse the artificial sympathy which we bring with us to the theatre, and determine upon the circumstances in which we accept and those in which we refuse to share imaginary joys and sorrows. There is an art of lulling sensibility to sleep and providing it with dreams, as happens in the case of a mesmerised person. And there is also an art of throwing a wet blanket upon sympathy at the very moment it might arise, the result being that the situation, though a serious one, is not taken seriously. This latter art would appear to be governed by two methods, which are applied more or less unconsciously by the comic poet. The first consists in *isolating*, within the soul of the character, the feeling attributed to him, and making it a parasitic organism, so to speak, endowed with an independent existence. As a general rule, an intense feeling successively encroaches upon all other mental states, and colours them with its own peculiar hue; if, then, we are made to witness this gradual impregnation, we finally become impregnated ourselves with a corresponding emotion. To employ a different image, an emotion may be said to be dramatic and contagious when all the harmonics in it are heard along with the fundamental note. It is because the actor thus thrills throughout his whole being that the spectators themselves feel the thrill. On the contrary, in the case of emotion that leaves us indifferent, and that is about to become comic, there is always present a certain *rigidity* which prevents it from establishing a connection with the rest of the soul in which it has taken up its abode. This rigidity may be manifested, when the time comes, by puppet-like movements, and then it will provoke laughter; but, before that, it had already alienated our sympathy: how can we put ourselves in tune with a soul which is not in tune with itself? In Molière's *L'Avare* we have a scene bordering upon drama. It is the one in which the borrower and the usurer, who have never seen each other, meet face to face and find that they are son and father. Here we should be in the thick of a drama, if only greed and fatherly affection, conflicting with each other in the soul of Harpagon, had effected a more or less original combination. But such is not the case. No sooner has the interview come to an end than the father forgets everything. On meeting his son again he barely alludes to the scene, serious though it has been: "You, my son, whom I am good enough to forgive your recent escapade, etc." Greed has thus passed close to all other feelings *absentmindedly*, without either touching them or being touched. Although it has taken up its abode in the soul and become master of the house, none the less it remains a stranger. Far different would be avarice of a tragic sort. We should find it attracting and absorbing, transforming and assimilating the divers energies of the man: feelings and affections, likes and dislikes, vices and virtues, would all become something into which avarice would breathe a new kind of life. Such seems to be the first essential difference between high-class comedy and drama.

There is a second, which is far more obvious and arises out of the first. When a mental state is depicted to us with the object of making it dramatic, or even merely of inducing us to take it seriously, it gradually crystallises into *actions* which provide the real measure of its greatness. Thus, the miser orders his whole life with a view to acquiring wealth, and the pious hypocrite, though pretending to have his eyes fixed upon heaven, steers most skilfully his course here below. Most certainly, comedy does not shut out calculations of this kind; we need only take as an example the very machinations of Tartuffe. But that is what comedy has in common with drama; and in order to keep distinct from it, to prevent our taking a serious action seriously, in short, in order to prepare us for laughter, comedy utilises a method, the formula of which may be given as follows: *instead of concentrating our attention on actions, comedy directs it rather to gestures.* By *gestures* we here mean the attitudes, the movements and even the language by which a mental state expresses itself outwardly without any aim or profit, from no other cause than a kind of inner itching. Gesture, thus defined, is profoundly different from action. Action is intentional or, at any rate, conscious; gesture slips out unawares, it is automatic. In action, the entire person is engaged; in gesture, an isolated part of the person is expressed, unknown to, or at least apart from, the whole of the personality. Lastly —and here is the essential point—action is in exact proportion to the feeling that inspires it: the one gradually passes into the other, so that we may allow our sympathy or our aversion to glide along the line running from feeling to action and become increasingly interested. About gesture, however, there is something explosive, which awakes our sensibility when on the point of being lulled to sleep and, by thus rousing us up, prevents our taking matters seriously. Thus, as soon as our attention is fixed on gesture and not on action, we are in the realm of comedy. Did we merely take his actions into account, Tartuffe would belong to drama: it is only when we take his gestures into consideration that we find him comic. You may remember how he comes on to the stage with the words: "Laurent, lock up my hair-shirt and my scourge." He knows Dorine is listening to him, but doubtless he would say the same if she were not there. He enters so thoroughly into the *rôle* of a hypocrite that he plays it almost sincerely. In this way, and this way only, can he become comic. Were it not for this material sincerity, were it not for the language and attitudes that his long-standing experience as a hypocrite has transformed into natural gestures, Tartuffe would be simply odious, because we should only think of what is meant and willed in his conduct. And so we see why action is essential in drama, but only accessory in comedy. In a comedy, we feel any other situation might equally well have been chosen for the purpose of introducing the character; he would still have been the same man though the situation were different. Now, we do not get this impression in a drama. Here characters and situations are welded together; or rather, events form part and parcel with the persons, so that were the drama to tell us a different story, even though the actors kept the same names, we should in reality be dealing with other persons.

To sum up, whether a character is good or bad is of little moment; granted he is unsociable, he is capable of becoming comic. We now see that the seriousness of the case is of no importance either: whether serious or trifling, it is still capable of making us laugh, provided that care be taken not to arouse our emotions. Unsociability in the performer and insensibility in the spectator—such, in a word, are the two essential conditions. There is a third, implicit in the other two, which so far it has been the aim of our analysis to bring out.

This third condition is automatism. We have pointed it out from the outset of this work, continually drawing attention to the following point: what is essentially laughable is what is done automatically. In a vice, even in a virtue, the comic is that element by which the person unwittingly betrays himself— the involuntary gesture or the unconscious remark. Absentmindedness is always comical. Indeed, the deeper the absentmindedness the higher the comedy. Systematic absentmindedness, like that of Don Quixote, is the most comical thing imaginable: it is the comic itself, drawn as nearly as possible from its very source. Take any other comic character: however unconscious he may be of what he says or does, he cannot be comical unless there be some aspect of his person of which he is unaware, one side of his nature which he overlooks; on that account alone does he make us laugh.[1] Profoundly comic sayings are those artless ones in which some vice reveals itself in all its nakedness: how could it thus expose itself were it capable of seeing itself as it is? It is not uncommon for a comic character to condemn in general terms a certain line of conduct and immediately afterwards afford an example of it himself: for instance, M. Jourdain's teacher of philosophy flying into a passion after inveighing against anger; Vadius taking a poem from his pocket after heaping ridicule on readers of poetry, etc. What is the object of such contradictions except to help us to put our

---

[1] When the humourist laughs at himself, he is really acting a double part; the self who laughs is indeed conscious, but not the self who is laughed at.

finger on the obliviousness of the characters to their own actions? Inattention to self, and consequently to others, is what we invariably find. And if we look at the matter closely, we see that inattention is here equivalent to what we have called unsociability. The chief cause of rigidity is the neglect to look around—and more especially within oneself: how can a man fashion his personality after that of another if he does not first study others as well as himself? Rigidity, automatism, absentmindedness and unsociability are all inextricably entwined; and all serve as ingredients to the making up of the comic in character.

In a word, if we leave on one side, when dealing with human personality, that portion which interests our sensibility or appeals to our feeling, all the rest is capable of becoming comic, and the comic will be proportioned to the rigidity. We formulated this idea at the outset of this work. We have verified it in its main results, and have just applied it to the definition of comedy. Now we must get to closer quarters, and show how it enables us to delimitate the exact position comedy occupies among all the other arts.

In one sense it might be said that all *character* is comic, provided we mean by character the *ready-made* element in our personality, that mechanical element which resembles a piece of clockwork wound up once for all and capable of working automatically. It is, if you will, that which causes us to imitate ourselves. And it is also, for that very reason, that which enables others to imitate us. Every comic character is a *type*. Inversely, every resemblance to a type has something comic in it. Though we may long have associated with an individual without discovering anything about him to laugh at, still, if advantage is taken of some accidental analogy to dub him with the name of a famous hero of romance or drama, he will in our eyes border upon the ridiculous, if only for a moment. And yet this hero of romance may not be a comic character at all. But then it is comic to be like him. It is comic to wander out of one's own self. It is comic to fall into a ready-made category. And what is most comic of all is to become a category oneself into which others will fall, as into a ready-made frame; it is to crystallise into a stock character.

Thus, to depict characters, that is to say, general types, is the object of high-class comedy. This has often been said. But it is as well to repeat it, since there could be no better definition of comedy. Not only are we entitled to say that comedy gives us general types, but we might add that it is the *only* one of all the arts that aims at the general; so that once this objective has been attributed to it, we have said all that it is and all that the rest cannot be. To prove that such is really the essence of comedy, and that it is in this respect opposed to tragedy, drama and the other forms of art, we should begin by defining art in its higher forms: then, gradually coming down to comic poetry, we should find that this latter is situated on the border-line between art and life, and that, by the generality of its subject-matter it contrasts with the rest of the arts. We cannot here plunge into so vast a subject of investigation; but we needs must sketch its main outlines, lest we overlook what, to our mind, is essential on the comic stage.

What is the object of art? Could reality come into direct contact with sense and consciousness, could we enter into immediate communion with things and with ourselves, probably art would be useless, or rather we should all be artists, for then our soul would continually vibrate in perfect accord with nature. Our eyes, aided by memory, would carve out in space and fix in time the most inimitable of pictures. Hewn in the living marble of the human form, fragments of statues, beautiful as the relics of antique statuary, would strike the passing glance. Deep in our souls we should hear the strains of our inner life's unbroken melody,—a music that is oft-times gay, but more frequently plaintive and always original. All this is around and within us, and yet no whit of it do we distinctly perceive. Between nature and ourselves, nay, between ourselves and our own consciousness a veil is interposed: a veil that is dense and opaque for the common herd,— thin, almost transparent, for the artist and the poet. What fairy wove that veil? Was it done in malice or in friendliness? We had to live, and life demands that we grasp things in their relations to our own needs. Life is action. Life implies the acceptance only of the *utilitarian* side of things in order to respond to them by appropriate reactions: all other impressions must be dimmed or else reach us vague and blurred. I look and I think I see, I listen and I think I hear, I examine myself and I think I am reading the very depths of my heart. But what I see and hear of the outer world is purely and simply a selection made by my senses to serve as a light to my conduct; what I know of myself is what comes to the surface, what participates in my actions. My senses and my consciousness, therefore, give me no more than a practical simplification of reality. In the vision they furnish me of myself and of things, the differences that are useless to man are obliterated, the resemblances that are useful to him are empha-sised; ways are traced out for me in advance along which my activity is to travel. These ways are the ways which all mankind has trod before me. Things have been classified with a view to the use I can derive from them. And it is this classification I perceive, far more clearly than the colour and the shape of things. Doubtless man is vastly superior to the lower animals in this respect. It is not very likely that the eye of a wolf makes any distinction between a kid and a lamb; both appear to the wolf as the same identical quarry, alike easy to pounce upon, alike good to devour. We, for our part, make a distinction between a goat and a sheep; but can we tell one goat from another, one sheep from another? The *individuality* of things or of beings escapes us, unless it is materially to our advantage to perceive it. Even when we do take note of it—as when we distinguish one man from another—it is not the individuality itself that the eye grasps, *i.e.* an entirely original harmony of forms and colours, but only one or two features that will make practical recognition easier.

In short, we do not see the actual things themselves; in most cases we confine ourselves to reading the labels affixed to them. This tendency, the result of need, has become even more pronounced under the influence of speech; for words—with the exception of proper nouns—all denote genera. The word, which only takes note of the most ordinary function and commonplace aspect of the thing, intervenes between it and ourselves, and would conceal its form from our eyes, were that form not already masked beneath the necessities that brought the word into existence. Not only external objects, but even our own mental states, are screened from us in their inmost, their personal aspect, in the original life they possess. When we feel love or hatred, when we are gay or sad, is it really the feeling itself that reaches our consciousness with those innumerable fleeting shades of meaning and deep resounding echoes that make it something altogether our own? We should all, were it so, be novelists or poets or musicians. Mostly, however, we perceive nothing but the out-ward display of our mental state. We catch only the impersonal aspect of our feelings, that aspect which speech has set down once for all because it is almost the same, in the same conditions, for all men. Thus, even in our own individual, individuality escapes our ken. We move amidst generalities and symbols, as within a tilt-yard in which our force is effectively pitted against other forces; and fascinated by action, tempted by it, for our own good, on to the field it has selected, we live in a zone midway between things and ourselves, externally to things, externally also to ourselves. From time to time, however, in a fit of absentmindedness, nature raises up souls that are more detached from life. Not with that inten-tional, logical, systematical detachment—the result of reflection and philosophy—but rather with a nat-ural detachment, one innate in the structure of sense or consciousness, which at once reveals itself by a virginal manner, so to speak, of seeing, hearing, or thinking. Were this detachment complete, did the soul no longer cleave to action by any of its percep-tions, it would be the soul of an artist such as the world has never yet seen. It would excel alike in every art at the same time; or rather, it would fuse them all into one. It would perceive all things in their native purity: the forms, colours, sounds of the physical world as well as the subtlest movements of the inner life. But this is asking too much of nature. Even for such of us as she has made artists, it is by accident, and on one side only, that she has lifted the veil. In one direction only has she forgotten to rivet the perception to the need. And since each direction corresponds to what we call a *sense*—through one of his senses, and through that sense alone, is the artist usually wedded to art. Hence, originally, the diversity of arts. Hence also the speciality of predispositions. This one applies himself to colours and forms, and since he loves colour for colour and form for form, since he perceives them for their sake and not for his own, it is the inner life of things that he sees appearing through their forms and colours. Little by little he insinuates it into our own perception, baffled though we may be at the outset. For a few moments at least, he diverts us from the prejudices of form and colour that come between ourselves and reality. And thus he realises the loftiest ambition of art, which here consists in revealing to us nature. Others, again, retire within themselves. Beneath the thousand rudimentary actions which are the outward and visible signs of an emotion, behind the commonplace, conventional expression that both reveals and conceals an individual mental state, it is the emotion, the original mood, to which they attain in its undefiled essence. And then, to induce us to make the same effort ourselves, they contrive to make us see something of what they have seen: by rhythmical arrangement of words, which thus become organised and animated with a life of their own, they tell us—or rather suggest—things that speech was not calculated to express. Others delve yet deeper still. Beneath these joys and sorrows which can, at a pinch, be translated into language, they grasp something that has nothing in common with language, certain rhythms of life and breath that are closer to man than his inmost feelings, being the living law—varying with each individual—of his enthusiasm and despair, his hopes and regrets. By setting free and emphasising this music, they force it upon our attention; they compel us, willy-nilly, to fall in with it, like passers-by who join in a dance. And thus they impel us to set in motion, in the depths of our being, some secret chord which was only waiting to thrill. So art, whether it be painting or sculpture, poetry or music, has no other object than to brush aside the utilitarian symbols, the conventional and socially accepted generalities, in short, everything that veils reality from us, in order to bring us face to face with reality itself. It is from a misunderstanding on this point that the dispute between realism and idealism in art has risen. Art is certainly only a more direct vision of reality. But this purity of perception implies a break with utilitarian convention, an innate and specially localised disinterestedness of sense or consciousness, in short, a certain immateriality of life, which is what has always been called idealism. So that we might say, without in any way playing upon the meaning of the words, that realism is in the work when idealism is in the soul, and that it is only through ideality that we can resume contact with reality.

Dramatic art forms no exception to this law. What drama goes forth to discover and brings to light, is a deep-seated reality that is veiled from us, often in our own interests, by the necessities of life. What is this reality? What are these necessities? Poetry always expresses inward states. But amongst these states some arise mainly from contact with our fellow-men. They are the most intense as well as the most violent. As contrary electricities attract each other and accumulate between the two plates of the condenser from which the spark will presently flash, so, by simply bringing people together, strong attractions and repulsions take place followed by an utter loss of balance, in a word, by that electrification of the soul known as passion. Were man to give way to the impulse of his natural feelings, were there neither social nor moral law, these outbursts of violent feeling would be the ordinary rule in life. But utility demands that these outbursts should be foreseen and averted. Man must live in society, and consequently submit to rules. And what interest advises, reason commands: duty calls, and we have to obey the summons. Under this dual influence has perforce been formed an outward layer of feelings and ideas which make for permanence, aim at becoming common to all men, and cover, when they are not strong enough to extinguish it, the inner fire of individual passions. The slow progress of mankind in the direction of an increasingly peaceful social life has gradually consolidated this layer, just as the life of our planet itself has been one long effort to cover over with a cool and solid crust the fiery mass of seething metals. But volcanic eruptions occur. And if the earth were a living being, as mythology has feigned, most likely when in repose it would take delight in dreaming of these sudden explosions whereby it suddenly resumes possession of its innermost nature. Such is just the kind of pleasure that is provided for us by drama. Beneath the quiet humdrum life that reason and society have fashioned for us, it stirs something within us which luckily does not explode, but which it makes us feel in its inner tension. It offers nature her revenge upon society. Sometimes it makes straight for the goal, summoning up to the surface, from the depths below, passions that produce a general upheaval. Sometimes it follows a flank movement, as is often the case in con-

temporary drama; with a skill that is frequently
sophistical it shows up the inconsistencies of society;
it exaggerates the shams and shibboleths of the
social law, and so indirectly, by merely dissolving
or corroding the outer crust, it again brings us back
to the inner core. But, in both cases, whether it
weakens society or strengthens nature, it has the
same end in view: that of laying bare a secret portion of ourselves, what might be called the tragic
element in our character. This is indeed the impression we get after seeing a stirring drama. What has
just interested us is not so much what we have been
told about others as the glimpse we have caught of
ourselves—a whole host of ghostly feelings, emotions
and events that would fain have come into real
existence, but, fortunately for us, did not. It also
seems as if an appeal had been made within us to
certain ancestral memories belonging to a far-away
past—memories so deep-seated and so foreign to our
present life that this latter, for a moment, seems
something unreal and conventional, for which we
shall have to serve a fresh apprenticeship. So it is
indeed a deeper reality that drama draws up from
beneath our superficial and utilitarian attainments;
and this art has the same end in view as all the
others.

Hence it follows that art always aims at what is
individual. What the artist fixes on his canvas is
something he has seen at a certain spot, on a certain
day, at a certain hour, with a colouring that will
never be seen again. What the poet sings of is a
certain mood which was his, and his alone, and which
will never return. What the dramatist unfolds before
us is the life-history of a soul, a living tissue of feelings and events—something, in short, which has
once happened and can never be repeated. We may,

indeed, give general names to these feelings, but they cannot be the same thing in another soul. They are *individualised.* Thereby, and thereby only, do they belong to art; for generalities, symbols, or even types form the current coin of our daily perception. How, then, does a misunderstanding on this point arise?

The reason lies in the fact that two very different things have been mistaken for each other: the generality of things and that of the opinions we come to regarding them. Because a feeling is generally recognised as true, it does not follow that it is a general feeling. Nothing could be more unique than the character of Hamlet. Though he may resemble other men in some respects, it is clearly not on that account that he interests us most. But he is universally accepted and regarded as a living character. In this sense only is he universally true. The same holds good of all the other products of art. Each of them is unique, and yet, if it bear the stamp of genius, it will come to be accepted by everybody. Why will it be accepted? And if it is unique of its kind, by what sign do we know it to be genuine? Evidently, by the very effort it forces us to make against our predispositions in order to see sincerely. Sincerity is contagious. What the artist has seen we shall probably never see again, or at least never see in exactly the same way; but if he has actually seen it, the attempt he has made to lift the veil compels our imitation. His work is an example which we take as a lesson. And the efficacy of the lesson is the exact standard of the genuineness of the work. Consequently, truth bears within itself a power of conviction, nay, of conversion, which is the sign that enables us to recognise it. The greater the work and the more profound the dimly apprehended truth, the longer may the effect be in coming; but, on the other hand, the more universal will that effect tend to become. So the universality here lies in the effect produced, and not in the cause.

Altogether different is the object of comedy. Here it is in the work itself that the generality lies. Comedy depicts characters we have already come across and shall meet with again. It takes note of similarities. It aims at placing types before our eyes. It even creates new types, if necessary. In this respect it forms a contrast to all the other arts.

The very titles of certain classical comedies are significant in themselves. Le Misanthrope, l'Avare, le Joueur, le Distrait, etc., are names of whole classes of people; and even when a character comedy has a proper noun as its title, this proper noun is speedily swept away, by the very weight of its contents, into the stream of common nouns. We say "a Tartuffe," but we should never say "a Phèdre" or "a Polyeucte."

Above all, a tragic poet will never think of grouping around the chief character in his play secondary characters to serve as simplified copies, so to speak, of the former. The hero of a tragedy represents an individuality unique of its kind. It may be possible to imitate him, but then we shall be passing, whether consciously or not, from the tragic to the comic. No one is like him, because he is like no one. But a remarkable instinct, on the contrary, impels the comic poet, once he has elaborated his central character, to cause other characters, displaying the same general traits, to revolve as satellites round him. Many comedies have either a plural noun or some collective term as their title. "*Les* Femmes savantes," "*Les* Précieuses ridicules," "*Le Monde* où l'on s'ennuie," etc., represent so many rallying points on the stage adopted by different groups of characters, all belonging to one identical type. It would be interesting to analyse this tendency in comedy. Maybe dramatists have caught a glimpse of a fact recently brought forward by mental pathology, viz. that cranks of the same kind are drawn by a secret attraction to seek each other's company. Without precisely coming within the province of medicine, the comic individual, as we have shown, is in some way absentminded, and the transition from absentmindedness to crankiness is continuous. But there is also another reason. If the comic poet's object is to offer us types, that is to say, characters capable of self-repetition, how can he set about it better than by showing us, in each instance, several different copies of the same model? That is just what the naturalist does in order to define a species. He enumerates and describes its main varieties.

This essential difference between tragedy and comedy, the former being concerned with individuals and the latter with classes, is revealed in yet another way. It appears in the first draft of the work. From the outset it is manifested by two radically different methods of observation.

Though the assertion may seem paradoxical, a study of other men is probably not necessary to the tragic poet. We find that some of the great poets have lived a retiring, homely sort of life, without having a chance of witnessing around them an outburst of the passions they have so faithfully depicted. But, supposing even they had witnessed such a spectacle, it is doubtful whether they would have found it of much use. For what interests us in the work of the poet is the glimpse we get of certain profound moods or inner struggles. Now, this glimpse cannot be obtained from without. Our souls are impenetrable to one another. Certain signs of passion are all that we ever apperceive externally. These we interpret—though always, by the way, defectively—only by analogy with what we have ourselves experienced. So what we experience is the main point, and we cannot become thoroughly acquainted with anything but our own heart—supposing we ever get so far. Does this mean that the poet has experienced what he depicts, that he has gone through the various situations he makes his characters traverse, and lived the whole of their inner life? Here, too, the biographies of poets would contradict such a supposition. How, indeed, could the same man have been Macbeth, Hamlet, Othello, King Lear, and many others? But then a distinction should perhaps here be made between the personality *we have* and all those we might have had. Our character is the result of a choice that is continually being renewed. There are points—at all events there seem to be—all along the way, where we may branch off, and we perceive many possible directions though we are unable to take more than one. To retrace one's steps, and follow to the end the faintly distinguishable directions, appears to be the essential element in poetic imagination. Of course, Shakespeare was neither Macbeth, nor Hamlet, nor Othello; still, he *might have been* these several characters, if the circumstances of the case on one hand, and the consent of his will on the other, had cause to break out into explosive action what was nothing more than an inner prompting. We are strangely mistaken as to the part played by poetic imagination if we think it pieces together its heroes out of fragments filched from right and left, as though it were patching together a harlequin's motley. Nothing living would result from that. Life cannot be recomposed; it can only be looked at and reproduced. Poetic imagination is but a fuller view of reality. If the characters created by a poet give us the impression of life, it is only because they are the poet himself,—a multiplication or division of the poet,— the poet plumbing the depths of his own nature in so powerful an effort of inner observation, that he lays hold of the potential in the real, and takes up what nature has left as a mere outline or sketch in his soul in order to make of it a finished work of art.

drama inwards

Altogether different is the kind of observation from which comedy springs. It is directed outwards. However interested a dramatist may be in the comic features of human nature, he will hardly go, I imagine, to the extent of trying to discover his own. Besides, he would not find them, for we are never ridiculous except in some point that remains hidden from our own consciousness. It is on others, then, that such observation must perforce be practised. But it will, for this very reason, assume a character of generality that it cannot have when we apply it to ourselves. Settling on the surface, it will not be more than skin-deep, dealing with persons at the point at which they come into contact and become capable of resembling one another. It will go no farther. Even if it could, it would not desire to do so, for it would have nothing to gain in the process. To penetrate too far into the personality, to couple the outer effect with causes that are too deep-seated, would mean to endanger, and in the end to sacrifice all that was laughable in the effect. In order that we may be tempted to laugh at it, we must localise its cause in some intermediate region of the soul. Consequently, the effect must appear to us as an average effect, as expressing an average of mankind. And, like all averages, this one is obtained by bringing to-

comedy outwards

gether scattered data, by comparing analogous cases and extracting their essence; in short by a process of abstraction and generalisation similar to that which the physicist brings to bear upon facts with the object of grouping them under laws. In a word, method and object are here of the same nature as in the inductive sciences, in that observation is always external and the result always general.

And so we come back, by a roundabout way, to the double conclusion we reached in the course of our investigations. On the one hand, a person is never ridiculous except through some mental attribute resembling absentmindedness, through something that lives upon him without forming part of his organism, after the fashion of a parasite; that is the reason this state of mind is observable from without and capable of being corrected. But, on the other hand, just because laughter aims at correcting, it is expedient that the correction should reach as great a number of persons as possible. This is the reason comic observation instinctively proceeds to what is general. It chooses such peculiarities as admit of being reproduced, and consequently are not indissolubly bound up with the individuality of a single person,—a possibly common sort of uncommonness, so to say,—peculiarities that are held in common. By transferring them to the stage, it creates works which doubtless belong to art in that their only visible aim is to please, but which will be found to contrast with other works of art by reason of their generality, and also of their scarcely confessed or scarcely conscious intention to correct and instruct. So we were probably right in saying that comedy lies midway between art and life. It is not disinterested as genuine art is. By organising laughter, comedy accepts social life as a natural environment; it even obeys an impulse of social life. And in this respect it turns its back upon art, which is a breaking away from society and a return to pure nature.

II

Now let us see, in the light of what has gone before, the line to take for creating an ideally comic type of character, comic in itself, in its origin, and in all its manifestations. It must be deep-rooted, so as to supply comedy with inexhaustible matter, and yet superficial, in order that it may remain within the scope of comedy; invisible to its actual owner, for the comic ever partakes of the unconscious, but visible to everybody else, so that it may call forth general laughter; extremely considerate to its own self, so that it may be displayed without scruple, but troublesome to others, so that they may repress it without pity, but immediately repressible, so that our laughter may not have been wasted; sure of reappearing under fresh aspects, so that laughter may always find something to do; inseparable from social life, although insufferable to society; capable —in order that it may assume the greatest imaginable variety of forms—of being tacked on to all the vices and even to a good many virtues. Truly a goodly number of elements to fuse together! But a chemist of the soul, entrusted with this elaborate preparation, would be somewhat disappointed when pouring out the contents of his retort. He would find he had taken a vast deal of trouble to compound a mixture which may be found ready-made and free of expense, for it is as widespread throughout mankind as air throughout nature.

This mixture is vanity. Probably there is not a single failing that is more superficial or more deep-rooted. The wounds it receives are never very seri-

ous, and yet they are seldom healed. The services
rendered to it are the most unreal of all services,
and yet they are the very ones that meet with lasting
gratitude. It is scarcely a vice, and yet all the vices
are drawn into its orbit and, in proportion as they
become more refined and artificial, tend to be nothing more than a means of satisfying it. The outcome
of social life, since it is an admiration of ourselves
based on the admiration we think we are inspiring
in others, it is even more natural, more universally
innate than egoism; for egoism may be conquered
by nature, whereas only by reflection do we get
the better of vanity. It does not seem, indeed, as if
men were ever born modest, unless we dub with
the name of modesty a sort of purely physical bashfulness, which is nearer to pride than is generally
supposed. True modesty can be nothing but a medi-
tation on vanity. It springs from the sight of others'
mistakes, and the dread of being similarly deceived.
It is a sort of scientific cautiousness with respect
to what we shall say and think of ourselves. It is
made up of improvements and aftertouches. In short,
it is an acquired virtue.

It is no easy matter to define the point at which
the anxiety to become modest may be distinguished
from the dread of becoming ridiculous. But surely,
at the outset, this dread and this anxiety are one and
the same thing. A complete investigation into the
illusions of vanity, and into the ridicule that clings
to them, would cast a strange light upon the whole
theory of laughter. We should find laughter performing, with mathematical regularity, one of its
main functions—that of bringing back to complete
self-consciousness a certain self-admiration which is
almost automatic, and thus obtaining the greatest
possible sociability of characters. We should see that

vanity, though it is a natural product of social life, is an inconvenience to society, just as certain slight poisons, continually secreted by the human organism, would destroy it in the long run, if they were not neutralised by other secretions. Laughter is unceasingly doing work of this kind. In this respect, it might be said that the specific remedy for vanity is laughter, and that the one failing that is essentially laughable is vanity.

While dealing with the comic in form and movement, we showed how any simple image, laughable in itself, is capable of worming its way into other images of a more complex nature, and instilling into them something of its comic essence; thus, the highest forms of the comic can sometimes be explained by the lowest. The inverse process, however, is perhaps even more common, and many coarse comic effects are the direct result of a drop from some very subtle comic element. For instance, vanity, that higher form of the comic, is an element we are prone to look for, minutely though unconsciously, in every manifestation of human activity. We look for it if only to laugh at it. Indeed, our imagination often locates it where it has no business to be. Perhaps we must attribute to this source the altogether coarse comic element in certain effects which psychologists have very inadequately explained by contrast: a short man bowing his head to pass beneath a large door; two individuals, one very tall, the other a mere dwarf, gravely walking along arm-in-arm, etc. By scanning narrowly this latter image, we shall probably find that the shorter of the two persons seems as though he were trying *to raise himself* to the height of the taller, like the frog that wanted to make itself as large as the ox.

III

It would be quite impossible to go through all the peculiarities of character that either coalesce or compete with vanity in order to force themselves upon the attention of the comic poet. We have shown that all failings may become laughable, and even, occasionally, many a good quality. Even though a list of all the peculiarities that have ever been found ridiculous were drawn up, comedy would manage to add to them, not indeed by creating artificial ones, but by discovering lines of comic development that had hitherto gone unnoticed; thus does imagination isolate ever fresh figures in the intricate design of one and the same piece of tapestry. The essential condition, as we know, is that the peculiarity observed should straightway appear as a kind of *category* into which a number of individuals can step.

Now, there are ready-made categories established by society itself, and necessary to it because it is based on the division of labour. We mean the various trades, public services, and professions. Each particular profession impresses on its corporate members certain habits of mind and peculiarities of character in which they resemble each other and also distinguish themselves from the rest. Small societies are thus formed within the bosom of Society at large. Doubtless they arise from the very organisation of Society as a whole. And yet, if they held too much aloof, there would be a risk of their proving harmful to sociability. Now, it is the business of laughter to repress any separatist tendency. Its function is to convert rigidity into plasticity, to readapt the individual to the whole, in short, to round off the corners wherever they are met with. Accordingly, we here find a species of the comic whose varieties might be calculated beforehand. This we shall call the *professional comic.*

Instead of taking up these varieties in detail, we prefer to lay stress upon what they have in common. In the forefront we find professional vanity. Each one of M. Jourdain's teachers exalts his own art above all the rest. In a play of Labiche there is a character who cannot understand how it is possible to be anything else than a timber merchant. Naturally he is a timber merchant himself. Note that vanity here tends to merge into *solemnity,* in proportion to the degree of quackery there is in the profession under consideration. For it is a remarkable fact that the more questionable an art, science, or occupation is, the more those who practise it are inclined to regard themselves as invested with a kind of priesthood and to claim that all should bow before its mysteries. Useful professions are clearly meant for the public, but those whose utility is more dubious can only justify their existence by assuming that the public is meant for them: now, this is just the illusion that lies at the root of solemnity. Almost everything comic in Molière's doctors comes from this source. They treat the patient as though he had been made for the doctors, and nature herself as an appendage to medicine.

Another form of this comic rigidity is what may be called *professional callousness.* The comic character is so tightly jammed into the rigid frame of his functions that he has no room to move or to be moved like other men. Only call to mind the answer Isabelle receives from Perrin Dandin, the judge, when she asks him how he can bear to look on when the poor wretches are being tortured:

Bah! cela fait toujours passer une heure ou deux.[2]

[2] Bah! it always helps to while away an hour or two.

Does not Tartuffe also manifest a sort of professional callousness when he says—it is true, by the mouth of Orgon:

> Et je verrais mourir frère, enfants, mère et femme
> Que je m'en soucierais autant que de cela![3]

The device most in use, however, for making a profession ludicrous is to confine it, so to say, within the four corners of its own particular jargon. Judge, doctor and soldier are made to apply the language of law, medicine and strategy to the everyday affairs of life, as though they had become incapable of talking like ordinary people. As a rule, this kind of the ludicrous is rather coarse. It becomes more refined, however, as we have already said, if it reveals some peculiarity of character in addition to a professional habit. We will instance only Régnard's *Joueur,* who expresses himself with the utmost originality in terms borrowed from gambling, giving his valet the name of Hector, and calling his betrothed

> Pallas, du nom connu de la Dame de Pique;[4]

or Molière's *Femmes savantes,* where the comic element evidently consists largely in the translation of ideas of a scientific nature into terms of feminine sensibility: Épicure *me plaît . . ."* (Epicurus is charming), *"J'aime* les tourbillons" (I dote on vortices), etc. You have only to read the third act to find that Armande, Philaminte and Bélise almost invariably express themselves in this style.

Proceeding further in the same direction, we discover that there is also such a thing as a professional

---

[3] Let brother, children, mother and wife all die, what should I care!

[4] Pallas, from the well-known name of the Queen of Spades.

logic, *i.e.* certain ways of reasoning that are customary in certain circles, which are valid for these circles, but untrue for the rest of the public. Now, the contrast between these two kinds of logic—one particular, the other universal—produces comic effects of a special nature, on which we may advantageously dwell at greater length. Here we touch upon a point of some consequence in the theory of laughter. We propose, therefore, to give the question a wider scope and consider it in its most general aspect.

IV

Eager as we have been to discover the deep-seated cause of the comic, we have so far had to neglect one of its most striking phenomena. We refer to the logic peculiar to the comic character and the comic group, a strange kind of logic, which, in some cases, may include a good deal of absurdity.

Théophile Gautier said that the comic in its extreme form was the logic of the absurd. More than one philosophy of laughter revolves round a like idea. Every comic effect, it is said, implies contradiction in some of its aspects. What makes us laugh is alleged to be the absurd realised in concrete shape, a "palpable absurdity";—or, again, an apparent absurdity, which we swallow for the moment only to rectify it immediately afterwards;—or, better still, something absurd from one point of view though capable of a natural explanation from another, etc. All these theories may contain some portion of the truth; but, in the first place, they apply only to certain rather obvious comic effects, and then, even where they do apply, they evidently take no account of the characteristic element of the laughable, that is, the *particular kind* of absurdity the comic contains when it does contain something absurd. Is an immediate proof of this desired? You have only to choose one of these definitions and make up effects in accordance with the formula: twice out of every three times there will be nothing laughable in the effect obtained. So we see that absurdity, when met with in the comic, is not absurdity *in general*. It is an absurdity of a definite kind. It does not create the comic; rather, we might say that the comic infuses into it its own particular essence. It is not a cause but an effect—an effect of a very special kind, which reflects the special nature of its cause. Now, this cause is known to us; consequently we shall have no trouble in understanding the nature of the effect.

Assume, when out for a country walk, that you notice on the top of a hill something that bears a faint resemblance to a large motionless body with revolving arms. So far you do not know what it is, but you begin to search amongst your *ideas*—that is to say, in the present instance, amongst the recollections at your disposal—for that recollection which will best fit in with what you see. Almost immediately the image of a windmill comes into your mind: the object before you is a windmill. No matter if, before leaving the house, you have just been reading fairy-tales telling of giants with enormous arms, for although common sense consists mainly in being able to remember, it consists even more in being able to forget. Common sense represents the endeavour of a mind continually adapting itself anew and changing ideas when it changes objects. It is the mobility of the intelligence conforming exactly to the mobility of things. It is the moving continuity of our attention to life.

But now, let us take Don Quixote setting out for

the wars. The romances he has been reading all tell
of knights encountering, on the way, giant adver-
saries. He therefore must needs encounter a giant.
This idea of a giant is a privileged recollection,
which has taken its abode in his mind and lies there
in wait, motionless, watching for an opportunity to
sally forth and become embodied in a thing. It *is
bent* on entering the material world, and so the very
first object he sees bearing the faintest resemblance
to a giant is invested with the form of one. Thus,
Don Quixote sees giants where we see windmills.
This is comical; it is also absurd. But is it a mere
absurdity,—an absurdity of an indefinite kind?

It is a very special inversion of common sense. It
consists in seeking to mould things on an idea of one's
own, instead of moulding one's ideas on things,—
in seeing before us what we are thinking of, instead
of thinking of what we see. Good sense would have
us leave all our memories in their proper rank and
file; then the appropriate memory will every time
answer the summons of the situation of the moment
and serve only to interpret it. But in Don Quixote,
on the contrary, there is one group of memories in
command of all the rest and dominating the character itself: thus it is reality that now has to bow to
imagination, its only function being to supply fancy
with a body. Once the illusion has been created, Don
Quixote develops it logically enough in all its consequences; he proceeds with the certainty and precision of a somnambulist who is acting his dream.
Such, then, is the origin of his delusions and such
the peculiar logic which controls this particular
absurdity. Now, is this logic peculiar to Don Quixote?

We have shown that the comic character always
errs through obstinacy of mind or of disposition,

through absentmindedness, in short, through automatism. At the root of the comic there is a sort of
rigidity which compels its victims to keep strictly to
one path, to follow it straight along, to shut their
ears and refuse to listen. In Molière's plays how many
comic scenes can be reduced to this simple type:
a character following up his one idea, and continually recurring to it in spite of incessant interruptions!
The transition seems to take place imperceptibly
from the man who will listen to nothing to the one
who will see nothing, and from this latter to the one
who sees only what he wants to see. A stubborn
spirit ends by adjusting things to its own way of
thinking, instead of accommodating its thoughts to
the things. So every comic character is on the high-
road to the above-mentioned illusion, and Don
Quixote furnishes us with the general type of comic
absurdity.

Is there a name for this inversion of common
sense? Doubtless it may be found, in either an acute
or a chronic form, in certain types of insanity. In
many of its aspects it resembles a fixed idea. But
neither insanity in general, nor fixed ideas in particular, are provocative of laughter: they are dis-
eases, and arouse our pity. Laughter, as we have
seen, is incompatible with emotion. If there exists a
madness that is laughable, it can only be one compatible with the general health of the mind,—a sane
type of madness, one might say. Now, there is a sane
state of the mind that resembles madness in every
respect, in which we find the same associations of
ideas as we do in lunacy, the same peculiar logic as
in a fixed idea. This state is that of dreams. So either
our analysis is incorrect, or it must be capable of
being stated in the following theorem: *Comic absurdity is of the same nature as that of dreams.*

The behaviour of the intellect in a dream is exactly what we have just been describing. The mind, enamoured of itself, now seeks in the outer world nothing more than a pretext for realising its imaginations. A confused murmur of sounds still reaches the ear, colours enter the field of vision, the senses are not completely shut in. But the dreamer, instead of appealing to the whole of his recollections for the interpretation of what his senses perceive, makes use of what he perceives to give substance to the particular recollection he favours: thus, according to the mood of the dreamer and the idea that fills his imagination at the time, a gust of wind blowing down the chimney becomes the howl of a wild beast or a tuneful melody. Such is the ordinary mechanism of illusion in dreams.

Now, if comic illusion is similar to dream illusion, if the logic of the comic is the logic of dreams, we may expect to discover in the logic of the laughable all the peculiarities of dream logic. Here, again, we shall find an illustration of the law with which we are well acquainted: given one form of the laughable, other forms that are lacking in the same comic essence become laughable from their outward resemblance to the first. Indeed, it is not difficult to see that any *play of ideas* may afford us amusement if only it bring back to mind, more or less distinctly, the play of dreamland.

We shall first call attention to a certain general relaxation of the rules of reasoning. The reasonings at which we laugh are those we know to be false, but which we might accept as true were we to hear them in a dream. They counterfeit true reasoning just sufficiently to deceive a mind dropping off to sleep. There is still an element of logic in them, if you will, but it is a logic lacking in tension and, for that

very reason, affording us relief from intellectual
effort. Many "witticisms" are reasonings of this kind,
considerably abridged reasonings, of which we are
given only the beginning and the end. Such play
upon ideas evolves in the direction of a play upon
words in proportion as the relations set up between
the ideas become more superficial: gradually we
come to take no account of the meaning of the words
we hear, but only of their sound. It might be instructive to compare with dreams certain comic scenes
in which one of the characters systematically repeats
in a nonsensical fashion what another character
whispers in his ear. If you fall asleep with people
talking round you, you sometimes find that what
they say gradually becomes devoid of meaning, that
the sounds get distorted, as it were, and recombine
in a haphazard fashion to form in your mind the
strangest of meanings, and that you are reproducing
between yourself and the different speakers the
scene between Petit-Jean and The Prompter.[5]

There are also *comic obsessions* that seem to
bear a great resemblance to dream obsessions. Who
has not had the experience of seeing the same
image appear in several successive dreams, assuming
a plausible meaning in each of them, whereas these
dreams had no other point in common. Effects of
repetition sometimes present this special form on
the stage or in fiction: some of them, in fact, sound
as though they belonged to a dream. It may be the
same with the burden of many a song: it persistently
recurs, always unchanged, at the end of every verse,
each time with a different meaning.

Not infrequently do we notice in dreams a particular *crescendo,* a weird effect that grows more

[5] *Les Plaideurs* (Racine).

pronounced as we proceed. The first concession ex-
torted from reason introduces a second; and this one,
another of a more serious nature; and so on till the
crowning absurdity is reached. Now, this progress
towards the absurd produces on the dreamer a very
peculiar sensation. Such is probably the experience
of the tippler when he feels himself pleasantly drifting into a state of blankness in which neither reason
nor propriety has any meaning for him. Now, consider whether some of Molière's plays would not
produce the same sensation: for instance, *Monsieur
de Pourceaugnac,* which, after beginning almost rea-
sonably, develops into a sequence of all sorts of absurdities. Consider also the *Bourgeois gentilhomme,*
where the different characters seem to allow themselves to be caught up in a very whirlwind of madness as the play proceeds. "If it is possible to find a
man more completely mad, I will go and publish it
in Rome." This sentence, which warns us that the
play is over, rouses us from the increasingly extravagant dream into which, along with M. Jourdain, we
have been sinking.

But, above all, there is a special madness that is
peculiar to dreams. There are certain special contradictions so natural to the imagination of a dreamer,
and so absurd to the reason of a man wide-awake,
that it would be impossible to give a full and correct
idea of their nature to anyone who had not experienced them. We allude to the strange fusion that a
dream often effects between two persons who henceforth form only one and yet remain distinct. Generally one of these is the dreamer himself. He feels he
has not ceased to be what he is; yet he has become
someone else. He is himself, and not himself. He
hears himself speak and sees himself act, but he feels
that some other "he" has borrowed his body and

stolen his voice. Or perhaps he is conscious of speaking and acting as usual, but he speaks of himself as a stranger with whom he has nothing in common; he has stepped out of his own self. Does it not seem as though we found this same extraordinary confusion in many a comic scene? I am not speaking of *Amphitryon,* in which play the confusion is perhaps suggested to the mind of the spectator, though the bulk of the comic effect proceeds rather from what we have already called a "reciprocal interference of two series." I am speaking of the extravagant and comic reasonings in which we really meet with this confusion in its pure form, though it requires some looking into to pick it out. For instance, listen to Mark Twain's replies to the reporter who called to interview him:

Question. Isn't that a brother of yours?

Answer. Oh! yes, yes, yes! Now you remind me of it, that *was* a brother of mine. That's William—*Bill* we called him. Poor old Bill!

Q. Why? Is he dead, then?

A. Ah! well, I suppose so. We never could tell. There was a great mystery about it.

Q. That is sad, very sad. He disappeared, then?

A. Well, yes, in a sort of general way. We buried him.

Q. Buried him! *Buried* him, without knowing whether he was dead or not?

A. Oh no! Not that. He was dead enough.

Q. Well, I confess that I can't understand this. If you buried him, and you knew he was dead—

A. No! no! We only thought he was.

Q. Oh, I see! He came to life again?

A. I bet he didn't.

Q. Well, I never heard anything like this. *Some-*

body was dead. *Somebody* was buried. Now, where was the mystery?

A. Ah! that's just it! That's it exactly. You see, we were twins,—defunct and I,—and we got mixed in the bath-tub when we were only two weeks old, and one of us was drowned. But we didn't know which. Some think it was Bill. Some think it was me.

Q. Well, that *is* remarkable. What do *you* think?

A. Goodness knows! I would give whole worlds to know. This solemn, this awful tragedy has cast a gloom over my whole life. But I will tell you a secret now, which I have never revealed to any creature before. One of us had a peculiar mark,—a large mole on the back of his left hand: that was *me. That child was the one that was drowned!* . . . etc., etc.

A close examination will show us that the absurdity of this dialogue is by no means an absurdity of an ordinary type. It would disappear were not the speaker himself one of the twins in the story. It results entirely from the fact that Mark Twain asserts he is one of these twins, whilst all the time he talks as though he were a third person who tells the tale. In many of our dreams we adopt exactly the same method.

V

Regarded from this latter point of view, the comic seems to show itself in a form somewhat different from the one we lately attributed to it. Up to this point, we have regarded laughter as first and foremost a means of correction. If you take the series of comic varieties and isolate the predominant types at long intervals, you will find that all the intervening varieties borrow their comic quality from their resemblance to these types, and that the types themselves are so many models of impertinence with regard to society. To these impertinences society retorts by laughter, an even greater impertinence. So evidently there is nothing very benevolent in laughter. It seems rather inclined to return evil for evil.

But this is not what we are immediately struck by in our first impression of the laughable. The comic character is often one with whom, to begin with, our mind, or rather our body, sympathises. By this is meant that we put ourselves for a very short time in his place, adopt his gestures, words and actions, and, if amused by anything laughable in him, we invite him, in imagination, to share his amusement with us; in fact, we treat him first as a playmate. So, in the laugher, we find a "hail-fellow-well-met" spirit—as far, at least, as appearances go—which it would be wrong of us not to take into consideration. In particular, there is in laughter a movement of *relaxation* which has often been noticed, and the reason of which we must try to discover. Nowhere is this impression more noticeable than in the last few examples. In them, indeed, we shall find its explanation.

When the comic character automatically follows up his idea, he ultimately thinks, speaks and acts as though he were dreaming. Now, a dream is a relaxation. To remain in touch with things and men, to see nothing but what is existent and think nothing but what is consistent, demands a continuous effort of intellectual tension. This effort is common sense. And to remain sensible is, indeed, to remain at work. But to detach oneself from things and yet continue to perceive images, to break away from logic and yet continue to string together ideas, is to indulge in play or, if you prefer, in *dolce far niente*. So, comic absurdity gives us from the outset the impression of playing with ideas. Our first impulse is to join in the game. That relieves us from the strain of thinking.

Now, the same might be said of the other forms of the laughable. Deep-rooted in the comic, there is always a tendency, we said, to take the line of least resistance, generally that of habit. The comic character no longer tries to be ceaselessly adapting and readapting himself to the society of which he is a member. He slackens in the attention that is due to life. He more or less resembles the absentminded. Maybe his will is here even more concerned than his intellect, and there is not so much a want of attention as a lack of tension: still, in some way or another, he is *absent*, away from his work, taking it easy. He abandons social convention, as indeed—in the case we have just been considering—he abandoned logic. Here, too, our first impulse is to accept the invitation to take it easy. For a short time, at all events, we join in the game. And that relieves us from the strain of living.

But we rest only for a short time. The sympathy that is capable of entering into the impression of the comic is a very fleeting one. It also comes from a lapse in attention. Thus, a stern father may at times forget himself and join in some prank his child is playing, only to check himself at once in order to correct it.

Laughter is, above all, a corrective. Being intended to humiliate, it must make a painful impression on the person against whom it is directed. By laughter, society avenges itself for the liberties taken with it. It would fail in its object if it bore the stamp of sympathy or kindness.

Shall we be told that the motive, at all events, may be a good one, that we often punish because we love, and that laughter, by checking the outer manifestations of certain failings, thus causes the person laughed at to correct these failings and thereby improve himself inwardly?

Much might be said on this point. As a general rule, and speaking roughly, laughter doubtless exercises a useful function. Indeed, the whole of our analysis points to this fact. But it does not therefore follow that laughter always hits the mark or is invariably inspired by sentiments of kindness or even of justice.

To be certain of always hitting the mark, it would have to proceed from an act of reflection. Now laughter is simply the result of a mechanism set up in us by nature or, what is almost the same thing, by our long acquaintance with social life. It goes off spontaneously and returns tit for tat. It has no time to look where it hits. Laughter punishes certain failings somewhat as disease punishes certain forms of excess, striking down some who are innocent and sparing some who are guilty, aiming at a general result and incapable of dealing separately with each individual case. And so it is with everything that comes to pass by natural means instead of happening by conscious reflection. An average of justice may show itself in the total result, though the details, taken separately, often point to anything but justice.

In this sense, laughter cannot be absolutely just. Nor should it be kind-hearted either. Its function is to intimidate by humiliating. Now, it would not succeed in doing this, had not nature implanted for that very purpose, even in the best of men, a spark of spitefulness or, at all events, of mischief. Perhaps we had better not investigate this point too closely, for we should not find anything very flattering to ourselves. We should see that this movement of relaxation or expansion is nothing but a prelude to laughter, that the laugher immediately retires within himself, more self-assertive and conceited than ever, and is evidently disposed to look upon another's personality as a marionette of which he pulls the strings. In this presumptuousness we speedily discern a degree of egoism and, behind this latter, something less spontaneous and more bitter, the beginnings of a curious pessimism which becomes the more pronounced as the laugher more closely analyses his laughter.

Here, as elsewhere, nature has utilised evil with a view to good. It is more especially the good that has engaged our attention throughout this work. We have seen that the more society improves, the more plastic is the adaptability it obtains from its members; while the greater the tendency towards increasing stability below, the more does it force to the surface the disturbing elements inseparable from so vast a bulk; and thus laughter performs a useful function by emphasising the form of these significant undulations.

Such is also the truceless warfare of the waves on the surface of the sea, whilst profound peace reigns in the depths below. The billows clash and collide with each other, as they strive to find their level. A fringe of snow-white foam, feathery and frolicsome, follows their changing outlines. From time to time, the receding wave leaves behind a remnant of foam on the sandy beach. The child, who plays hard by, picks up a handful, and, the next moment, is astonished to find that nothing remains in his grasp but a few drops of water, water that is far more brackish, far more bitter, than that of the wave which brought it. Laughter comes into being in the self-same fashion. It indicates a slight revolt on the surface of social life. It instantly adopts the changing forms of the disturbance. It, also, is a froth with a saline base. Like froth, it sparkles. It is gaiety itself. But the philosopher who gathers a handful to taste may find that the substance is scanty, and the aftertaste bitter.

THE MEANINGS OF COMEDY

★

Wylie Sypher

1. *Our New Sense of the Comic*

Doubtless Meredith and Bergson were alike wearied
by the "heavy moralizings" of the nineteenth century,
with its "terrific tonnage," and thus sought relief in
comedy of manners. For both really confine their
idea of comedy within the range of comedy of
manners; and they have given us our finest, most
sensitive theory of that form. Comedy, says Bergson,
is a game—a game that imitates life. And in writing
the introduction to *The Egoist,* Meredith thinks of
this game as dealing with human nature in the
drawing room "where we have no dust of the struggling outer world, no mire, no violent crashes." The
aftertaste of laughter may be bitter, Bergson grants,
but comedy is itself only "a slight revolt on the surface of social life." Its gaiety happens like froth along
a beach, for comedy looks at man from the outside:
"It will go no farther."

For us, today, comedy goes a great deal farther—
as it did for the ancients with their cruel sense of
the comic. Indeed, to appreciate Bergson and Meredith we must see them both in a new perspective,
now that we have lived amid the "dust and crashes"
of the twentieth century and have learned how the
direst calamities that befall man seem to prove that
human life at its depths is inherently absurd. The
comic and the tragic views of life no longer exclude
each other. Perhaps the most important discovery
in modern criticism is the perception that comedy
and tragedy are somehow akin, or that comedy can
tell us many things about our situation even tragedy
cannot. At the heart of the nineteenth century
Dostoevsky discovered this, and Søren Kierkegaard

spoke as a modern man when he wrote that the comic and the tragic touch one another at the absolute point of infinity—at the extremes of human experience, that is. Certainly they touch one another in the naïve art of Paul Klee, whose "little scrawls" tell the ridiculous suffering of modern man. Klee adopts the child's drawing because there is a painful wisdom in the hobgoblin laughter of children: "The more helpless they are, the more instructive are the examples they offer us." The features of modern man, whose soul is torn with alarm, are to be seen in Klee's daemonic etching, Perseus, The Triumph of Wit Over Suffering, of which the artist himself said: "A laugh is mingled with the deep lines of pain and finally gains the upper hand. It reduces to absurdity the unmixed suffering of the Gorgon's head, added at the side. The face is without nobility—the skull shorn of its serpentine adornment except for one ludicrous remnant." In our sculpture, too, the image of modern man is reduced to absurdity—in, for example, Giacometti's figures, worn thin to naked nerve patterns and racked by loneliness.

Our comedy of manners is a sign of desperation. Kafka's novels are a ghastly comedy of manners showing how the awkward and hopelessly maladroit hero, K, is inexorably an "outsider" struggling vainly somehow to "belong" to an order that is impregnably closed by some inscrutable authority. Kafka transforms comedy of manners to pathos by looking, or feeling, from the angle of the alien soul. He treats comedy of manners from the point of view of Dostoevsky's "underground man," and his heroes are absurd because their efforts are all seen from below, and from within. In his notebooks Kafka described the anxiety with which his characters try to bear up under a perpetual judgment life passes upon them: "Watching, fearing, hoping, the answer steals round the question, peers despairingly in her enigmatic face, follows her through the maddest paths, that is, the paths leading farthest away from the answer." Kafka is a modern Jeremiah laughing in feverish merriment, prophetically writing the incredible—the depraved—comedy of our concentration camps, which are courts where the soul of contemporary man undergoes an absurd Trial by Ordeal. His comedy reaches the stage of the inarticulate, as tragedy does when Lear frets about the button.

Our new appreciation of the comic grows from the confusion in modern consciousness, which has been sadly wounded by the politics of power, bringing with it the ravage of explosion, the atrocious pain of inquisitions, the squalor of labor camps, and the efficiency of big lies. Wherever man has been able to think about his present plight he has felt "the suction of the absurd." He has been forced to see himself in unheroic positions. In his sanest moments the modern hero is aware that he is J. Alfred Prufrock, or Osric, an attendant lord—"Almost, at times, the Fool." Or else Sweeney, the apeneck, seeking low pleasures while death and the raven drift above.

We have, in short, been forced to admit that the absurd is more than ever inherent in human existence: that is, the irrational, the inexplicable, the surprising, the nonsensical—in other words, the comic. One of the evidences of the absurd is our "dissociation of sensibility," with the ironic lack of relation between one feeling and another; and the artist now must, as Eliot once said, accept the chaos which serves for our life, span the unstable consciousness of the ordinary man: "The latter falls in love or reads Spinoza, and these two experiences have nothing to do with each other, or with the noise of the typewriter or the smell of cooking." The fragmentary lives we live are an existential comedy, like the intense schizoid lives of Dostoevsky's characters. In *The Brothers Karamazov,* Ivan says, "Let me tell you that the absurd is only too necessary on earth. The world stands on absurdities, and perhaps nothing would have come to pass without them." In our modern experiences the ethical "golden mean" seems to have broken down, and man is left face to face with the preposterous, the trivial, the monstrous, the inconceivable. The modern hero lives amid irreconcilables which, as Dostoevsky suggests, can be encompassed only by religious faith—or comedy.

The sense of the absurd is at the root of our characteristic philosophy—existentialism. The existential religious hero is Kierkegaard, who wrote "In truth, no age has so fallen victim to the comic as this." Kierkegaard, like Kafka, finds that "the comical is present in every stage of life, for wherever there is life there is contradiction, and wherever there is contradiction the comical is present." Kierkegaard's highest comedy is the comedy of faith; since the religious man is the one who knows by his very existence that there is an endless, yawning difference between God and man, and yet he has the infinite, obsessive passion to devote himself to God, who is all, whereas man is nothing. Without God man does not exist; thus "the more thoroughly and substantially a human being exists, the more he will discover the comical." Finite man must take the full risk of encountering an infinite God: "Existence itself, the act of existing, is a striving, and is both pathetic and comic in the same degree." Faith begins with a sense of "the discrepancy, the contradiction, between the infinite and the finite, the eternal and that which becomes." So the highest form of comedy is that "the infinite may move within a man, and no one, no one be able to discover it through anything appearing outwardly." The earnestness of one's faith is tested by one's "sensitiveness to the comical," for God is all and man is nothing, and man must come to terms with God. If one exists *as* a human being, he must be hypersensitive to the absurd; and the most absurd contradiction of all is that man must risk everything without insurance against losing everything. This is precisely what ordinary "Christians" refuse to do, Kierkegaard finds; they wish to find a "safe" way to salvation, to find God without being tormented, and to base their faith on what is probable, reasonable, assured. This is itself ludicrous—the despicable comedy of "Christendom," which requires religion to be comforting and "tranquilizing." Even in his religious life man is always being confronted with the extreme hazard in the guise of the absurd.

This sense of having to live amid the irrational, the ludicrous, the disgusting, or the perilous has been dramatized by the existentialists; and it has also been boldly exploited by propagandists and those who seize power by using "the big lie," that most cynical form of modern political comedy. For all our science, we have been living through an age of Un-reason, and have learned to submit to the Improbable, if not to the Absurd. And comedy is, in Gautier's words, a logic of the absurd.

In his notebooks Kafka explained that he wanted to exaggerate situations until everything becomes clear. Dostoevsky has this sort of comic clarity—a frightening clarity of the grotesque, reducing life, as totally as tragedy, by means of a perspective that foreshortens everything, to absurdity. From this perspective, which is often Goya's or Picasso's, man looks puppetlike, and his struggles diminish to pathos. For example, in the closing pages of *The Brothers Karamazov* when Ilusha is buried, Snegiryov runs distracted about the corpse of his boy, strewing flowers on the coffin, scattering morsels of bread for sparrows on the little grave. These scenes cause a laughter so raw that it brings grimaces hardly to be distinguished from tragic response. The force of this comic "shock" is like the "qualm" stirred by tragedy; it can disorient us, "disturb" us as confusingly as tragic calamity. Melville's tormented Captain Ahab sets his course headlong "outward," driven on by the modern "delight in foundering." Like Conrad's character Kurtz, he is a madman in the grip of "merciless logic for a futile purpose." We are now more sensitive to these absurd calamities than to tragic recognitions. We appreciate Rouault, who sees man as a Clown. In its style Picasso's giant Guernica, that premonition of total war, is a shocking comic strip in black and white, showing how the ridiculous journalese of painting can be an idiom for modern art.

Guernica is like a bad dream; and Kafka's novels are nightmares. The dream is nonsensical and free, having none of the logic and sobriety of our waking selves; the very incongruity of the dream world is comic. Freud interprets the dream and the jest as a discharge of powerful psychic energies, a glimpse into the abyss of the self. We have learned to read our dreams to tell us what we really are, for we now find that the patterns of our conscious life have meanings that can be explained only by looking below them into the chaos of the unconscious life always there, old, irrational, and inarticulate except in the language of the sleeping self when, as Banquo warned Macbeth, the instruments of darkness tell us truths. By exploiting the dream, surrealism plays the comedy of modern art, and psychoanalysis plays the comedy of modern medical practice.

Freud is not the only one to suggest that the joke, like the dream, is an upsurge from the unconscious, a mechanism for releasing powerful archaic impulses always there below the level of reason.[1] The caricaturist and the masters of grotesque art have long employed a kind of dreamwork, charged with the spell of mania, like medieval gargoyles or paintings by Bosch and Gruenewald, where there is fiendish zest in wracking man's body. Expressionist art has always been one of the most potent forms of caricature, whether it be paintings by Van Gogh and Kokoschka or Michelangelo's unfinished sculptures. The caricaturist and expressionist use comic distortions that often are the overstatements of a soul shaken by neurosis. Long before Di Chirico and Yves Tanguy painted their dream-fantasies, Bergson guessed that comic automatism resembles the automatism of the dream: *"L'absurdité comique est de même nature que celle des rêves."* Bergson adds: "Whenever the comic personage mechanically holds his idea, he ends by thinking, speaking, acting as if he dreamed." Surrealism is "dream play" (*les jeux du rêve*) since the surrealist painter represents the involuntary "free" associations of the hidden life, which have their own "absurdity" and "improbability." As Bergson remarked, psychological automatism is as comic as the physical automatism of gesture. Dickens is the great artist of physical automatism with his Uriah Heeps and his Mrs. Gamps. Molière is not the only great artist of psychological automatism, for Dostoevsky's "split" characters have the mechanism of surrealist art. His people move, as we do in dreams, by involuntary impulses; they make "psychological gestures." Surrealism surprises us with the *imprévu,* the unexpected psychic gesture controlled by the Id.

Thus the comic gesture reaches down toward the Unconscious, that dim world usually assigned to tragedy, the midnight terrain where Macbeth met the witches. The joke and the dream incongruously distort the logic of our rational life. The joke and the dream are "interruptions" in the pattern of our consciousness. So also, possibly, is any truly creative work of art a form of "interruption" of our normal patterns or designs of seeing and speaking, which are mere formulas written on the surface layer of the mind. Underneath this surface layer is the pattern-free (non-Gestalt) activity of the unconscious, undisciplined self, which cannot be expressed by the forms consciousness imposes on our vision and thought. The deepest "meanings" of art therefore arise wherever there is an interplay between the patterns of surface-perception and the pressures of depth-perception. Then the stated meanings will fringe off into unstated and unstatable meanings of great power, felt dimly but compellingly. Behind the trim scaffolding of artistic "form" and logic there whispers, for a moment, the wild voice of the unconscious self—using the disturbed language of the dream and the jest, as well as the language of tragedy. This uncivilized but knowing self Nietzsche once called Dionysian, the self that feels archaic pleasure and archaic pain. The substratum of the world of art, Nietzsche says, is "the terrible wisdom of Silenus," and Silenus is the satyr-god of comedy leading the ecstatic "chorus of natural beings who as it were live ineradicably behind every civilization." The confused statements of the dream and the joke are intolerable to the daylight, sane, Apollonian self.

No doubt the tragic experience reaches deeply down into the "interruptions" of conscious life, conjuring up our grim disinherited selves and expressing the "formless" intimations of archaic fear and archaic struggle. But in an artist like Dostoevsky the comic experience can reach as deeply down, perhaps because the comic artist begins by accepting the absurd, "the improbable," in human existence. Therefore he has less resistance than the tragic artist to representing what seems incoherent and inexplicable, and thus lowers the threshold of artistic perception. After all, comedy, not tragedy, admits the disorderly into the realm of art; the grotesque depends upon an irrational focus. Ours is a century of disorder and irrationalism.

Is it any wonder that along with our wars, our machines, and our neuroses we should find new meanings in comedy, or that comedy should represent our plight better than tragedy? For tragedy needs the "noble," and nowadays we seldom can assign any usable meaning to "nobility." The comic now is more relevant, or at least more accessible, than the tragic. As Mephisto explains to God, one cannot understand man unless one is able to laugh: "For man must strive, and striving, he must err."

Man has been defined as a social animal, a tool-making animal, a speaking animal, a thinking animal, a religious animal. He is also a laughing animal (Malraux takes the "archaic smile" in sculpture as a sign man has become aware of his soul). Yet this definition of man is the obscurest of all, for we do not really know what laughter is, or what causes it. Though he calls his essay "Laughter," Bergson never plumbs this problem. We have never agreed about the motives, mechanism, or even the temper of laughter. Usually the Greeks laughed to express a disdain roused by seeing someone's mischance, deformity, or ugliness. One of the least agreeable scenes in classical literature is the cruel, casual slaying of wretched Dolon, a Trojan spy caught skulking one night by Diomedes and Ulysses near the Greek camp; after tormenting Dolon with a hint he can save his life, the gleeful Ulysses, smiling no doubt an archaic smile, watches Diomedes strike off the head of their captive, "green with fear." There is also scandalous Homeric mirth among the Olympians themselves when lame Hephaistos calls the gods together to ridicule his wife Aphrodite, lying trapped with brazen Ares, god of war. To be laughed at by the ancients was to be defiled.

Malice, however, is only one of the many obscure motives for laughing, which has been explained as a release from restraint, a response to what is incongruous or improper, or a sign of ambivalence—our hysteric effort to adjust our repulsion from, and our attraction to, a situation. Certainly laughter is a symptom of bewilderment or surprise. Sometimes it is said that a laugh detonates whenever there is a sudden rupture between thinking and feeling.[2] The rupture occurs the instant a situation is seen in another light. The shock of taking another point of view causes, in Bergson's words, a momentary "anesthesia of the heart."

During the Middle Ages people seem to have laughed at the grotesque as when, for instance, Chrétien de Troyes brings among the dainty knights and ladies of his romance *Yvain* a rustic lout whose "ears were big and mossy, just like an elephant's," or when Dante's gargoylelike demons caper through the lower circles of hell making obscene noises. In

pious legends like "The Tumbler of Our Lady"
medieval laughter is charitable, becoming almost
tender in anecdotes about Friar Juniper, that tattered
soul who in meekness and humility played seesaw
with children.

Renaissance laughter was complex. Sometimes it
was like Cellini's, swaggering with contempt—
sprezzatura. When Machiavelli laughs he almost
sneers, notably in his play *Mandragola*, showing how
a stupid old husband is cuckolded. We can fancy
that his Prince would laugh somewhat like a Borgia.
Then there is Erasmus' satire, quiet and blighting;
less boisterous than Rabelais' monstrous glee. Ben
Jonson's plays ridicule the classic-bourgeois "types"
(as Bergson would call them) who, like Rabelais'
mammoths, are laughable because they have an
excess of one "humor" in their disposition or "com-
plexion." Shakespeare's theatre is filled with medi-
cally "humorous" persons like Falstaff, who raise a
laugh at once brutal, loving, and wise. The laughter
in Cervantes' *Quixote* is gentler and more thoughtful,
and not so corrosive as Hamlet's wit, which is tinged
with Robert Burton's melancholy.

Hamlet's "disturbed" laughter was very "modern,"
as was also the strained, joyless grimace of Thomas
Hobbes, who explained laughter as a sense of "sudden glory" arising from our feeling of superiority
whenever we see ourselves triumphantly secure
while others stumble. Hobbes brings in the note of
"biological" laughter, for he takes life to be a struggle
for power waged naturally in a brutish combat
"where every man is enemy to every man." Some
three hundred years later Anthony M. Ludovici
rephrased Hobbes's theory in Darwinian form by
supposing that a laugh is man's way of showing his
fangs.[3] And man needs, like any animal, to show

his fangs only when he is threatened; we laugh in self-defense and bare our teeth to recruit our sinking spirits or to ease our aching sense of inferiority or danger. Laughter is a tactic for survival, a mark of "superior adaptation" among gregarious animals. The weak and the savage both laugh. Ludovici agrees with Nietzsche that man laughs only because he can suffer excruciatingly; and his direst, most inward sickness is the thwarting of his will.

On this latter theme we can play every variation of modern comedy with all its satanic ironies and romantic dreamwork. The "genial" romantics of the early nineteenth century assumed, with Charles Lamb, that laughter is an overflow of sympathy, an amiable feeling of identity with what is disreputably human, a relish for the whimsical, the odd, the private blunder. Carlyle (of all people!) cheerfully supposed that the man who smiles is affectionate. But there were the diabolic romantics, too, driven by the Will to Power or consumed by their own poisons, and they laughed menacingly, frantically. Baudelaire's laugh, heard in the dark bohemian world of Paris—the Paris which drove men desperate and betrayed their ideals—is "a nervous convulsion, an involuntary spasm," a proof of man's fallen state.[4] The feverish laugh of Baudelaire's hero sears his lips and twists his vitals; it is a sign of infinite nobility and infinite pain. Man laughed only after the Exile, when he knew sin and suffering; the comical is a mark of man's revolt, boredom, and aspiration. "The laugh is satanic; it is likewise deeply human." It is the bitter voice of nineteenth-century disillusion. Schopenhauer was the first to define the romantic irony in this desolate laugh of the "underground man": laughter "is simply the sudden perception of incongruity" between our ideals and the actualities before us. Byron jested "And if I laugh at any mortal thing / 'Tis that I may not weep."

The mirth of the disenchanted and frustrated idealist, frenzied by his sense of the impassable distance between what might be and what is, reaches its shrillest pitch in Nietzsche, the scorpion-philosopher, exempt from every middle-class code, whose revolt is, unlike Bergson's comedy of "slight revolt on the surface of social life," savage. Nietzsche is able to transvalue all social values by pain, disgust, fury. This sickly laughter of the last romantics is the most confused and destructive mirth Western man has ever allowed himself. It has all the pessimism which Bergson chose not to consider. Rimbaud's laugh is a symptom of anguish and a glimpse into the abyss of the self. It is a terrifying scorn, a shameless expense of lust, an eruption of the pleasure-principle in a world where pleasure is denied. Nietzsche's laughter is a discharge far more "possessed" than the Freudian sexual release.

So Bergson's analysis of laughter is incomplete, which may explain why he thinks comedy works only from "the outside." Comedy may, in fact, not bring laughter at all; and certain tragedies may make us laugh hysterically. It was Shelley who found the comedy in *King Lear* to be "universal, ideal, and sublime." Ben Jonson himself noted "Nor is the moving of laughter always the end of comedy." When Coleridge lectured on *Hamlet* and *Lear* he pointed out that terror is closely joined with what is ludicrous, since "The laugh is rendered by nature itself the language of extremes, even as tears are." Thus *Hamlet* "will be found to touch on the verge of the ludicrous," because "laughter is equally the expression of extreme anguish and horror as of joy." The grimace of mirth resembles the grimace of suffering; comic and tragic masks have the same distortion. Today we know that a comic action sometimes yields tragic values.[5] In Balzac's *human* comedy (*Comédie humaine*) we meet Old Goriot and Cousin Pons, those heroes of misery.

If we have no satisfactory definition of laughter, neither do we have any satisfactory definition of comedy. Indeed, most of the theories of laughter and comedy fail precisely because they oversimplify a situation and an art more complicated than the tragic situation and art. Comedy seems to be a more pervasive human condition than tragedy. Often we are, or have been, or could be, Quixotes or Micawbers or Malvolios, Benedicks or Tartuffes. Seldom are we Macbeths or Othellos. Tragedy, not comedy, limits its field of operation and is a more closely regulated form of response to the ambiguities and dilemmas of humanity. The comic action touches experience at more points than tragic action. We can hardly hope that our various definitions of comedy will be more compatible than our definitions of laughter; yet each of the many definitions has its use in revealing the meanings of comedy. Bergson's alone will not suffice, or Meredith's either; and they both will mean more when seen against the full spectrum of comic values.

Ordinarily we refer to "high" and "low" comedy; but we cannot speak of "low" tragedy. All tragedy ought to be "high." There are, of course, various orders of tragic action, such as *drame* and "heroic tragedy"; however, as tragedy falls away from its "high" plane it tends to become something else than tragedy. Tragedy is indeed "an achievement peculiarly Greek"—and needs a special view of man's relation to the world.[6] But comedy thrives everywhere and fearlessly runs the gamut of effects from "high" to "low" without diminishing its force or surrendering its values or even jeopardizing them. Once Mme. de Staël said: "Tragedies (if we set aside some of the masterpieces) require less knowledge of the human heart than comedies." What a strange opinion! Yet which of Shakespeare's plays really shows a more profound knowledge of the hearts of fathers and children: *Lear,* or *Henry IV,* 1 and 2, and *Henry V?* Is not the crisis luridly overstated in *Lear* and met with greater insight in the figures of Henry IV, Hal, Hotspur, and Falstaff? Can we honestly claim that Shakespeare reveals more about life in the tragedy of Lear than in the conflicts between Henry and his wild son? Are not many of the problems raised in the great tragedies solved in the great comedies?

Mme. de Staël continues: "The imagination without much difficulty can represent what often appears —the features of sorrow. Tragic characters take on a certain similiarity that blurs the finer distinctions between them, and the design of a heroic action determines in advance the course they must take." (Whereas Bergson claims it is comedy that deals with types.) Surely the comic action is more unpredictable, and delight is an emotion quite as individual as grief, remorse, or guilt.

Further, and illogically, "low" comedy is as legitimate as "high." In fact, the lower the range, the more authentic the comedy may be, as we know when we behold the Wife of Bath, that slack daughter of Eve, or Falstaff, that ruffian always on the point of untrussing. At the bottom of the comic scale—where the human becomes nearly indistinguishable from the animal and where the vibration of laughter is longest and loudest—is the "dirty" joke or the "dirty" gesture. At this depth comedy unerringly finds the lowest common denominator of human response, the reducing-agent that sends us reeling back from our proprieties to the realm of old Pan. The unquenchable vitality of man gushes up from the lower strata of Rabelais' comedy, inhabited by potbellied monsters who tumultuously do as they wish in a world built entirely with the apparatus of a gargantuan pedagogy. There we drop the mask which we have composed into the features of our decent, cautious selves. Rabelais strips man of his breeches; he is the moral *sans-culotte*. Psychologists tell us that any group of men and women, no matter how "refined," will, sooner or later, laugh at a "dirty" joke, the question being not whether they will laugh but when, or at precisely what "dirty" joke; that is, under exactly what co-efficient of stress a code of "decency" breaks apart and allows the human being to fall steeply down to the recognition of his inalienable flesh.

Yet laughter at the obscenest jest forever divides man from animal, because the animal is never self-conscious about any fleshly act whatever; whereas man is not man without being somehow uneasy about the "nastiness" of his body. One of the deepest paradoxes in comedy thus reveals itself in obscenity, which is a threshold over which man enters into the human condition; it is a comic equivalent to the religious state of original sin or of tragic "error," and man may as justly be thought human because of his sense of what is "dirty" as because of his sense of what is "evil," "sinful," or fearful. This elemental self-awareness—this consciousness of shame at one's flesh—sets one of the lowest margins for civilization; and, conversely, a hypersensitivity to what is "obscene" is a mark of a decadent society. The paradox in comic filth was madly intensified in the satire of Jonathan Swift, that puritan pornographer, who wrote in his notebook that "A nice man is a man of nasty ideas." Swift forces comic obscenity to its extremes in Gulliver's disgust at the Yahoos; his fastidiousness is insane when Gulliver is frightened by the red-haired female Yahoo who stands gazing and howling on the bank, inflamed with desire to embrace his naked body.

As we move "up" the scale of comic action, the mechanisms become more complex but no more "comic."[7] Physical mishaps, pratfalls, and loud collisions are the crudest products of Bergson's comic "automatism." It is hard to distinguish these pleasures from our glee at physical deformity; and here we detect the cruelty inherent in comedy, which may perhaps be another form of the cruelty inherent in tragic disaster. Essentially our enjoyment of physical mishap or deformity springs from our surprise and delight that man's motions are often absurd, his energies often misdirected. This is the coarsest, most naïve, comedy of manners. Another sort of mechanical comedy is the farce—mistaken identities, coincidences, mistimings—which can be a very complicated engine of plot devices. In this range of comedy the characters need only be puppets moved from the outside, as events require. There is the right key to the wrong door, or the wrong key to the right door; and it does not matter very much who is inside, provided it is the unexpected figure. In these comic vehicles fate takes the guise of happy or unhappy chance, which is, of course, only a tidy arrangement of improbable possibilities. On this sort of artificial framework comedy displays some of its most glittering designs.

Or comedy can be a mechanism of language, the repartee that sharply levels drama and life to a sheen of verbal wit. Congreve's cool, negligent persons like Fainall are beings who have a *verbal* existence, of extremely delicate taste, and able to refine all their pleasures to raillery: "I'd no more play with a man that slighted his ill fortune than I'd make love to a woman who undervalued the loss of her reputation." The transparent Mrs. Fainall lives and moves in the same dry atmosphere and speaks with the same brittle tongue: "While I only hated my husband, I could bear to see him; but since I have despised him, he's too offensive." Such comedy of manners does not hesitate to sacrifice humanity to dialogue. Or rather, the dialogue itself may be a fragile mechanism of wit to elevate the comedy to "intellectual" heights. Shakespeare's intricate wit in *Love's Labour's Lost,* with its "flowers of fancy, the jerks of invention," demands of us an agility that makes the brain spin. The play is a thin fabric of banter dazzling us with preciosity, its quick venue of phrase—"snip, snap, and home." At its gilded moments this comedy feeds upon dainties, delights to drink ink, to eat paper, to replenish the spirit with joy, to come to honorable terms with a code of manners, and to leave trudging far behind those who are sensible only in the duller parts.

But it is more than a parterre of devices: it is a drama played by those odd, lovable Shakespearean creatures for whom Bergson seems to have so little feeling—they are "characters" in the British sense of the word. Berowne and Don Armado are among them, and they inhabit the higher domain of comedy where we meet Fielding's Squire Western, Chaucer's Monk, Cervantes' Quixote, Sterne's Uncle Toby, and Dickens' Sam Weller. Such persons cannot exist in the dry seclusion of farce. They require the mellow neighborhood of a comedy of humors

which gathers into its action spirits of strong and
perverse disposition and convincing weight. These
characters thrive at more genial latitudes than Ben
Jonson allowed them in his comedy of humors,
which was too harshly satiric. English literature is,
as Taine said, the native province of these unruly
creatures whose life blood pulses richly, whose features are odd, and whose opinions, gestures, vices,
and habits control the mechanism of the plot in
which they happen to be cast. Indeed, such dispositions may temper the whole climate in which events
happen and constantly threaten to wreck the tight
logic of a fiction. Mercutio and Benedick are incor-
rigible fellows of this sort. We never take seriously
the action in which they have a role; but we take
them seriously. They live for us as Falstaff lives; for
Falstaff is more than a sack of guts. He moves the
whole play from within; he is a temperamental as
well as an anatomical grotesque.

These "characters" realized in depth stand at the
threshold of "high" comedy, which is really a transformation of comedy of manners. Whenever a society becomes self-conscious about its opinions, codes,
or etiquette, comedy of manners may serve as a sort
of philosophic engine called "comedy of ideas." Frail
as they are, and known best in their moments of
raillery, Millamant and Mirabell raise Congreve's
Way of the World to a bolder order of comedy of
manners: "Let us," says Millamant to Mirabell, "be
as strange as if we had been married a great while,
and as well bred as if we were not married at all."
The edge of this comedy is sharpened by sanity as
well as verbal wit, and, as Meredith clearly saw,
Molière magnified comedy of manners to the dimensions of a criticism of life. Our most provoking social
critic is Shaw, although Pirandello soars farther into

a crystalline sphere of ideas. The world of Aristophanes could have been shaped only in the sophisticated theatre of an Athens that had begun to examine its own conventions. Aristophanes is like
Erasmus or Gide, who serve as the intellectual conscience of a nervous and self-scrutinizing society
where all is not now so well as it might be or has
been or seems to be.

At the radiant peak of "high" comedy—a peak we
can easily sight from Meredith's essay—laughter is
qualified by tolerance, and criticism is modulated
by a sympathy that comes only from wisdom. Just
a few writers of comedy have gained this unflinching but generous perspective on life, which is a
victory over our absurdities but a victory won at a
cost of humility, and won in a spirit of charity and
enlightenment. Besides Shakespeare in, perhaps,
The Tempest, one might name Cervantes and Henry
James and Jane Austen, or Thomas Mann in his
Magic Mountain, when pliable, diseased Clavdia
yields carelessly to the stricken Hans Castorp in
a scene where the grimness of human life, its folly
and its error, are seen clearly and with a perverse tenderness: *"Petit bourgeois!"* she says to
him—*"Joli bourgeois à la petite tache humide."*
For they both know that the body, love, and death
are all three the same thing, and that the flesh is sickness and desire, and life only a fever in matter. This
is how "high" comedy chastens men without despair,
without rancor, as if human blunders were seen from
a godlike distance, and also from within the blun-
dering self. The deep humiliation and reassurance
in Don Quixote's madness and recovery, with his
resignation, detachment, and self-awareness, are all
confirmed by the experience of Shakespeare's Benedick—to whom Meredith appealed. After proving

himself as foolish as the rest of the world, Benedick comes to a vision of the human condition: "For man is a giddy thing, and this is my conclusion." Benedick speaks without bitterness, bias, or pride; and has learned, like Hans Castorp, to accept the insufficiency of man without being damaged.

So the range of comedy is more embracing than the range of tragedy; and if tragedy occurs at some middle point in ethical life where failure is weighed against man's nobility of spirit, comedy ventures out into the farther extremes of experience in both directions, toward the bestial or "obscene," and at the other end of the spectrum toward the insane heroics of Nietzsche or the vision of Prospero, who sees sin as the last mistake of all our many mistakes, dispelled before our clearer reason whenever hate seems more absurd than charity.

We may prefer one theory of comedy to another; but we shall find it hard to get along without the other. In *Winter's Tale*, Autolycus meditates on his lot: "I am courted now with a *double occasion*." The phrase is useful, for comedy is built upon double occasions, double premises, double values. "Nothing human is alien to me," says the character in Terence. Nothing human is alien to comedy. It is an equivocal art. If we now have trouble isolating comedy from tragedy, this is not because comedy and tragedy are identical, but rather because comedy often intersects the orbit of tragic action without losing its autonomy. Instead, comedy in its own right, boldly and illogically, lays claim to some of the values that traditionally are assigned to tragedy alone. Think, for example, of Henry James's "Beast In the Jungle," which really is comedy of manners suddenly consumed in the flame of Marcher's grief that he has lost May forever through his own selfishness. Here is comedy seen ruthlessly "from within" as Bergson did not allow. Marcher is a fool—but a sinister fool, an egoist far more barbaric than Meredith's sleek Sir Willoughby Patterne. And James's London, a society of genteel manners and frail nerves, is a scene where savage eyes glare behind the social simper.

II. *The Ancient Rites of Comedy*

In fact, to interpret the complications and contradictions in comedy, we must look far backward toward Aristotle and the Greeks; for the meanings in comedy are tribally old, and Bergson and Meredith refine almost beyond recognition the primitive violence of comedy, which, curiously, reappears again in James, Kafka, and "us moderns."

The notion of an affinity between tragedy and comedy would not be strange to the Greeks: not to Socrates, we know, because of what happens in *The Symposium,* a very dramatic dialogue where Plato brings together in debate the comedian Aristophanes, the tragedian Agathon, and along with them the goat-faced Socrates, the philosophic clown, a figure who stands near the center of all the larger problems of comedy. In the course of this night-long dialogue Socrates is described by Alcibiades as looking "exactly like the masks of Silenus." He turns to Socrates and asks: "You will not deny that your face is like that of a satyr? And there is a resemblance in other points too. For example, you are a bully." Yet Socrates makes the notorious Alcibiades ashamed of his misdeeds. Alcibiades complains, "Mankind are nothing to him; all his life is spent in mocking and flouting at them." This Socrates, resembling a caricature of a man, is the person who alone is able to make the dissolute Athenians care for their souls; his words "amaze and possess the soul of every man." Plato reports that by daybreak only Aristophanes and Agathon are still awake to hear Socrates insisting that anyone who can write tragedy can also write comedy because the craft (*techne*) of writing comedy is the same as the craft of writing tragedy.

Surely Socrates, comedian and martyr, mocker and moralist, was the proper one to hold this notion, which has gained new implication now that the social anthropologists have discovered what Aristotle already knew—namely, that comedy is a primal rite; a rite transformed to art. As F. M. Cornford puts it, comedy is "a scene of sacrifice and a feast."[8] Aristotle intimated as much in the *Poetics* by stating that at first both tragedy and comedy were improvisations, the one rising from the Dithyramb, the other from phallic songs "still used as ritual in many of our cities." These improvisations having evolved in different ways, each found its "natural form," the comic writer presenting men as "worse than they are," the tragic writer as "better," and the comic being a version of the Ludicrous—which in turn is a variety of the Ugly without being painful or destructive. Comedy, he adds, has no history—that is, it passed unnoticed for a long time, although it had definite "forms" (*schemata*) even in the early poets. Aristotle thinks that tragedy gained its "magnitude" after it passed its "satyric" phase and took on a "stately manner" at a "late phase" of its history. Thereafter tragedy imitated "noble actions" of "noble personages," whereas comedy dealt with the "meaner sorts of actions among the ignoble." He also says that comedy turned from an early use of "invective" to a "dramatizing of the ridiculous." In early satyric dramas, poetry was adapted to dancing.

However cryptic Aristotle's comment may be, it is clear that he traces the origins of drama to some sort of fertility rite—Dionysiac or phallic—the primitive "sacrifice and feast" mentioned by Cornford. It is now accepted that art is born of rites and that the comic and tragic masks are themselves archetypal symbols for characters in a tribal "semantics of ritual." Behind tragedy and comedy is a prehistoric death-and-resurrection ceremonial, the rite of killing the old year (the aged king) and bringing in the new season (the resurrection or initiation of the adolescent king). Associated with killing the old king and devouring his sacrificial body was the ancient rite of purging the tribe by expelling a scapegoat on whose head were heaped the sins of the past year. Frazer describes what happened during this "public expulsion of evils" at a season when there was an "oblation of first fruits":

. . . the time of year when the ceremony takes place usually coincides with some well-marked change of season. . . . this public and periodic expulsion of devils is commonly preceded or followed by a period of general license, during which the ordinary restraints of society are thrown aside, and all offences, short of the gravest, are allowed to pass unpunished. (*Golden Bough*)

At this public purging or catharsis the scapegoat was often the divine man or animal, in the guise of victim, to whom were transferred the sins and misfortunes of the worshipers. Eventually the divine character of the scapegoat was forgotten; as Frazer notes, he became an ordinary victim, a wretch who was a condemned criminal perhaps, actually as well as ritually guilty. This ancient death-and-resurrection rite, then, seems to have had a double meaning: the killing of the god or king to save him and the

tribe from the sterility of age, and the expulsion of
evils (or devils) amid rejoicing of a people who
were redeemed by the sacrifice of a hero-victim.

From this rudimentary sacrifice-and-feast evolved
comic and tragic poetry, using a "canonical" plot
formula older than either art, an elemental folk
drama from which derived in obscure ways the "action" (myth) of the Athenian theatre. In its typical
form the archaic fertility ceremony—involving the
death or sacrifice of a hero-god (the old year), the
rebirth of a hero-god (the new year), and a purging
of evil by driving out a scapegoat (who may be
either god or devil, hero or villain)—requires a contest or *agon* between the old and new kings, a slaying of a god or king, a feast and a marriage to com-
memorate the initiation, reincarnation, or resurrection of the slain god, and a final triumphal
procession or *komos,* with songs of joy. Behind the
marriage ceremonial probably lies the myth of the
primal union between the earth-mother and the
heaven-father. Following this revelation of the mysteries of life, the new hero-king is proclaimed and
elevated: there is an "apotheosis," epiphany, or
manifestation of the young hero-god (a theophany).

The rites may take the guise of an initiation or
testing of the strength of the hero or his fertility,
perhaps in the form of a "questioning" or catechism,
after which there comes to him a "discovery" or
"recognition"—an *anagnorisis* or new knowledge. Or
else the sacrifice may be interrupted by an unwelcome intruder (an *alazon*) who views the secret
rites; he is a profaner of the mysteries, an alien. This
character must be put to flight or else confounded
in a "struggle" that may also occur in the form of a
catechism, to which he does not know the proper
answers. In either case there is a debate, a dialec-

tic contest, which is preserved in Aristophanes'
Clouds, for instance, as an argument between
"Right Logic" and "Wrong Logic." Thus again the
comic action is double, since it is both a rational
debate and a phallic orgy. Logic and passion appear
together in the primal comic formula.

In Cornford's opinion the dramatic form known
as tragedy eventually suppressed the sexual magic
in this canonical plot, leaving only the portrayal of
the suffering and death of the hero, king, or god.
Comedy, however, kept in the foreground the erotic
action, together with the disorderly rejoicing at the
rebirth or resurrection of the god-hero who survives
his *agon.* In this sense comedy preserves the archaic
"double occasion" of the plot formula, the dual and
wholly incompatible meanings of sacrifice and feast,
cruelty and festival, logic and license. So much we
may read into Aristotle's remark that comedy was,
like tragedy, originally an improvisation, its "action"
being a procession of the devotees of Phales carrying
the emblem of the god, that profane and sacred
symbol, the ithyphallus, the *penis erectus.* After
pausing at the place of sacrifice to pray to Dionysus
they continued their procession to the burden of
phallic songs.

If this indeed be the origin of comedy we can
guess why Aristotle said that "tragedy advanced by
slow degrees, and having passed through many
changes, found its natural form and then stopped
evolving." Unlike comedy, tragedy is a "closed" form
of art, with a single, fixed, and contained meaning
(by contrast to the disorderly relaxed meanings in
comedy). Tragedy demands a law of necessity or
destiny, and a finality that can be gained only by
stressing a logic of "plot" or "unified action" with a
beginning, middle, and end. Within the confines of

this action the hero is given to sacrifice or death. That is, tragedy performs the sacrificial rite without the festival—which means that it is a less complex, less ambiguous form of drama than comedy. Retaining its double action of penance and revel, comedy remains an "improvisation" with a loose structure and a precarious logic that can tolerate every kind of "improbability."

The coherent plot is vital to tragic theatre (Aristotle says that plot is the very soul of tragedy); and a tragic action needs to convey a sense of destiny, inevitability, and foreordination. The tragic poet often implies there are unchanging moral laws behind the falling thunderbolt. The fate of a tragic hero needs to be made "intelligible" as the comic hero's fate does not; or at least tragic fate has the force of "necessity" even if it is not "intelligible." Somehow tragedy shows what "must" happen, even while there comes a shock of unsurmised disaster. As Aristotle said, in tragedy, coincidence must have an air of probability. Then too, tragedy subordinates "character" to the design of the plot; for the purpose of tragedy, says Aristotle, is not to depict "character," but, rather, to show "men in action," so that the "character" of a tragic hero reveals itself in a deed which expresses his moral disposition. Comedy, on the contrary, can freely yield its action to surprise, chance, and all the changes in fortune that fall outside the necessities of tragic myth, and can present "character" for its own sake.

Following what Aristotle implied, Cornford is able to say that if tragedy requires plot first of all, comedy is rooted so firmly in "character" its plot seems derivative, auxiliary, perhaps incidental. Unlike tragedy, comedy does not have to guard itself by any logic of inevitability, or by academic rules.

Comedy makes artistic all the unlikely possibilities that tragic probability must reject. It keeps more of the primitive aspect of *play* than does tragedy.

From the anthropologist's view the tragic action, however inspiring and however perfect in artistic form, runs through only one arc of the full cycle of drama; for the entire ceremonial cycle is birth: struggle: death: resurrection. The tragic arc is only birth: struggle: death. Consequently the range of comedy is wider than the tragic range—perhaps more fearless—and comic action can risk a different sort of purgation and triumph.[9] If we believe that drama retains any of the mythical values of the old fertility rite, then the comic cycle is the only fulfilled and redemptive action, and, strange to think, the death and rebirth of the god belong more fittingly to the comic than to the tragic theatre. Is this the reason why it is difficult for tragic art to deal with Christian themes like the Crucifixion and the Resurrection? Should we say that the drama of the struggle, death, and rising—Gethsemane, Calvary, and Easter—actually belongs in the comic rather than the tragic domain? The figure of Christ as god-man is surely the archetypal hero-victim. He is mocked, reviled, crowned with thorns—a scapegoat King.

If the authentic comic action is a sacrifice and a feast, debate and passion, it is by the same token a Saturnalia, an orgy, an assertion of the unruliness of the flesh and its vitality. Comedy is essentially a Carrying Away of Death, a triumph over mortality by some absurd faith in rebirth, restoration, and salvation. Originally, of course, these carnival rites were red with the blood of victims. The archaic seasonal revel brought together the incompatibles of death and life. No logic can explain this magic vic-

tory over Winter, Sin, and the Devil. But the
comedian can perform the rites of Dionysus and his
frenzied gestures initiate us into the secrets of the
savage and mystic power of life. Comedy is sacred
and secular.

Thus it happens that from the earliest time the
comic ritual has been presided over by a Lord of
Misrule, and the improvisations of comedy have the
aspect of a Feast of Unreason, a Revel of Fools—a
Sottie. Comedy is a release, a taking off the masks
we have put on to deal with others who have put on
decent masks to deal with us. The Church herself
knew how salutary is this comic rite of unmasking,
for near the season of Lent the monks used to ap-
point one of their number to be Lord of Unreason
and chant the liturgy of Folly, during which an Ass
was worshiped and the mass parodied in a ceremony
no less religious, in its profane way, than the Dionysian and Saturnalian revels of Greece and Rome.[10]
During these *ludi inhonesti* the monks at vespers
gave the staff of office to a Lord of Misrule
while they chanted *"deposuit potentes de sede, et
exultavit humiles."* In performing the mock mass the
celebrants brayed the responses. The first Herod of
the mystery plays may have been *Rex Stultorum,*
and we know that medieval drama never excluded
the comic from its religious ritual. Those in the thrall
of carnival come out, for a moment, from behind the
façade of their "serious" selves, the façade required
by their vocation. When they emerge from this
façade, they gain a new perspective upon their
official selves and thus, when they again retire behind their usual *personae,* they are more conscious
of the duplicity of their existence. That is why Freud
thought of the comic as an "unmasking," a mechanism that allows, whether we watch or play it, a "free

discharge" of impulses we daily have to repress. The carnival is an hour when we are permitted to recover our "lost infantile laughter" and to rejoice again with the pleasure of a child. It redeems us from our "professional" life.

Aristotle said that tragedy works a purgation or "catharsis" and carries off harmful passions by means of an allowed public cleansing of the self, enabling us to face with poise the calamities of life. Tragedy has been called "mithridatic" because the tragic action, inoculating us with large doses of pity and fear, inures the self to the perils we all face. Comedy is no less mithridatic in its effects on the self, and has its own catharsis. Freud said that nonsense is a toxic agent acting like some "poison" now and again required by the economy of the soul. Under the spell of this intoxication we reclaim for an instant our "old liberties," and after discharging our inhibited impulses in folly we regain the sanity that is worn away by the everyday gestures. We have a compulsion to be moral and decent, but we also resent the obligations we have accepted. The irreverence of the carnival disburdens us of our resentment and purges our ambivalence so that we can return to our duties as honest men. Like tragedy, comedy is homeopathic. It cures folly by folly.

The tragic law works a transformation: from sin and suffering come calm of mind and resistance to disaster, to fears that weaken us. The transformations in comedy are equally miraculous: from license and parody and unmasking—or putting on another mask—come renewed sanity and responsibility, a confidence that we have looked at things from a lower angle and therefore know what is incorruptible. In Shakespeare's play the madness of midsummer night is necessary to purge doting and in-

constant lovers. After the fierce vexation of their
dreams comes the bright Athenian dawn, with secure judgment. As Hippolyta says:

> And all their minds transfigured so together,
> More witnesseth than fancy's images,
> And grows to something of great constancy;
> But howsoever, strange and admirable.

The comic perspective can be reached only by
making game of "serious" life. The comic rites are
necessarily impious, for comedy is sacrilege as well
as release. That is one reason why comedy is intolerable to the sober moralist Rousseau, who gravely
protests that the women of Geneva will be corrupted by going to the theatre to see how Molière
satirizes virtuous men like Alceste. Plato has the
same puritan timidity, despising the art that stirs up
"the rebellious principle" in men, "especially at a
public festival when a promiscuous crowd is as-
sembled in a theatre" where passions are roused and
fed. Plato's high-minded snobbism, like Rousseau's
petty-bourgeois "seriousness," is brought to bear
chiefly against tragedy; yet both have an abiding
fear of the carnival, which has the power "of harm-
ing even the good" by its contagious impieties. Plato
warns his Guardians of the ideal State not to be
given to laughter, for "violent laughter tends to provoke an equally violent reaction." He especially
fears buffooneries or any "impulse to play the clown"
—"and by encouraging its impudence at the theatre
you may be unconsciously carried away into playing
the comedian in your private life." But Freud saw
what this impudence means, for the comic action is
a mode of "representation through the opposite,"
and man must periodically befoul the holy and reduce himself to folly. We find ourselves reflected in

the comedian, who satisfies our need for impieties.

Nietzsche believed that we discover truth in the excesses of a Dionysiac orgy, which is ecstasy as well as pain. This orgy takes place in the theatre he calls "epidemic" because it sweeps the individual into the tide of a mass emotion. In *The Birth of Tragedy* Nietzsche says that Greek drama was played at a point of conflict between our Apollonian and our Dionysian selves. The Apollonian self is reason (*logos*), while the unruly Dionysiac self finds its voice in song (*melos*)—the song of the chorus. Who are the chorus, singing before the actors (who stand apart to speak their dialogue)? They are the satyr-selves, the natural beings madly giving out cries of joy and sorrow that arise from the vast cosmic night of primordial existence. "Is it possible," Nietzsche asks, "that madness is not necessarily a symptom of degeneration, of decline, of a decadent culture? Perhaps this is a question for alienists—there are neuroses of *health?*" Nietzsche finds the substratum of both comedy and tragedy in the old satyr-self: "Our deepest insights must—and should—appear as follies, and under certain circumstances as crimes." So Zarathustra rejoices in the Ass-Festival: "A little valiant nonsense, some divine service and ass-festival, some old joyful Zarathustra-fool, some blusterer to blow your souls bright." When he sings the wild songs of Bacchus, man loses his personal identity, his "differentiation," and ceases to be a thinker. He becomes the Dionysiac hero, the archetypal Reveller. In the epidemic theatre there is a metamorphosis, for civilized man finds again his archaic being among the throng.

The Dionysiac theatre consecrates truth by outbursts of laughter. Comedy desecrates what it seeks to sanctify. The orgiastic cleansing of the self and the tribe is ritually performed in Shakespeare's *Henry IV*, 1 and 2, which is a Feast of Unreason ceremonially held in the taverns of Eastcheap, with Falstaff presiding as Lord of Misrule. The Lancastrian king Henry IV, Bolingbroke, has under the guise of just causes usurped the throne and slain the anointed king, Richard II. After this stroke of power politics Henry has ventured to put on the mask of repute and piety; but behind this decent royal *persona* is the "shadow" self of the old unscrupulous Bolingbroke, and he confesses to Hal:

> . . . God knows, my son,
> By what by-paths and indirect crookt ways
> I met this crown; and I myself know well
> How troublesome it sat upon my head . . .

Henry cannot wear the royal garments easily because he has come to his throne by the unholy cunning of the opportunist. Richard's blood will not out, and like a tragic guilt it stains the grace of Henry's rule. Yet Bolingbroke cannot drop the mask. So Hal's heritage is tainted, and the Lancastrian line must be purged. This false righteousness can be washed away only by rites acted hilariously on Gadshill, where Hal connives at another, baser thievery that is detected—a parody of his father's practice. In the depths of bohemia, amid whores, parasites, and cowards, a realm where Falstaff is king and priest, young Hal is initiated into the company of Fools and Rogues. Falstaff asks the ruthless question: "What is honor?" The Lancastrians must answer before they are legitimate kings. With all the lewdness of the comedian Falstaff reduces to absurdity the lineage of Bolingbroke when he jests at the parentage of young Harry and knows him to be his father's son only by a villainous hanging lip, which proclaims him honestly begot. In this pit of degradation Hal cleanses himself and his line from the policy of his ancestors, and by coming out from behind the façade of Lancastrian pompousness he proves that he is, indeed legitimately, the heir apparent. By stooping to Doll Tearsheet, Harry makes himself eligible to woo Kate of France. Falstaff is at once devil and priest, coward and hero, tempter and scapegoat, and essentially the satyr who lives ineradicably behind the façade of every culture. Without his ribaldry, his drunken wisdom, Britain cannot be redeemed.

III. *The Guises of the Comic Hero*

Hence the range of comic action is far wider than Bergson supposed when he remarked that the comic is something mechanical encrusted on what is living and that the comic hero is dehumanized because he makes only gestures, automatic motions, which look ridiculous when they are "interrupted." Bergson, perhaps following Stendhal's notion that we remain untouched by the plight of the comic figure, saw him from only one angle, treating him as if he were a toy manikin which, wound up, is geared to execute the same motion wherever he is put. Bergson's comic hero is only a caricature of a man. Yet Don Quixote, even while making mechanical gestures, enters the realm of *human* action as a figure like Tartuffe cannot. In Dickens and Dostoevsky, too, the characters are geared to make a few stormy gestures, but are not merely comic machines like Tartuffe and Harpagon, who by contrast merely gesticulate. Chaucer's Wife of Bath is another creature capable of only a few responses who is, nevertheless, more than an automaton.

Above all other comic heroes, perhaps, Falstaff is

a grotesque who has by no means disqualified himself from being a man; in fact, he has a kind of massive "probability" and authentic selfhood-in-depth. Behind his great belly there is an ample personality, and his gesticulations, mechanical as they seem, are comparable to the moral "action" of a tragic hero. Nor is Falstaff isolated from us like Tartuffe, even when his cowardly motions are "interrupted" as he is caught red-handed at Gadshill or on the field at Shrewsbury. Exactly when Falstaff is driven into the tightest corner—when like Tartuffe he is "caught" firmly in the mechanical trap of comedy—he asks his most troublesome questions: What is honor? What is so much like a counterfeit man as a dead hero? Tartuffe does not have this ingenuity, this power to come to grips with us at close quarters. Falstaff is never so dangerous as when he is at bay —which proves that he has an existence of his own apart from the intrigue in which he has a role. Some of Dostoevsky's grotesque people who have obsessive notions also have this power to challenge us as we stand outside the comic arena and watch them from a position of presumed safety. The sickly hero of *Notes from the Underworld* faces us with some very awkward problems which a character so absurd and artificial has no right to raise. Furthermore, at the basest level of his "low" comedy Falstaff ventures to address himself directly to us, making us doubt Bergson's opinion that only "high" comedy is close to life. Indeed, Falstaff shows how narrow the margin sometimes is between high and low comedy, for he was doubtless born a comic machine of a very low order—the *miles gloriosus*—yet as if by a leap he traverses the whole distance between "low" and "high" and is able to dwell disturbingly among us in his own libertine way.

The truth is that the comic hero has a complexity of character Bergson and Meredith did not suspect. Falstaff and Hal are both comedians who take part in the ancient ritual of feast and sacrifice, orgy and debate. In the oldest comedy there was a struggle, or *agon*, with the Impostor (or *alazon*) who looked with defiling eye upon the sacred rites that must not be seen. The alazon was put to flight after a contest with either the young king or with a character known as the *eiron*, "the ironical man." The alazon is a boaster who claims, traditionally, more than a share of the agonist's victory. It was the duty of the eiron, who often professed ignorance, to reduce the alazon, to bring him to confusion. Sometimes the king himself assumed the character of the eiron— "the ironical buffoon"—to deflate the boaster or "unwelcome intruder" who appeared to know more than he actually did. Thus somewhere at the heart of old comedy—ritual comedy—was a combat of the king-eiron against the impostor-intruder-alazon.

This ancient struggle was still being waged in Aristotle's *Ethics* (II, 7; IV, 7, 8) in the contrast between the boaster (alazon) and the self-depreciator (eiron); and midway between these two characters is the "straightforward" man who neither exaggerates nor understates. Here, as in old comedy, the alazon is the alter ego of the eiron. The two extremes appear together.

Aristotle mentions Socrates as the "mock-modest" character who understates things; and, in fact, Socrates is a kind of alter ego to Falstaff, the boaster-buffoon. The double nature of the comic hero is symbolized in these two: Falstaff and Socrates. They are of opposite disposition, yet not so unlike as we might think. The essential character of the eiron is incarnate in Socrates, who was "ignorant" and who

also had the disposition of the "buffoon" or "fool," the
features of the comic spirit itself, the coarse, ugly
mask of the satyr or clown. The Socratic method is
a tactic of winning victory by professing ignorance,
by merely asking questions of the "impostors," the
so-called "wise" men of Athens. Irony "defeats the
enemy on his own ground," for in the course of the
comic debate the supposed wisdom of the alazon is
reduced to absurdity, and the alazon himself becomes a clown. Thus Socrates, without risking any
dogmatic answers, corrects the folly of those sophists who claimed to know the truth, or who were ignorant enough to presume there is no truth. So the
ironical man by his shrewd humility ("lying low beneath the gods and saying nothing") proves to be
wiser than the wisdom of the world. Irony has been
called one of the faces of shame. Yet we must remember that Falstaff the buffoon and impostor used
the same sort of interrogation Socrates the ironist
used. He asks the same sort of questions: What is
honor? Socrates asked: What is justice?

Socrates, like Falstaff, is both ironist and buffoon;
he is the questioner using a philosophic buffoonery
to seek the truth. In *The Republic* Thrasymachus
speaks of Socrates' "shamming ignorance" in his "im-
becile way." Socrates is a sort of supersophist who
inquires or doubts, and thus again resembles Falstaff. He has a double or triple character, for he is,
as Falstaff was, both victor and victim—a victim,
eventually, of the unthinking Athenians who re-
fused to have their creed unsettled. He was finally
condemned to drink the hemlock because he asked
too many impious questions. And Falstaff is rejected
by King Hal. The eiron himself, with the rude face
of the satyr, is at last, like the king in the fertility
rite, sacrificed by the tribe. Socrates is a kind of ala-

zon too, since he did claim to have his "wisdom," given him by his daemon, a still small voice he held sacred. When he is condemned to death by the court he stubbornly insists that if they kill him they will injure themselves far more than they injure him, for they will not find another like him, a gadfly given to the city by God. This is a considerable claim. He adds, "I know but little, and I do not suppose that I know. But I do know that injustice and disobedience to a better, whether God or man, is evil and dishonorable." Here we need to recall that Aristotle classified comic characters as being of three kinds: buffoon, ironist, and impostor. Socrates is all three —and so is Falstaff.

Thus is revealed the deep ambiguity in the comic hero: the Impostor, the enemy of God, is not only the alter ego of the ironist; he is, in Cornford's phrase, the double of the very god himself. The god must be slain and devoured; therefore the guilt feeling of the tribe arising from sacrificing their god-king is transferred to the figure of the alazon, the antagonist and profaner who serves as scapegoat for the injury done the god during the fertility cere-mony. The impostor profanes the rites; then he is beaten and driven out. So the tribe rationalizes its sin by persecuting the One Who Dares To Look. Cornford says: "The reviling and expulsion of the Antagonist-Impostor is the darker counterpart of the Kômos, which brings in the new God, victorious over him in the Agon." The god who is savior must be hated and slain. He has a double nature: he who is venerated, he who is reviled. Before the resurrec-tion there is the crowning with thorns. The alazon is one of the disguises worn by the god-hero before he is sacrificed; he is also, by the same token, the "antagonistic" self that must be disowned before the worshiper is "possessed" by the god. Hence the ambivalence toward the comic hero.

Or the alazon-eiron may be simply the agent of God, like Goethe's Mephisto, who explains how he is "the spirit that endlessly denies" but is also "part of a power that would alone work evil, but engenders good." The Impostor, Profaner, or Devil is a "darkness that is part of light." Evil is inherent in Good, and to reach salvation man must pass through a "negation of negation." Therefore Faust finds himself bound to the impudent spirit who is only his darker self. Faust exclaims: "Why must I be fettered to this infamous companion who battens upon mischief and delights in ruin?" He does not yet know that the one who goads him—the Tempter—is a deputy of God. And the eiron, who can put on the features of the buffoon and scapegoat, is, in his other self, a mocker, blasphemer, and Offender. He embodies, again, the side of the god that must be rebelled against before the god can be worshiped. God must be hated before he can be loved, denied before he is believed. The comedian plays the role of Doubting Thomas. He is at once a stone rejected by the builder, and the cornerstone of the temple. Comedy is destructive and creative. So Falstaff, like Socrates, has a double nature and a double fate: eiron and alazon, tempter and clown, hero and knave, the great god Pan and also Pharmakos—he who is expelled with communal sins heaped on his head.

Falstaff is a central image in comedy. Symbolically he is the Fool; and the province of the Fool is the whole wide circuit of life and death, laughter and tears, wisdom and ignorance.[11] The fool is comic man. He is no mechanical figure. His gestures have daemonic power, and he carries his scepter by right of ancient rule. We fear him as god; we laugh at him as clown. All the ambiguities and ambivalences of comic action pivot on this archetypal hero of many guises. The fool wears motley—the particolor of human nature—and quickly changes one mask for another, putting on indifferently and recklessly the shifting features of man, playing with gusto more roles than are suitable to the tragic hero. The fool at last proves to be the clown; and the clown is He Who Gets Slapped—and "is none the worse for his slapping." He is resilient with a vitality lacking to the tragic hero, who must accept his misfortune and his responsibility with a stoic face, with a steadier logic than the absurd logic of comedy.

In general one may distinguish two orders of fool, natural and artificial. The natural fool is the archaic victim who diverts the wrath of the gods from the anointed figure of the king. He is the alter ego of the Successful Man, who needs to exempt himself from the jealousy and ill will of the Olympians and who therefore provides himself with someone insolent or ignorant, whom the gods smite. The fool is vicarious Sufferer. He is reviled, beaten, and stricken; but he has the privilege of vilifying the Prosperous Man; he is free to humble the Exalted by mockery. The fool saves the hero from the awful sin of pride (*hubris*). He is the Ugly One who by slandering, guards the king, or even the priest, from the evil eye. He may be dwarfed and deformed; he may be an idiot. But the idiot has the wisdom of innocence and the naïveté of the child.

To this order of natural fools belongs Friar Juniper, the holy clown of the Franciscan order, whose antics were a token of grace, who had great power against the Devil and went about in ragged cowl, greatly comforted when the people called him blockhead.

In his mind the fool bears the stigmata of holiness. Dostoevsky's saintly prostitutes like Sonia, or his "idiots" like Muishkin and Alyosha, have a close kinship with the natural fool. Kafka's heroes—those anonymous abused innocents known only as K—are natural fools who behold their own affliction with wide, credulous eyes. Everything strikes K with wonder and surprise, since he is the amateur in living who cannot be sophisticated by custom, who never learns his way around. For him life is always astonishment, effort, and uncertainty.

At his most contemptible the artificial fool may be the parasite of the old Greco-Roman comedies, a servile instrument in the hands of wealth and power. These fools use the oily manners of Rosencrantz and Guildenstern, or Osric, that yeasty, superserviceable knave spacious only in the possession of dirt.

But the fool can also be the seer, the prophet, the "possessed," since the madness of the fool is oracular, sibylline, delphic. He may be the voice crying in the wilderness, an Evangelist or Baptist, or an Imbecile-Prince like Muishkin, whose friends toll him he will always be a child, and who has revelations: "The recognition of God as our Father, and of God's joy in men as His own children, which is the chief idea of Christ." The fool may be the godly Dolt like the medieval Tumbler of Our Lady, or the poetic Seer like Rimbaud. He may, like Touchstone, look askance at life with a cool reluctance to commit himself. Sometimes his intuition is tragic, like the naïve cynicism of Lear's Fool, who sees the folly of playing Machiavellian games in a world rent by tempest. In the Sermon on the Mount, Jesus tells us with the voice of Innocence that we must accept the ridiculous as the basis of morality: "Blessed are the meek, for they shall inherit the earth."

The comedian is indeed a "revolutionary simpleton." No modern has claimed this more emphatically
than Kierkegaard, who saw how the religious man
must first of all be a comedian: "The religious individual has as such made the discovery of the comical
in largest measure." Kierkegaard's religious man is
not necessarily the comic poet or actor, but he is
the one who has seen that our deepest experiences
come to us in the form of contradictions. Therefore
he is afflicted with the "higher madness" that is the
comedy of faith, a passionate belief in the absurd.
The knight of faith knows that the pathetic is
inherent in the comic, that suffering is a mark of
blessedness: "And hence it comes about that one is
tempted both to weep and to laugh when the
humorist speaks." Kierkegaard restates in another
key the theme of Nietzsche's existential comedy:
that one who suffers "by virtue of his suffering *knows
more* than the shrewdest and wisest can ever know."
Like a modern saint Nietzsche writes: "Suffering
makes noble: it separates."

Thus in almost all his roles the fool is set apart,
dedicated, alienated, if not outcast, beaten, slain.
Being isolated, he serves as a "center of indifference,"
from which position the rest of us may, if we will,
look through his eyes and appraise the meaning of
our daily life. Archimedes is said to have promised
"Give me a place to stand, and I will move the earth."
In art, in ethics, in religion the fool finds a place to
stand, for he is the detached spectator who has been
placed, or has placed himself, outside accepted
codes. From this point "outside"—this extrapolated
fulcrum—he takes his leverage on the rest of us, and
from his point of vantage can exclaim with Puck,
the comic avenger, "Lord, what fools these mortals
be."

There is something malign in Puck's spirit; he is scornful and delights in confusion. When this scorn is fierce enough we have the comic spirit of Swift, who frightens us out of laughter into dismay, if not despair. Just as Kierkegaard discovers the extreme absurdities of faith by extrapolating the attitude of the humorist, so Jonathan Swift leads us to the verge of a gulf of hopelessness by extrapolating the mischievous attitude of Puck. His Majesty of Brobdingnag tells Gulliver, after deliberation, "I can not but conclude the bulk of your natives to be the most pernicious race of little odious vermin that nature ever suffered to crawl upon the surface of the earth." The most galling of all comic figures are Swift's loathsome Yahoo-men, who reduce us all to intolerable shame.

There is something Puckish, also, in Hamlet's spirit, taunting and curious as it is. Amid the rottenness of Denmark the Prince serves as a philosophic and temperamental fool, a center of "indifference." He stands apart from gross revelry under his own melancholy cloud; and from his distance he is able to perceive more things than philosophy can dream; for the dust of great Alexander may stop a bunghole, and however thick my lady paints, she comes to a foul grave, the noisome state of Yorick, who is eaten by the same worms that feed upon Polonius, that duller fool. Hamlet is humorist and sufferer existing alone with his disdainful soul. He allows himself every incaution, and with midsummer lunacy puts an antic disposition on. Some of Hamlet's motives are devilish—Mephistophelian; his vocation is picaresque, to ask impudent questions and lead us along the narrow ledge where the immoralist walks, making us quarter our thoughts with an obsessive guile. Hamlet, Mephisto, Byron, Stendhal, Nietzsche, and

Gide are heroes who belong in a comic theatre
where man is goaded and teased, led down the
dimmest passes of sin, to see what is learned by evil.

When he appears as tempter, the fool—the comic
hero who stands "outside"—must put on the mask.
He disguises himself as clown or devil, wearing as
need arises the garb of buffoon, ironist, madman. He
must lead us, finally, to the witches' kitchen and the
Walpurgis Night; or to the wilderness where we
meet our "shadow" selves face to face, although we
have disowned these selves in our public life. There
in the wilderness or on the Brocken the god in us
is confronted by the Adversary, our "other" self, who
lays before us illusions of pomp, knowledge, and
pleasure. In tempting us the Adversary must have
the features of innocence, must charm us with man-
nerly good will, gaiety, finesse, and high spirits. He
may seem as honest as Iago, whose motiveless ma-
lignity wears the bland mask of friendship. Iago is
the Socratic interrogator who destroys us with our
own ideals; yet he is an illusion: "I am not what I
am," he says. This Adversary may speak folly or
profanity; or jest insanely, as did Nietzsche, who
tempted the whole respectable middle class with
his madness. His Satyr-Heroes have recognized Dionysus as god and they "*revert* to the innocence of
the beast-of-prey conscience, like jubilant monsters,
who perhaps come from a ghostly bout of murder,
arson, rape, and torture with bravado and moral
equanimity, as though merely some wild student's
prank had been played."

The rebel, the immoralist, the free and licensed
self in this terrible comedy of the future has passed
"beyond" and looks back from a new and daring perspective upon the morality of the herd, which is hollow. Nietzsche's comic hero is the Despiser, the

Blond Beast; or else he is the Great Sick Man over-
come by his disgust, his nausea as he examines, from
his point "outside," the premises of a morality we
have never examined. To feel the spell of this
Tempter we must take the awful risk of entering
into a "boundary-situation" where nothing is taken
for granted and where all our values must be found
anew without help from "the others." Here we walk
alone upon the margin of Reason. The Adversary
goes with us to this highest precipice of comedy, the
edge of the abyss where we glance with Nietzsche
into Chaos. There we must stand on the brink of
Nonsense and Absurdity and not be dizzy. If we do
not fall, or plunge, we may be saved. Only by taking
this risk can we put Satan behind us. Only thus can
the Rebel learn what is Good. The comic Feast of
Unreason is a test and a discovery, and our season
spent mumming with the Lord of Misrule can show
what will redeem us. The Adversary must be expelled. The Tempter must perish. That is, we must
sacrifice him to save ourselves.

Young Hamlet, late from Wittenberg, stands alone
on the brink of this abyss, sees himself as a ridiculous fellow crawling between heaven and earth with
more sins at his beck than he has time to act. So he
puts on the antic disposition of the fool. And if a
sense of contradiction and absurdity is a cause of
comedy, then Hamlet is a profoundly comic character. He encounters what Kierkegaard calls either/or
choices, the extremes that cannot be mediated but
only transcended. That is, the comic hero and the
saint accept the irreconcilables in man's existence.
Both find themselves face to face with the Inexplicable and the Absurd. When, for example, as
Kierkegaard points out, Abraham holds the knife
above Isaac and at the command of God is about to

slay his son, he places himself outside and beyond all moral norms and is either, quite simply, a murderer or a believer. He stands alone in a situation that allows no middle term whatever. He meets an extreme peril that cannot be related to "virtue" or any human ethic. His dilemma can only be transcended by a "perspective from infinity"—looking at it from the infinite distance of faith, a perspective so far extrapolated beyond ethics that it extends from "eternity." Then Abraham is rescued from the irreconcilables in his crisis.

The comic hero finds himself in situations like Abraham's because comedy begins from the absurd and the inexplicable and, like faith, tolerates the miraculous. Dostoevsky, as usual, begins with the Unaccountable when old man Karamazov lies with Stinking Lizaveta and begets Smerdyakov, who is as truly his son as the saintly Alyosha. In the same way Miranda in *The Tempest* knows that good wombs have borne bad sons: Antonio is proof. Prospero accepts these incompatibles in reality, then transcends them by his "perspective from infinity," for at the farthest reaches of his magical vision life is like some dream that seems to come and fade. Precisely because he is face to face with the Inexplicable the comic hero is eligible for "rescue," like Don Quixote, who is mad to the degree of pouring curds over his poor head but who dies, like a saint, in a state of grace.

Often the comic hero is rescued because Improvisation and Uncertainty are the premises of comic action, and the goddess Fortuna presides over great tracts of the comic scene. But the law of Inevitability or Necessity bears heavily on the tragic hero, who is not eligible for rescue because in tragedy man must somehow take responsibility for the flaws in the nature of things or at least pay a penalty for them. To be sure, the tragic hero meets the Inexplicable—by what logic does Oedipus happen to confront his father on the road to Thebes and kill him in a narrow pass? Behind tragedy, too, is a riddle of the Sphinx, the warning of oracles only hoarsely spoken. In any case the tragic poet feels some compulsion to look backwards across the gulf of disaster and help us understand why the hero met his doom. Or he must fortify us against the Inexplicable and reassure us that Justice is not wrecked by it; whereas the comic artist can accept absurdities as the open premises of his account of life and not be troubled by them. The comedian practices an art of exaggeration, or overstatement.

The tragic hero, however, must heed some "golden mean" between extremes; he does not dare *play* with life as the comic hero does. The tragic hero meets either/or dilemmas but must pay some penalty for not being able to conciliate incompatibles. His only refuge from despair is a stoic endurance between those incompatibles; he must somehow prove himself adequate to the disasters he suffers. The tragic poet cannot, like the comic artist or the religious hero, look at man's struggle from infinite distances and revise its human weight or its penalties. Tragedy is a form of ethical heroism, suggesting that "man is the measure," even between desperate choices.

The tragic hero, noble and magnified, can be of awesome stature. The comic hero refuses to wear the trappings of moral or civil grandeur, usually preferring motley, or the agility of the clown. He is none the less man, and Hamlet more than once rouses our suspicion that the tragic hero is eligible for comic roles: or is it the other way round, that Hamlet is a comic hero who generates tragic values? The Prince touches his deepest meanings when he has on his antic humor. Then he needs no grandeur to hide his weakness, which is laughably naked.

Under the auspices of Fortuna comedy allows a play of character impossible in tragedy, which requires a hero "greater and better than most men" but capable of "error." As Aristotle says, the tragic hero cannot be either "depraved" or simply a victim of "bad luck." Comedy, however, delights to deal with those who are victims of bad luck, along with those who are "depraved" or "vicious"—by means of the grotesque. By disfiguring the hated person in caricature, comedy is able to elevate hatred to art. Swift evidently saw man as depraved and vicious, and projected his hatred into the grotesques called Yahoos. At the severest phase of grotesque we can behold the unnatural figures of King Lear and his daughters, who seem to have reduced life to horrors from which tragedy turns away. The crazy Lear wails:

> When we are born, we cry that we are come
> To this great stage of fools.

In this savage play men seem to be puppets (but not automatons).

Cornford tells us why comedy can utilize the grotesque. In Greece and Rome comedy was gradually transmuted from religious Mystery to theatrical Mime. So when comedy lost its appearance of being what originally and essentially it was, a fertility celebration, the characters tended to become grotesques, and the comedian continued using many of the stock masks tragedy had discarded. The original chorus of celebrant animal-figures gave a name to some of Aristophanes' comedies like *The Birds* and

The Wasps. The old goat-chorus and satyr-masks invaded the final comic unit of the tetralogy. The Impostor, particularly, became a stylized, stereotyped figure, like the Vice in medieval plays with his lath dagger and his sortie from Hell-Mouth. In this way the comic personality did indeed become dehumanized when it was a vehicle for making certain gestures—the automatic gestures of Punch and Pierrot. Are not these lively creatures the ancestors of Tartuffe and other caricatures? They are born of Mime and live the repetitive existence of Bergson's manikins, oscillating between life and art. Yet we must once more remind ourselves that Falstaff, born of a "mask," generates a personality and temperament more human than his gestures entitle him to.

iv. *The Social Meanings of Comedy*

The tradition of Mime, Mask, and Caricature, then, explains why Bergson thought, with Stendhal, that comedy requires a certain rigidity in the comic personage, an *insociabilité* in the hero and a degree of *insensibilité* in the spectator. But Falstaff breaks down this insensibility and offers us a sort of release and purgation Pierrot cannot. Falstaff proves what Freud suspected: that comedy is a process of safeguarding pleasure against the denials of reason, which is wary of pleasure. Man cannot live by reason alone or forever under the rod of moral obligation, the admonition of the superego. In the person of Falstaff the superego "takes a holiday." The comedian is the self behaving as prodigal and bohemian. From its earliest days comedy is an essential pleasure mechanism valuable to the spectator and the society in which he lives. Comedy is a momentary and publicly useful resistence to authority and an escape from its pressures; and its mechanism is a free discharge of repressed psychic energy or resentment through laughter. Its purpose is comparable to the release of the dream, except that the dream is private and asocial, whereas the comic uproar is "infectious." Freud goes so far as to say "The comical appears primarily as an unintentional discovery in the social relations of human beings." Meredith, of course, emphasized more strongly than Bergson that comedy is "the ultimate civilizer."

The ambivalence of comedy reappears in its social meanings, for comedy is both hatred and revel, rebellion and defense, attack and escape. It is revolutionary and conservative. Socially, it is both sympathy and persecution.

One of the strongest impulses comedy can discharge from the depths of the social self is our hatred of the "alien," especially when the stranger who is "different" stirs any unconscious doubt about our own beliefs. Then the comedian unerringly finds his audience, the solid majority, itself a silent prey to unrecognized fears. He can point out our victim, isolate him from sympathy, and cruelly expose him to the penalty of our ridicule. In this role the comic artist is a "conservative" or even a "reactionary" who protects our self-esteem. Wherever comedy serves as a public defense mechanism, it makes all of us hypocrites: we try to laugh our doubts out of existence. Wherever comedy is a symptom of fear, our mirth indicates the zeal with which we are maltreating our scapegoat. Certainly the laugh of the satirist is often a sneer; and there is an undercurrent of satire in most comedy.

To this extent the comic response is tribal and, if it is malicious, uncivilized. Any majority secretes venom against those who trouble it, then works off

this venom in mocking some figure like Shylock the
Jew, the Usurer, hated by right-thinking Christians
precisely because he lives in the free and open
market on a premise of ruthless competition. Shylock is the naked image of renaissance "initiative,"
whose thrift is called greed only because he is He-
brew. "And thrift," Shylock protests, "is blessing if
men steal it not." Could any gentile entrepreneur
put it better? The inconsistency is implied by the
shadow of pathos falling across Shylock's ugly figure.
Let us avoid the old dispute whether Shylock is
tragic: it is clear enough that according to the confused premises of the play a Christian without
money is tragic and a Jew without money is funny.
And Jews should be without money. Unless the Jew
is Jessica, who becomes Christian by gilding herself
with ducats.

Granted that Shakespeare sees his victim in double perspective (for Shylock the monster becomes
Shylock the man when he asks "If you prick us, do
we not bleed?"), the Elizabethan audience probably
did not see the Jew in this double way but took his
grotesque figure to be a hateful and hated image of
greed. The higher the social charge in comedy, the
less the audience is likely to care about distinguish-
ing truth from prejudice. The classical instance
would be *The Clouds,* a play in which Aristophanes
evidently leads a pack of right-minded Athenians in
hounding down sophists who have insulted the gods
and shaken the ordinary pieties. Never mind what
questions the sophists really asked; never mind
whether we can answer their questions—we must
quell these troublemakers:

Strike, smite them, spare them not, for many reasons:
BUT MOST BECAUSE THEY HAVE BLASPHEMED THE GODS.

The attack in Molière's *Highbrow Ladies* is not so blunt, but it is none the less based on the premise that women are not entitled to be foppish; they must be conveniently stupid.

Usually the comedian will address us with most assurance when he is conservative, when he affirms the security of any group already unsure of itself. In middle-class societies, particularly, the comic artist often reassures the majority that its standards are impregnable or that other standards are not "normal" or "sane." Then the comedian banishes doubt by ridicule and is the "diplomatic artist."[12]

Yet this defense of the *status quo* occurs in a society where there is a hidden conflict in social standards; and the comedian may appear on the other side of the barricades, with the revolutionaries. Falstaff gleefully invites us to join him in making bohemian sallies among the ranks of the Philistines, bringing confusion to their hosts. The very appearance of Shylock as a sympathetic villain indicates the malaise in Elizabethan society about "rugged individualism." Similarly the figure of Tartuffe is a focus for the conflict between an ideal of personal integrity and the unscrupulous piety of an acquisitive class. In despising Tartuffe we despise our own hypocrisy, whether it be a false puritan asceticism or the slippery indulgence of the Jesuits. Tartuffe could be born only in a society anxious about its honesty. He is a sign of what we reject.

Or else the comedian can evade the conflict, relieving the stress between competing ideals by laughter. He may enable us to "adjust" incompatible standards without resolving the clash between them. Thus we laugh when Tartuffe brings our conflict into the open, because we may not wish to recognize that we, too, seek power, women, and money, and that all these may be more desirable than piety. We laugh at Tartuffe because we do not intend to see clearly what he means. We may also laugh at Falstaff because we do not—must not—grant that good sherris sack is, after all, the real value of life, and honor only a word. Falstaff raises questions we wish to blink, and we laugh at him to prevent his damaging our convictions which are taboo.

In its boisterous moods comedy annihilates the power of evil in the person of the scapegoat. Yet we have already seen that this triumphant laughter is a mode of defense, because the enemy who has power over us must be neutralized by transforming him into a harmless victim.[13] Falstaff, we have said, has the sacred power of a god of fertility; therefore he must be disguised before he can be laughed out of existence, lest he threaten us too closely. Comedy is at once a defense against the Enemy and a victorious assault upon Him. He vanishes in an explosion of choral mirth.

At its most triumphant moments comic art frees us from peril without destroying our ideals and without mustering the heavy artillery of the puritan. Comedy can be a means of mastering our disillusions when we are caught in a dishonest or stupid society. After we recognize the misdoings, the blunders, we can liberate ourselves by a confident, wise laughter that brings a catharsis of our discontent. We see the flaws in things, but we do not always need to concede the victory, even if we live in a human world. If we can laugh wisely enough at ourselves and others, the sense of guilt, dismay, anxiety, or fear can be lifted. Unflinching and undaunted we see *where we are*. This strengthens us as well as society.

When comic art is generous enough, it is a triumphant affirmation of truth—which, we see, cannot be damaged by our failures. "Great comic artists assume that truth may bear all lights."[14] In this belief lies the heroic courage of the comedian. The unvanquishable Falstaff is an ageless witness that truth can bear all lights: this comic giant proves that honor cannot be sullied in Eastcheap or on Gadshill. He breaks down our unreliable attitudes—unreliable because they are overguarded. His obscene questions strip us of our linen decencies and free us from the iron yoke of conformity. This high priest of comedy is doing us the service John Milton gravely did in *Areopagitica* when he protested against fugitive and cloistered virtues. "That which purifies us is trial," Milton writes, "and trial is by what is contrary." Milton requires trial by "dust and heat." Falstaff challenges us from alleys and bawdy houses. He asks us to walk out of the whited sepulchre we have made into our world; and when we walk abroad with Falstaff we discover what John Milton discovered: that truth is strong next to the Almighty and will not be put to the worse when she grapples with falsehood in open encounter.

To be able to laugh at evil and error means that we have surmounted them. Comedy may be a philosophic, as well as a psychological, compensation. Whenever we become aware that this is not the best of possible worlds, we need the help of the comedian to meet the "insuperable defects of actuality."[15] We escape with him into a logical order by laughing at the imperfections of the world about us; the comic artist releases us from the limitations in things as they are. Chafed by the deficiencies in reality the comedian may be more intransigent than the tragedian. Tragedy accepts the flaw in the world as it is, then ventures to find nobility in "the inexorable march of actual situations." If the tragic illusion is potent enough we are reconciled to the tears at the heart of things. But unless he is in his "diplomatic" mood, the comedian refuses to make these concessions to actuality and serves, instead, as chief tactician in a permanent resistance movement, or rebellion, within the frontiers of human experience. By temperament the comedian is often a fifth columnist in social life.

An outrageous rebel is that same picaresque knave Falstaff, who dares us to stride with him across the boundaries of caution into the Walpurgis Night of a new philosophic order where one lives completely at ease. Even the rococo comedy in *Tristram Shandy* is daring, for Sterne trespasses smirkingly against every decency for the sake of liberating his exquisite feelings. One of the annoying intransigents in our own society was André Gide, who temperamentally was unable to write tragedy but insisted on publishing, in the teeth of his "serious" friends, his diabolical *Corydon*. Gide kept saying, "My function is to disturb." He is the classic type of comic artist who is *agent provocateur*. In Gide and Goya and Swift the tenor of comedy is uncompromising, irreverent.

In her own quiet way Jane Austen devastates our compromises and complacencies—especially male complacency. It is said one can read her novels and never guess that France was red with terror or that British troops were dying at Waterloo. She leaves all that turmoil to the "romantics." Meanwhile Miss Austen placidly undermines the bastions of middle-class propriety. Her irreverence is calm, but she knows better than the "romantics" that one must not compromise one's honesty. She is not the less dangerous because she operates inconspicuously. There she resembles Henry James, who lays bare in his overbred prose the shameless vulgarity of the *haute bourgeoisie*. We must not be deceived, either, about Miss Austen's cool disposition, which seems defensive, wary of being taken in. She is using the caution native to those comic artists who contrive to protect themselves against scorn while they are making us scorn others. Her contempt is polite.

This is comedy near its "highest," which, Bergson and Meredith agree, is a game played in social life. In *Two Sources of Morality and Religion* Bergson described two orders of society, the one unchanging, mechanical, stratified, conservative, and "closed"; the other mobile, organic, fluid, and "open." A colony of insects is a "closed" order, alert for danger, attack, defense. It is a society with Spartan efficiency and, ability to survive. The members of a closed society care nothing for humanity but live untroubled by dreams or doubts. The open society has a different morality because it is sensitive to the fringe of intuition, "vague and evanescent," that envelops every clear idea. Those living in an open society are self-aware, responsive to the nuance, the not-wholly-formulated. The open society gives play to individuality, true selfhood. Stendhal's hero Julien Sorel belongs in an open society but is trapped within the confines of a closed caste system. So his adventures become a picaresque comedy played at the expense of the insensitive people about him and of his own malaise.

To expand Bergson's idea a little, we may say that the "lower" the comedy, the more it needs a "closed" social order, and the "higher" the comedy, the more the situation is "open" socially and morally. The mechanics of Shakespeare's *Comedy of Errors* are possible in a situation firmly "closed," where events exactly balance each other in a series of neatly arranged coincidences. The moral rigidity in this world is suggested by the Duke's mechanical, paralyzing ethic which causes him to say to Aegeon: "For we may pity, though not pardon, thee."

The situation in *Twelfth Night* seems to be more "open" but really is not. Behind the delicate manners in Illyria is a tightly closed social order, as the aspiring Malvolio finds, to his distress and our delight. The fellow is a bounder; his eye is fixed hard on Olivia; he is the butler who woos his mistress. The man is a yellow-stockinged fool; and he is a fool first of all because he wishes to leap the barriers, which are far too high. At all costs Malvolio must not climb. Obviously Malvolio is an ass—obviously. Yet no more so than Sir Andrew Aguecheek, at whom we laugh, but not malignly as we do at Malvolio. Sir Andrew has a prerogative of asininity in virtue of his birth. He is a natural, not a bounder. Hard-mindedly we identify our scapegoat, Malvolio parading cross-gartered, even if we do not choose to see him for what, socially, he is: the Impostor who must be expelled with a vengeance. Sir Andrew cannot be devalued by the sneer alone, because he is guarded by his rank. But Malvolio the popinjay rouses our archaic wrath at the Pretender—who is, in this event, our own social alter ego to be publicly tormented, disclaimed, icily denied. Comedy of manners often releases the cruelty in a closed society; and the stiff ranks in this society put us in unnatural positions.

At the height of comedy the whole situation "opens" in many directions. *Love's Labour's Lost* begins as if it were to be a "closed" comedy like *Twelfth Night,* for the scene is the fastidious Academe in Navarre where some precious fools are pledging themselves to an ascetic life for three years, depriving themselves of sleep, food, and love.

Berowne alone protests, in the name of "grace."
Then one by one the lordly fantasticoes fall in love
with very frail women and break their vows, yield-
ing to the flesh. These wits bring themselves face to
face with human realities. But before they can re-
adjust, the King of France dies, and they all find
themselves standing at the mouth of the grave,
where they must pause. The entire company disperses with a curiously somber and hesitant bene-
diction: "You that way, we this way." The play shows
how the movement of high comedy is expanding,
scattering itself from situation to situation always
farther abroad, opening toward other possibilities,
holding all in suspense.[16] Berowne is one of those
who, with Benedick and Mercutio and Hamlet, cannot be at home in a closed plot, a closed society, a
closed ethic.

Shakespeare's most "open" comedy—nearly mystic
in Bergson's sense—is *The Tempest*, where all the
machinery of plot is suspended in evanescent meanings that are almost musical. This play disperses into
unknown modes of being, where even Caliban can
seek for grace. The act of forgiveness is the moral
pole of this comedy, and under the spell of Prospero's sea-change we are able to look as if from afar,
backward upon the wrongs done in the dark abysm
of the past. Evil is there, in Antonio and Sebastian,
in Stephano and Trinculo and Caliban; but at these
moral latitudes we can see even the vicious Antonio
as if he were only a troubling recollection. Amid devouring shows and strange noises human nature is
transfigured. Prospero's magic is the godlike charity
of understanding, thus enduring, all. Using the tolerance of high comedy, and its confidence, Prospero
speaks gently to those who tried to kill him. In this
larger perspective sin seems to be the last delusion

of man's mind, an error that is absurd. Prospero's vision of life is not tragic because sin is seen from distances that exempt man from disastrous penalties. All miracles are performed at this height of comedy, which brings us into a shifting, open world that continuingly transforms itself without being emptied of the cruelest actualities. Antonio is eager to murder with his three inches of obedient steel; yet these failings in men cannot damage the illusion that is truth. The vile Antonio cannot destroy what is good. Tragic danger is here cancelled by a feat of moral insight. The drama of Prospero's isle, the farthest reach of comedy, is an insubstantial pageant. It is also a triumphant revision of life, a politics of illusion.

Bergson must have seen life as Prospero did, since he described this politics of illusion in *Two Sources of Morality and Religion:*

The open society is the society which is deemed in principle to embrace all humanity. A dream dreamt, now and again, by chosen souls, it embodies on every occasion something of itself in creations, each of which, through a more or less far-reaching transformation of man, conquers difficulties hitherto unconquerable.

Prospero's charity is the imaginative fulfillment of an ethic such as Bergson mentions. There is nothing in actuality to justify his mercy, his confidence, or his vision; yet these master the failings of nature and work a change in man. Comedy is, indeed, like a dream, as even Bergson perhaps did not suspect. In saying that life is rounded with a sleep, Prospero is but repeating the words spoken by Theseus, king of a realm where there were midsummer-night dreams; for when Theseus saw the silly interlude rudely played by the mechanicals in honor of him and Hippolyta he explained: "The best in this kind

are but shadows, and the worst are no worse if imagination amend them." Theseus saw that the drama
was there, even if it was badly played; and he was
grateful to the wretched players, who gained their
triumph not on their poor stage but in Theseus'
fancy.

The high comic vision of life is humane, an
achievement of man as a social being. Meredith addressed himself to "our united social intelligence,
which is the Comic Spirit." He suspected that comedy is "the ultimate civilizer." If Prospero's comedy
is transcendentally "open," Meredith's social comedy remains a worldy discipline with, nevertheless,
full moral overtones. In all civilized societies, Meredith insists, the comic spirit must hover overhead,
its lips drawn in a slim, hungry smile, wary and
tense, thoughtfully eager to see the absurdities of
polite men and women. Kierkegaard might have
been describing Meredith's faun when he said the
"comic spirit is not wild or vehement, its laughter
is not shrill." For Kierkegaard, too, the highest comedy, like the highest pathos, rarely attracts attention
by making great shows. Only the "lower forms of the
comical do show themselves by something extrinsic.
The highest in life does not make a showing, because
it belongs to the last sphere of inwardness." No society is in good health without laughing at itself
quietly and privately; no character is sound without
self-scrutiny, without turning inward to see where it
may have overreached itself. The perception of the
self as comic touches the quick; and honest self-in-
spection must bring a sense of the comical. This kind
of awareness is an initiation into the civilized condition; it lightens the burden of selfishness, cools the
heat of the ego, makes us impressionable by others.

So the comic spirit keeps us pure in mind by requiring that we regard ourselves skeptically. Indeed this spirit is an agent of that civilizing activity Matthew Arnold called "criticism," which is essential to "culture." It is an activity necessary to middle-class society, where we gravitate easily toward that dead center of self-satisfaction, the Philistine. Arnold tells us why criticism brings salvation, and why culture *is* criticism:

And thus culture begets a dissatisfaction, which is of the highest possible value in stemming the common tide of men's thoughts in a wealthy and industrial community, and which saves the future, as one may hope, from being vulgarized, even if it cannot save the present. (*Culture and Anarchy*)

Shakespeare's plays, says Meredith, are saturated with the golden light of comedy—the comedy that is redemptive as tragedy cannot be. Consider what happens in *Much Ado About Nothing* when Benedick makes the startling comic discovery that he himself, together with the other mistaken people in the play, is a fool. Here is a moral perception that competes with tragic "recognition." The irony of Benedick's "recognition" is scorching, for he has boasted, all along, that he cannot find it in his heart to love any of Eve's daughters, least of all Beatrice. And Beatrice, for her part, has avowed she will never be fitted with a husband until God makes men of some other metal than earth. Both these characters are too deep of draught to sail in the shoal waters of sentimentality, and both have bravely laid a course of their own far outside the matchmaking that goes easily on in Messina. Each is a mocker, or eiron; but in being so, each becomes the boaster (alazon) betrayed into the valiant pose that they are exempt from love. Then they both walk, wide-eyed, like "proud" Oedipus, into the trap they have laid for themselves. There they see themselves as they are. When Benedick hears himself called hard-hearted he suffers the bewilderment of comic discovery and knows that his pose as mocker is no longer tenable. So he turns his scornful eye inward upon his own vanity: if Beatrice is sick for love of his ribald self he must give up his misogyny and get him a wife. He yields himself, absurdly, to Beatrice, saying "Happy are they that hear their detractions and can put them to mending." At the extreme of his own shame Benedick is compelled to see himself as he sees others, together along a low horizon. Thus occur the comic purgation, the comic resignation to the human lot, the comic humbling of the proud, the comic ennobling after an act of blindness. Those who play a comic role, like Benedick or Berowne or Meredith's Sir Willoughby Patterne, wrongheadedly are liable to achieve their own defeat and afterwards must hide their scars. The comic and the tragic heroes alike "learn through suffering," albeit suffering in comedy takes the form of humiliation, disappointment, or chagrin, instead of death.

There is a comic road to wisdom, as well as a tragic road. There is a comic as well as a tragic control of life. And the comic control may be more usable, more relevant to the human condition in all its normalcy and confusion, its many unreconciled directions. Comedy as well as tragedy can tell us that the vanity of the world is foolishness before the gods. Comedy dares seek truth in the slums of Eastcheap or the crazy landscape Don Quixote wanders across or on the enchanted Prospero isle. By mild inward laughter it tries to keep us sane in the drawing room, among decent men and women. It tells us that man is a giddy thing, yet does not despair of men.

Comedy gives us recognitions healing as the recognitions of tragic art. They are sometimes revelations and come in the moonlit forest of a summer night; then Bottom, with his ass head, is transformed to a Seer, a Visionary, and Bottom's Dream is apocalyptic. For Bottom, the poor weaver, reports: "I have had a dream; past the wit of man to say what dream it was. Man is but an ass if he go about to expound this dream." After this midnight dream everything is seen from a new distance; as Hermia says:

> Methinks I see these things with parted eye
> When every thing seems double.

Tragedy needs a more single vision than comedy, for the comic perception comes only when we take a double view—that is, a human view—of ourselves, a perspective by incongruity. Then we take part in the ancient rite that is a Debate and a Carnival, a Sacrifice and a Feast.

Wylie Sypher

1. Most of what I say about Freud's interpretation of comedy derives from *Wit and Its Relation to the Unconscious*. But I have also drawn upon Ernst Kris: *Psychoanalytic Explorations in Art* (1952) to describe what the unconscious contributes to comic art, especially the grotesque; and also on A. P. Rossiter: *English Drama from Early Times to the Elizabethans* (1950), which has some useful passages on caricature. The remarks upon art as an "interruption" in normal consciousness are based on Anton Ehrenzweig: *Psycho-Analysis of Artistic Vision and Hearing*, 1953.

2. This theory of laughter as being due to a "bisociation" of sensibility is discussed at length in Arthur Koestler: *Insight and Outlook*, 1949.

3. Anthony M. Ludovici: *The Secret of Laughter*, 1932.

4. Probably the most important discussion of "satanic" laughter is Baudelaire's brief essay "On the Essence of Laughter, and In General, On the Comic in the Plastic Arts," which appeared as early as 1855 and was reprinted in *Aesthetic Curiosities*.

5. According to L. C. Knights "comedy is essentially a serious activity" ("Notes on Comedy" in *Determinations*, ed. F. R. Leavis, 1934).

6. As Edith Hamilton says in *The Greek Way*.

7. The "scale" of comic effects is arranged in Alan Reynolds Thompson: *The Anatomy of Drama*, 1942, Chapter VI. I have modified Thompson's scale in certain ways.

8. Behind my whole discussion of this rite and my whole account of the inconsistent theories necessary to explain comedy is Francis M. Cornford: *The Origin of Attic Comedy*, 1914. Cornford's interpretation seems to me to offer our only means of under-

standing the incompatibles in comedy without laying ourselves open to a charge of willful illogicality. These incompatibles in comedy are also dealt with effectively in Johan Huizinga: *Homo Ludens* and in Élie Aubouin: *Technique et psychologie du comique*. See also Northrop Frye: "The Argument of Comedy" in *English Institute Essays, 1948*.

9. Gertrude Rachel Levy in *The Gate of Horn* (1948), p. 319 ff., stresses this interpretation; but, again, my primary debt is to Cornford.

10. This parody is described in A. P. Rossiter: *English Drama from Early Times to the Elizabethans*, 1950.

11. In discussing the nature of the Fool and his many roles, I have relied heavily on Enid Welsford: *The Fool*, 1935, as well as on Kris: *Psychoanalytic Explorations in Art*, 1952, and J. A. K. Thomson: *Irony*, 1927.

12. In *The Dark Voyage and the Golden Mean* Albert Cook advances the ingenious but somewhat narrow-gauge theory that tragedy ventures to make the Dark Voyage toward Risk and Wonder, whereas comedy stays safely within the limits of a Golden Mean. This is a tenable argument, certainly; however, the distinction can hardly be made this simply, and the comedian is often a "revolutionary" as well as a "diplomatic" artist.

13. The best discussion of the complicated psychology behind this sort of comedy seems to me Hugh Dalziel Duncan: *Language and Literature in Society*, 1953, which I have utilized in the following comments.

14. So argues Duncan, p. 53 ff. Ernst Cassirer has also written a major comment on the "sympathetic vision" of the great comic artists who, he says, bring us close to the realities of our human world and dissolve our scorn in a laughter that liberates us (*Essay on Man*).

15. James Feibleman: *In Praise of Comedy*, p. 178 ff., develops this view and shows how comedy is a form of "rebellion" against "things as they are."

16. The point is made by Paul Goodman: *The Structure of Literature*, 1954, p. 89 ff.

BIBLIOGRAPHICAL NOTE

The following are the chief secondary sources on which I have based my discussion of the complex meanings of comedy:

Aubouin, Élie: Technique et psychologie du comique, 1948

Bullitt, John M.: Jonathan Swift and the Anatomy of Satire, 1953

Cook, Albert S.: The Dark Voyage and the Golden Mean, 1949

Cooper, Lane: An Aristotelian Theory of Comedy, 1922

Cornford, Francis M.: The Origin of Attic Comedy, 1914

Duncan, Hugh Dalziel: Language and Literature in Society, 1953

Feibleman, James: In Praise of Comedy, 1939

Fergusson, Francis: The Idea of a Theatre, 1949, 1953

Frye, Northrop: "The Argument of Comedy" (English Institute Essays, 1948)

Goodman, Paul: The Structure of Literature, 1954

Greig, J. Y. T.: The Psychology of Laughter and Comedy, 1923

Harrison, Jane: Themis, 1912, 1927

Huizinga, Johan: Homo Ludens, 1944, 1955

Koestler, Arthur: Insight and Outlook, 1949

Kris, Ernst: Psychoanalytic Explorations in Art, 1952

Levy, Gertrude Rachel: The Gate of Horn, 1948

Michiels, Alfred: Le Monde du comique et du rire, 1886

Piddington, Ralph: The Psychology of Laughter, 1933

Potts, L. J.: Comedy, 1949

Rossiter, A. P.: English Drama from Early Times to the Elizabethans, 1950

Seward, Samuel S.: The Paradox of the Ludicrous, 1930

Smith, Willard M.: The Nature of Comedy, 1930

Thompson, Alan Reynolds: The Anatomy of Drama, 1942

———: The Dry Mock, 1948

Thomson, George: Aeschylus and Athens, 1941

Thomson, J. A. K.: Irony, 1927

Victoria, Marcos: Ensayo preliminar sobre lo cómico, 1941

Villiers, André: La psychologie du comédien, 1942

Weisinger, Herbert: Tragedy and the Paradox of the Fortunate Fall, 1953

Welsford, Enid: The Fool, 1935